product design review

a method for error-free product development

product design review

a method for error-free product development

COMPILED BY TAKASHI ICHIDA

edited by Edward C. Voigt

PUBLISHER'S MESSAGE BY NORMAN BODEK

CRC Press is an imprint of the
Taylor & Francis Group, an **informa** business
A PRODUCTIVITY PRESS BOOK

Originally published as *Deizain Rebyu Jireishu*, © 1989 by Takashi Ichida.

First published 1996 by Productivity Press, Inc

Published 2019 by CRC Press
Taylor & Francis Group
6000 Broken Sound Parkway NW, Suite 300
Boca Raton, FL 33487-2742

ISBN 13: 978-1-56327-041-3 (hbk)

Visit the Taylor & Francis Web site at
http://www.taylorandfrancis.com

and the CRC Press Web site at
http://www.crcpress.com

Cover and text design by Shannon Holt

Library of Congress Cataloging-in-Publication Data

Deizain rebyū jireishū. English.
Product design review : a method for error-free product development / compiled by Takashi Ichida ; edited by Edward C. Voigt
p. cm.
Includes index.
ISBN 1-56327-041-2
1. Design, Industrial. 2. New products. 3. Reliability (Engineering)
I. Ichida, Takashi, 1920-1993. II. Voigt, Edward C. III. Title
TS171.D4313 1996
658.5'75—dc20 96-3637
CIP

CONTENTS

PUBLISHER'S MESSAGE

Quality control on the manufacturing shop floor is capable of revolutionizing work processes everywhere. The quality movement is spreading quickly beyond manufacturing to hospitals, government agencies, financial institutions, and business offices in most organizations. But it still has not quite reached the catacombs of product design and development departments. In product development, quality programs like QFD (quality function deployment) and concurrent engineering have begun to change the focus of new product definition to include production engineers, suppliers, marketing departments, and especially the customer in the product definition process. Yet the design process itself often abounds with rework, duplicated efforts between teams, confusion among computer languages, and many other hindrances to high quality designs. Product design for most companies is consequently the costliest phase of new product cycle time.

At Productivity Press, we have begun to address the needs of product design teams with a series of books to support improvement in design and development processes. This latest in the series, *Product Design Review: A Method for Error-Free Product Development* focuses on a method for keeping errors out of the design process while insuring target costing and timely delivery. Design review (DR) does not focus only on the product definition phase but is a method of reviewing the quality of the design throughout the life cycle of the product, concluding with customer feedback for incorporation in the next product development cycle.

The Union of Japanese Scientists and Engineers (JUSE) has led many companies through the training and implementation process of design review. This book summarizes the tremendous results those companies have achieved by using DR, while also reflecting the difficulties they encountered in getting it underway. It therefore serves as a valuable guide to learning, including case studies from the experiences of a number of these successful companies. DR has several generic phases, but companies must modify the process to suit their culture, product types, manufacturing approaches, and customer requirements. Consequently, only by reading the stories of companies who use this method can one begin to understand the many ways design review can be employed to support the QCD strategies of the organization.

Chapter 1 describes the essential elements of DR from product concept, definition and design, through production, delivery, and customer use. Chapter 2 presents the results of a survey conducted by JUSE of companies implementing DR. Part 2 includes case studies from six companies, each from a different industry, who have successfully applied DR and won recognition from the Union of Japanese Scientists and Engineers (JUSE) as a result of their efforts. These case studies highlight the method while showing readers how DR can be modified to suit the individual culture, product type, and customer requirement of each company. Design review is a method that can be shaped by the unique needs of any organization. In Part 3, Mr. Ichida has included several essays placing DR in the context of other process innovations: artificial intelligence as a tool in product design, checklists, quality function deployment, Taguchi methods, and configuration control.

We wish to thank JUSE Press for allowing us to translate and publish this fine book in the West. In addition we want to acknowledge the efforts of the many people who made this high quality book: Diane Asay, editor in chief, for overseeing the project through completion; Bruce Talbot for the translation; Edward Voigt for his excellent development work; Karen Sandness for copyediting; Shannon Holt for the text and cover design; Susan Swanson for production management; Caroline Berg-Kutil for typesetting; and Catchword for the index.

Norman Bodek
Publisher

PREFACE

Japan's first design review (DR) organizations were developed among its more advanced companies in the early 1970s. The JUSE (Union of Japanese Scientists and Engineers) formed a "Design Review Committee" in 1976 to study some of the successes of these groups. Our main interest was in promoting this approach and better tailoring it to other Japanese companies. Committee members were Messrs. Shin'ichi Takahashi (an NEC employee at the time), Sadashige Morikawa (Toshiba), Katsuyoshi Yamada (Toyota Motor), the late Tetsuji Makino (National Space Development Agency), and myself.

The following is part of a policy statement we drafted to clarify our understanding of design reviews:

> *Design review is a system that involves gathering and evaluating objective knowledge about product design quality and the concrete plans for making it a reality, suggesting improvements at each point, and confirming that the process is ready to proceed to the next phase.*

JUSE published our committee's findings in the 1977 *Design Review Guide* (in Japanese). Many authors contributed to the case studies and essays, and we also received much assistance from companies in conducting surveys and compiling response data. We used the *Guide* as the springboard for a series of JUSE-sponsored design review seminars. Fifty-nine of these seminars were held in the next dozen years, with a total of over 6,500 participants.

In 1981 the late Mr. Tetsuji Makino and I co-authored the JUSE publication *Design Review* (also in Japanese), which, I am grateful to note, won the Nikkei Quality Control Prize for that same year. This book went into more detail on the section in the *Design Review Guide* titled "Fundamentals of DR," which Mr. Makino and I had also coauthored. Among the subjects we addressed were approaches to design, design analysis methods, and design evaluation. To the extent that *Design Review* describes the fundamentals and methods of DR, it can still be a useful reference today.

However, before instituting DR, any company must first tailor DR methods and procedures to its own needs. This is where case studies of other companies' experiences are often helpful. Hence I have compiled the present volume, in which representatives from various industries describe their ongoing DR activities and the successful results they have achieved. I can confidently recommend this book as an accurate description of current DR activities in Japan.

Design Review Case Studies includes the following:

- A summary of responses to a DR-related survey that the JUSE Design Review Committee conducted in 1987 (Part 1, Chapter 2).
- Recent case studies from six companies (Part 2).
- Essays by DR experts on five related topics (Part 3).

I would like to offer my heartfelt thanks to those who so kindly contributed the case studies and essays. I would also like to express profound gratitude to everyone associated with the JUSE Design Review Committee who helped conduct the survey and organize the results, particularly Mr. Yasuhiko Tateyama of JUSE and my colleague Dr. Keiichi Sakai of Kanazawa Industrial College.

Finally, I would like to thank the hardworking editorial staff at JUSE for their assistance in producing this book.

Takashi Ichida
November 15, 1989

product design review

a method for error-free product development

PART 1

DR IN JAPAN TODAY

In recent years Western companies have paid close attention to Japanese theories and practices, but mostly in the manufacturing arena (quality, productivity, JIT). They know much less about how we design and develop products. The first part of this book thus examines the principles that define DR in Japan.

Takashi Ichida
Kanazawa Industrial College

1 DR overview

In its simplest sense, DR is just what its name implies: design review. It involves basic principles that can be applied many ways. Indeed, the survey responses and case studies in this book reflect a wide variety of approaches and methods. For instance, the numbers and names of product development phases and DR meetings vary from one company to the next. Some of the variation stems from differences in organization and policy, some from the type of product and market.

We included this first chapter as an overview of DR to clarify the terminology and tie the rest of the book together. This is not a list of do's and don'ts, just a concise summary of what DR is all about. It ends with selected responses to one item in a 1987 survey on problems encountered, general observations, and follow-up items with respect to carrying out DR.

DEFINING DR

Companies around the world, Japan included, face increasing complexity and decreasing time available for bringing products to market. DR offers a systematic way to manage this process better. It helps ensure that product design quality reflects and meets customer requirements, within cost and time constraints.

Here are two more formal definitions of DR:

1. Japanese Industrial Standard JIS Z 8115-1981:

"Judgment and improvement of an item at the design phase, reviewing the design in terms of function, reliability, and other characteristics, with cost

and delivery as constraints and with the participation of specialists in design, inspection, and implementation."

2. **JUSE Design Review Committee (see preface):**

"Design review is a system that involves gathering and evaluating objective knowledge about product design quality and the concrete plans for making it a reality, suggesting improvements at each point, and confirming that the process is ready to proceed to the next phase."

DR FUNDAMENTALS

But what is so special about design reviews? Engineers and designers have been conducting them for ages on both new product and construction projects. What we call DR here is in some ways the same thing. The difference lies more in *how* it is carried out. Here are the essential principles driving DR:

- At *every* stage until a product reaches the market, use DR to evaluate its design in terms of quality, cost, and delivery (QCD).
- Make the best of available knowledge and technology from both in-house and outside sources.
- Do everything possible to resolve problems as they arise; do not pass them downstream.

DR CONTENT

While DR comes in many shapes and sizes, all reviews should follow this basic pattern:

- Collecting and compiling information
- Defining quality targets
- Evaluating product and process designs and supporting operations
- Proposing improvements
- Defining subsequent actions
- Confirming readiness for the next stage

FORMAL AND INFORMAL DR

Within the above boundaries, there are two types of DR:

Formal design review (FDR), for which companies have standard policies and procedures. Each such review is a key event in the process of product development and production planning. The development schedule clearly shows the days designated for DR within each phase, and those responsible carry it out thoroughly, particularly at the beginning of a phase. FDR is essential for consistent quality results.

Informal design review (IDR), developed and conducted by individual design reviewers. IDR is used only as needed, and its effectiveness can vary greatly. It is a review tool that can be incorporated into any planning or design step as time and resources allow.

Although Chapter 2 includes frequent references to IDR, all the case studies in Part 2 revolve around FDR, so for the remainder of the book, "DR" will refer to the formal version unless otherwise stated.

DR AND PHASES

Companies are learning to apply DR throughout product development, as opposed to the traditional one or two reviews confined to the design phase.

Phase-specific management divides a product's life cycle into major phases for managing QCD factors and may break it down further into incremental steps. This is also known as "step management " in quality control circles.

The author of each case study in Part 2 describes the phases and steps peculiar to his company and product. Many use the term "stage," focusing on the actual transition from one phase to the next.

Figure 1-1 is just one of this book's many illustrations of product development phases.

Details vary from one company to the next, but new product development generally follows this outline:

- Product Planning (identify what the product must do to satisfy the customer)
  - Concept
  - Definition
- Product Design (figure out how to build a product that will do that)

- General design
- Detailed design
- Prototype build
- Tests and revisions

- Production (build the product)
    - Process design
    - Pilot build
    - Full production
- Marketing (satisfy the customer and learn how to do it better)
    - Sales and service
    - Customer feedback

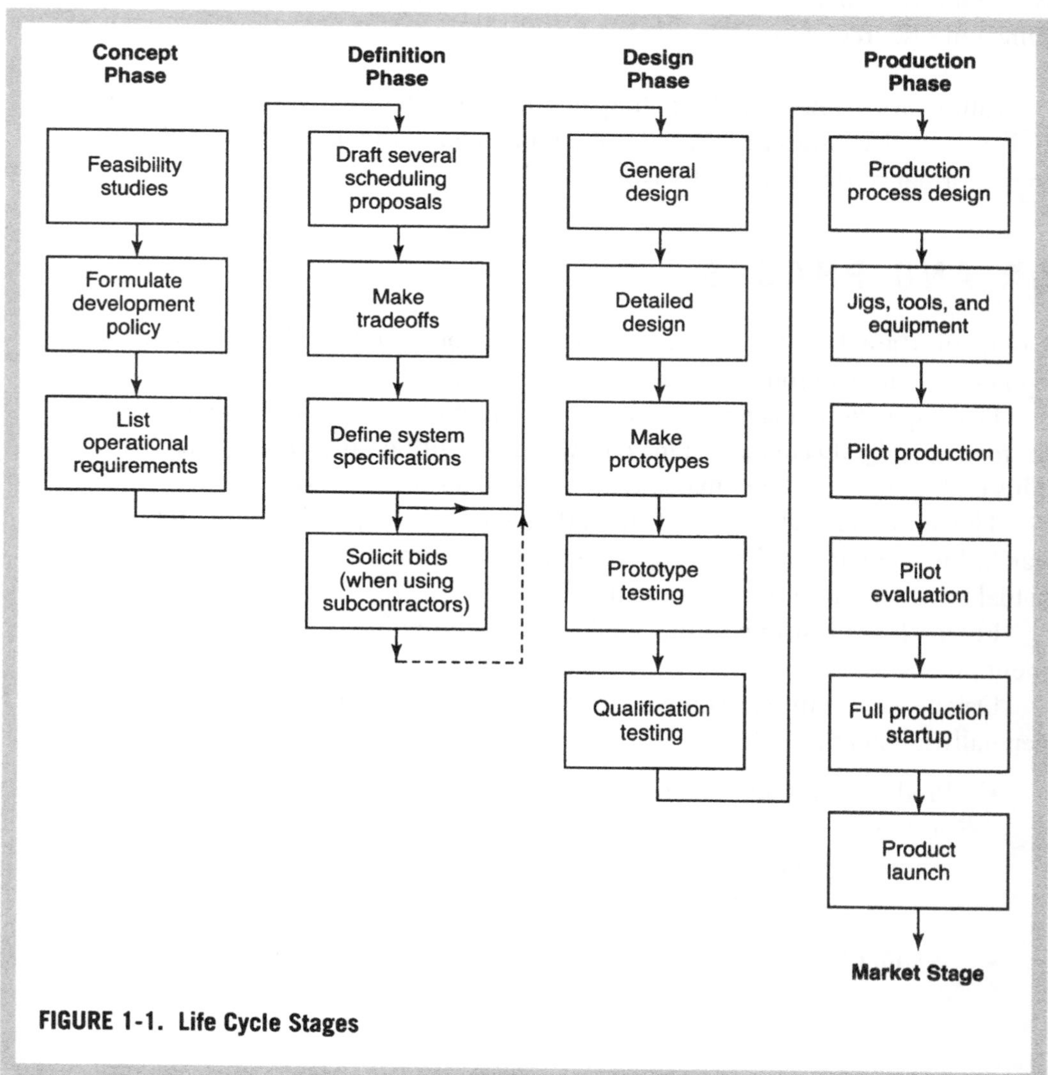

FIGURE 1-1. Life Cycle Stages

Like product development itself, DR is cyclical, not linear, so in many cases the final round of DR—evaluating customer feedback during the market phase—doubles as the first planning session for the next development cycle.

As we will see later in our discussion of survey questions Q7 and Q8 (Chapter 2), DR is applied most often at the general design stage, and to a lesser degree, at the detailed design and pilot building stages.

DR AND GROUP DECISION MAKING

Group decision making is deeply ingrained in Japanese life. Many of our companies have been quick to embrace DR because it is primarily a group activity.

When group activities go well, the group's collective strength is greater than the sum of what the members could exercise individually. We can expect such synergistic effects from DR, which should be regarded as more than "just reviewing designs." (One of the QC movement's major accomplishments was a shift in philosophy away from "just inspecting parts." We now recognize that quality comes not from inspections, but from each manufacturing process.)

The increasing sophistication and variety of product functions and consumer values have made design work more complicated. This applies not just to designers, but also to the planners who must build quality into designs and evaluate them. Therefore product designs must often be reviewed by groups of specialists.

Several years ago I wrote an article titled "Team Chess and Design Review." Team chess is one variation of Japanese chess *(shogi)* in which either two teams of players compete or a single player plays against a team of players. Team members consult together to decide each move. I had spoken with Mr. Naito, a top-ranked Japanese professional chess player. He once played a televised game against a team of three professionals and was roundly defeated. Looking back on the match he made this observation:

> *"One advantage of team play is that at least one member will likely recognize when a suggested move is bad, so there are very few bad moves. At the same time, team decision making may also miss the best possible move, since the majority may not recognize it as such. The general result though, is moves that are slightly above average. Since the first cardinal rule of Japanese chess is to avoid making bad moves, any team that consistently achieves this result is likely to win."*

The mental activity behind product design work can be categorized as follows:

1. Generating design ideas
2. Screening, combining, and improving design ideas
3. Evaluating and correcting design ideas

These are usually done in sequence. Idea-generating methods (like brainstorming) and VE (value engineering) both emphasize keeping the first two steps separate.

Returning to the analogy of team chess, Step 1 (generating design ideas) ends when the team members finish suggesting moves. At this point the team has several alternatives. They next carry out Steps 2 and 3 together, eliminating the bad suggestions. Unfortunately, some unorthodox but clever suggestions are often rejected as well. This typically results when the team moves on to Step 3 without doing Step 2 thoroughly enough.

Steps 1 and 2 correspond to the daily work of the Design Department and others within the organization. The functions of DR fall entirely within Step 3: examining the work, finding gaps and errors, and providing technical expertise.

The first cardinal rule of Japanese chess—to avoid making bad moves—also applies to product development. The famous space scientist Dr. Werner von Braun once said, "The better is the enemy of the good." When developing something under time constraints, before trying to fine-tune your designs, be sure that the designs you have decided are good are also designs that can be produced.

DR is a powerful tool, not for generating excellent ideas, but for making good ideas work. It separates the critical from the creative, thus avoiding bad moves without missing a lot of good ones in the process.

DR AND THE DESIGN DEPARTMENT

The manufacturing sector has long viewed Design, Manufacturing, and Inspection as its three main pillars, each having its own independent authority, as do the three main branches of government in both the United States and Japan. In this tradition the Design Department makes sure that both the Manufacturing and Inspection divisions turn out products that strictly adhere to their drawings and specifications.

Unfortunately, these drawings and specifications alone are not sufficient for production. People in Manufacturing must come up with additional documents such as shop drawings and operating procedures. This is where problems arise. First of all, those who make the shop drawings are usually given a fairly free hand, and conflicts with the design drawings are common. Likewise, Inspection often develops standards of its own, which it imposes on top of those from Design and Manufacturing.

So while the natural focus of DR is on the design phase, it must continue through the full production process to reconcile these discrepancies.

Let us now examine possible relationships between DR and the design department.

DR DOMINATED BY THE DESIGN DEPARTMENT

The DR team may include specialists and support people from other areas, but it belongs to the design department.

Advantages: You can introduce DR with minimal resistance. Design people can better prevent infringements upon their authority, thus also preserving their sense of pride and ownership.

Disadvantages: Those in Design will more likely guard their own turf when determining DR action items, subjects to be addressed, scheduling, preparation, and follow-up work.

DR OFFICE ADVISING THE DESIGN DEPARTMENT

The company establishes an independent DR office that communicates its findings and recommendations to Design via meeting minutes and research reports. Although the Design people retain the final authority to approve design, they are still obliged to respond to these communications. They must also submit and explain design plans and other documents to the DR office and handle any questions or suggestions.

Advantages: As with the first option, Design people can prevent infringements upon their authority. Under this system, however, a more impartial group determines DR action items, subjects to be addressed, scheduling, preparation, and follow-up work.

Disadvantages: There is a certain amount of difficulty in gaining sufficient understanding from both the design department and the DR office staff about the underlying philosophy and necessity of this mode of DR.

SHARED DR AUTHORITY

This relationship is similar to the previous one except that the DR office is elevated to a joint decision-making role with the design department.

Advantages: This is well suited to phase-specific or step management, since the two groups have to work together to move development along. You also still have the benefit of an impartial approach to the DR process.

Disadvantages: With even less sense of ownership, the design department easily overlooks routine procedures such as inspecting drawings and cross-checking specifications. Even so, you would further erode their authority by handing these tasks over to the DR office.

PROJECT MANAGEMENT RELATIONSHIP

Unlike the traditional model, this structure is built around projects instead of functional organizations. Product development is directed from one office with clearly defined assignments, resources, and deadlines. The product/project manager is in a position to ensure that all project responsibilities are met. As project complexity increases and time available for completion decreases, sophisticated techniques such as DR become invaluable.

The company carries out DR thoroughly and systematically. Each product development project has its own project manager (PM), as well as a DR group that includes appropriate department chiefs. The PM decides when the project is ready to advance to the next phase or step, based on evaluation of the DR reports and other status information. In many cases the DR managers represent a higher level within this type organization than the PM, so they make the final call on project advancement.

DR is not about criticizing the work of design engineers and making lists of faults and errors. It is a cooperative undertaking in which people from other areas contribute their expertise to produce better designs from the start. From this perspective, the second organizational mode listed—an independent DR office advising the design department—is usually the best option for Japanese manufacturers. The first organizational mode may work out for companies that are just introducing DR, but before long the disadvantages become too great to ignore.

The project management model is far more common in the United States than in Japan. In terms of balancing synergy and ownership, it is the approach perhaps most compatible with DR, but if your company does not already accommodate matrix organizations, you are looking at major changes that reach well outside the confines of product development.

In response to survey question Q34, "How much authority is granted to DR committee members?", 32 percent of DR committee members reported having final decision-making authority on designs, while 62 percent said they were given only an advisory role. Most responses in the latter group were from companies that had established a DR office supporting the Design Department.

SURVEY RESULTS

Chapter 2 discusses the results of a DR-related survey that the JUSE Design Review Committee conducted in 1987. However, one of the questions (the last one, Q41) was open ended, so it cannot be represented statistically. Instead we have set it apart as a fitting conclusion to this chapter.

Q41: Do you have any other opinions or thoughts on DR, such as common misunderstandings, problems encountered, general observations, or follow-up items? Please enter them in the space provided below.

Nearly all of the 278 respondents provided comments. Few reported any actions to correct misunderstandings of DR, but many described problems encountered during execution. Others mentioned issues for follow-up, DR goals and current DR conditions at their companies, and various requests for the JUSE Design Review Committee.

Some of the most frequently cited concerns were time and scheduling constraints, lack of staff experience in DR, inadequate preparation, and shortfalls in communication, cooperation, and commitment.

Here are the responses:

PROBLEMS ENCOUNTERED DURING DR EXECUTION

- Staff are unevenly matched in knowledge and skills. It is a challenge to keep daily activities on schedule.
- Product developers tend to press forward on their own, with little communication among related departments. This frustrates establishment of a system for disseminating and using information beginning with the concept phase.
- Due to the short development period, we do not always have time to make DR-based changes. We are also having a hard time carrying out cross-functional development within the organization, not even knowing how far it should extend.
- The need for organizational changes and transfers has complicated the selection of DR managers. Lack of DR experience among those selected has also slowed our progress.
- People outside Design often ask too much. They expect perfect satisfaction of market demands without allowing for the extra costs, and the designers sometimes feel like whipping boys within the DR organization.
- Our company is having trouble determining how far to extend decision-making authority and how to deal with problems such as technology gaps and lack of know-how.
- During the concept phase of new product development, DR meetings are little more than explanatory sessions, since hardly anyone has feedback to offer. The DR staff needs more advance preparation for this phase.
- Design managers consider DR separate from "real" design work, allowing their designers little time to prepare for it. Consequently, needed drawings and specifications are often not ready in time for DR meetings.

- DR is placing too much extra work on the shoulders of the design and engineering departments. Our designers end up putting in a lot of overtime.
- Our company does architectural design, and the builder typically requests changes at every stage of the design process. This makes it difficult to reserve time for DR activities.
- Our manufacturing department is always very busy, so they tend to let their DR work slide. We need to find ways to get them more involved in DR.
- It is hard for us to adjust our schedule in response to specialists' requests.

GENERAL OBSERVATIONS AND FOLLOW-UP ITEMS

- We have seen good results from cooperation among departments. However, there has been little substantive output from reviews of specific parts at the design and testing levels, mainly due to time constraints.
- We determine the frequency of DR meetings according to the complexity of the development process. (We divide it into several courses of action.) However, even though we determine these courses of action based on the anticipated complexity of the project, there are times when problems arise despite our having anticipated a simple process. We are now giving more thought to choosing our courses of action.
- Our company has not had much success with DR from a productivity standpoint (preventing the need for changes after the final design is issued). There are always minor design changes right up to full production. We assign DR priority to products according to extent of innovation and originality, but we will only succeed as we become more efficient. Part of the problem is that very few department chiefs are involved in DR.
- The content of our development projects is always both broad and deep. We try to run DR by company guidelines, which lag behind current technology. Thus we do not adjust to changing conditions very well. In light of this problem, we are looking into increased use of computers for better information management.

- Even though DR is in place, we are still having quality problems right up through product launch. We suspect that this may be due to oversights during the DR process.
- We have had difficulty establishing a DR system for our construction projects, due mainly to lack of case studies for reference. One area we would like to improve is analyzing reliability and failure modes.
- DR has become more important for our company as we have modified our products and added new ones. We have just been introduced to the concept and want to start applying it in the near future.
- Our company has had problems with documents not being ready for preliminary DR studies. Sometimes we run out of time for DR meetings. Also, our DR committee has a high absentee rate (or members often send others as substitutes).
- At our company, DR is becoming just a formality that eats up development time, and people struggle to be objective when evaluating data on new technologies. We acknowledge the need for DR relating to software, but we are searching for effective ways to do it.
- Our design department has yet to fully grasp what DR is all about, so we are still dealing with various problems that DR could have predicted. Right now our reviews go no farther than the design people feel is necessary. A more comprehensive and multifaceted program is still a long way off. For now we will try once more to persuade others of the need for more thorough DR.

RECAP

Once again, DR is not about creating *great* designs. It is about getting *good* designs *right*, making them work, and bringing them to market quickly and profitably.

Takashi Ichida
Kanazawa Institute of Technology

2
analysis of DR survey results

PREFACE

The JUSE Design Review Committee initiated a DR survey in September 1987. In early 1988 we compiled the results and sent them to the participating companies. We also summarized these results within a panel discussion at JUSE's 18th Reliability and Safety Symposium. This survey was much broader in scope than a similar one done in 1976:

Year	Fiscal 1976 (4/76 - 3/77)	Fiscal 1987 (4/87 - 3/88)
Companies surveyed	170	1,876
Companies responding	91	352
Response rate	54%	19%
Respondents practicing DR	74	278
Percent of surveyed companies practicing DR	44%	15%

In 1976 only a narrow range of high-tech companies were using DR for new products, and all those surveyed had already sent people to JUSE reliability seminars. The committee covered a much wider field in 1987, including some from the service sector, by sending questionnaires to all JUSE supporting members.

The following people helped plan the survey, formulate questions, arrange for compilation, and analyze the results:

- Takashi Ichida, Kanazawa Institute of Technology
- Katsuyuki Shimodaira, National Space Development Agency (NASDA)
- Shin'ichi Takahashi, Research Center for Development of Resource Exploration and Surveying Systems
- Kenji Horii, Japan Aero Engines Association
- Ayatomo Kanno, Science University of Tokyo
- Kiyokazu Suzuki, Kajima Corporation
- Keizo Nukada, Nitto Electric Works
- Katsuyoshi Yamada, Toyota Motor Company
- Sadashige Morikawa, Tabai Espec

The 41 survey questions and their responses are listed below (except Q41, which we reviewed in the last chapter).

CLASSIFICATION OF RESPONDENTS

Q1: In which of the following industries is your company most active?

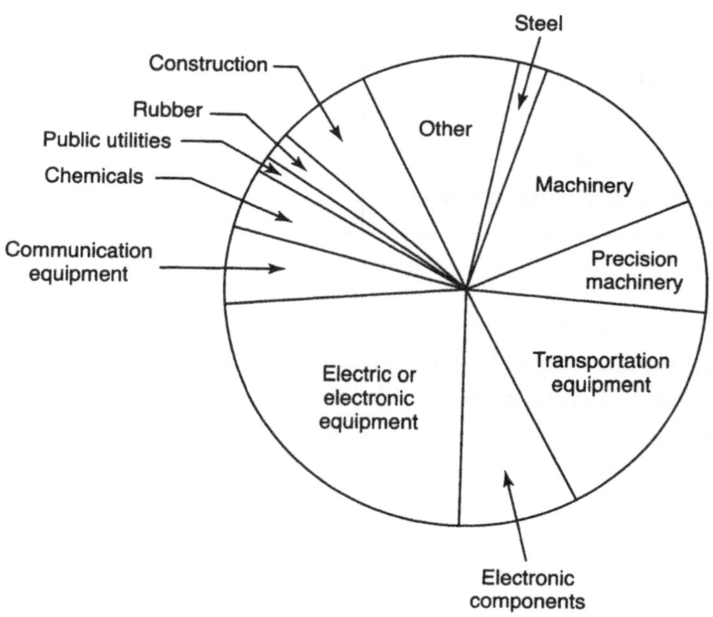

We have since reduced the number of categories from twelve to six by combining the ones with few responses:

- Materials processing and utilities (1, 8, 9, 10)
- Machinery (2, 3)
- Transportation equipment (4)
- Electrical and electronic (5, 6, 7)
- Construction (11)
- Other (12)

Companies in the construction industry, not even included in the 1976 survey, proved to be especially active in DR. While some of their terminology is different, they have picked up DR rather quickly and with good results.

Q2: *Please estimate the percentage of your products fitting each of these three categories (make sure they add up to 100 percent):*

1. Private use _____% 2. Industrial use _____% 3. Other _____%

We reclassified the responses, changing "other" to "research or special projects" and including a fourth "mixed" category for companies that did not indicate 50 percent or higher in any of the others. The following table shows the combined results from Q1 and Q2:

	Private use	Mixed	Industrial use	Research or special projects	Total
Process and utilities	6210 0 18				
Machinery	14346 1 64				
Transportation equipment	19322 2 46				
Electrical and electronic	341252 3 101				
Construction	483 1 16				
Other	1759 2 33				
Total	9433142 9 278				

SUMMARY OF DR-RELATED RESPONSES

The committee broke down all the responses by industry and product categories. In this book we will only look at those numbers for Q4, Q5, Q15, Q16, and Q17, sticking to pie chart representations for the rest. Also, "other" categories are only shown for questions where they accounted for more than five percent of the responses.

Q3: Does your company run DR before approving new product designs?

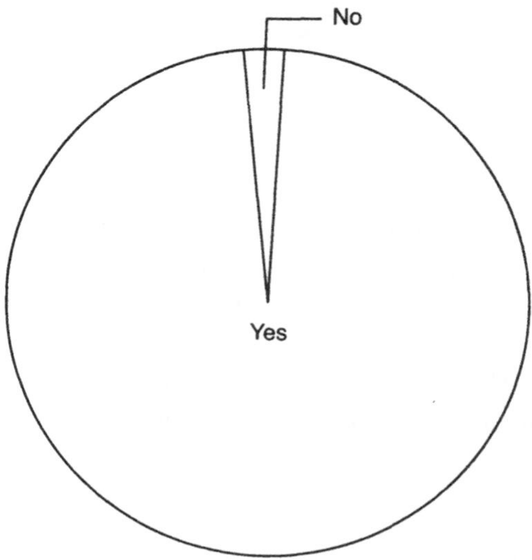

Note: Those responding "No" probably still use DR in other areas, such as planning full production startups or inspecting newly installed equipment.

Q4: If you responded "Yes" to Q3, what percentage of items subject to design approval has to go through DR?

TABLE 2-1. DR Coverage of Critical Design Items

	Maximum	Minimum	Average	No. of responses
Process and utilities	100	10	72	17
Machinery	100	5	69	58
Transportation equipment	100	1	63	40
Electrical and electronic	100	2	66	98
Construction	100	10	61	12
Other	100	3	58	28
Total	100	1	65	253

	Maximum	Minimum	Average	No. of responses
Private use	100	5	69	83
Mixed	100	7	61	28
Industrial use	100	1	64	133
Research or special projects	100	3	69	9
Total	100	1	65	253

Q5: How long has your company been practicing DR?

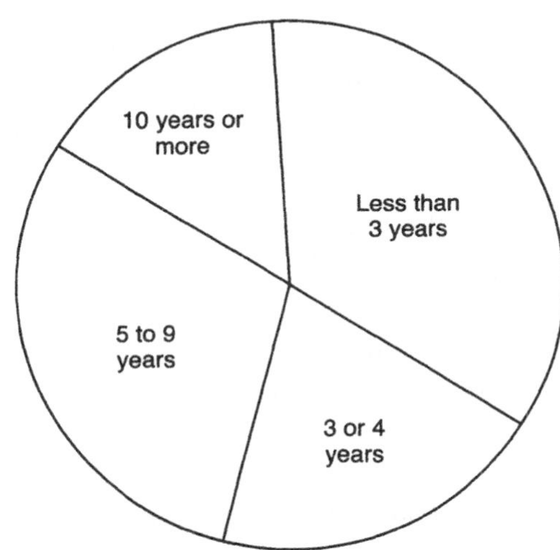

Q6: What was your company's original reason for introducing DR?

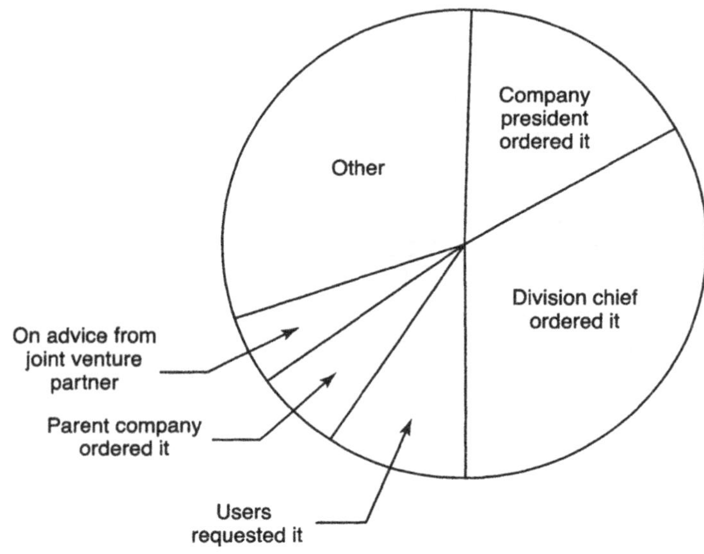

Thirty-two percent (89 of 278) of the respondents gave "other," and it included the following:

	Response	Number of responses	Percent of "other" category	Percent of all Q6 responses
1	Part of TQC or QA	30	34	11
2	On own initiative	20	22	7
3	Requested by design, engineering, or product development departments	10	11	4
4	Ordered by upper management	6	7	2
5	Followed general trend	3	3	1
6	Recommended by customer complaint department	3	3	1
7	Other	17	19	7
	Total	89	99	33

Both the pie chart and the fourth reason in this list showed us that Q6 was not framed clearly enough. What we had wanted to know was why the company had adopted DR, not who had ordered it.

Looking back at the distinction between formal and informal design reviews in Chapter 1, we can conclude that responses 1, 3, or 4 are from companies using FDR.

Q7: During which phase or phases does your company conduct DR? (Multiple responses are allowed.)

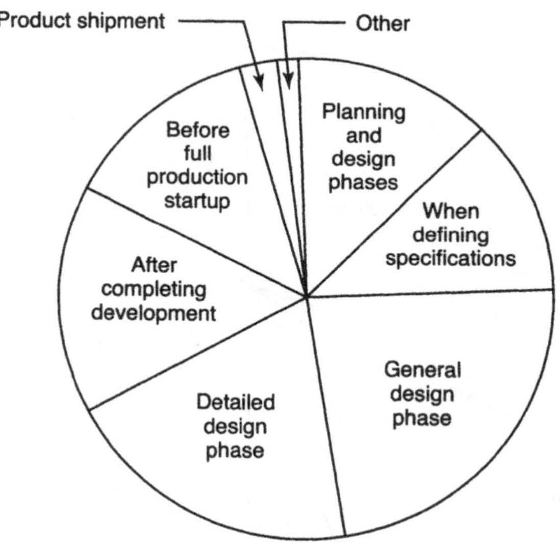

Q8: Please identify the manufacturing steps or processes during which your company conducts DR. (Multiple responses are allowed.)

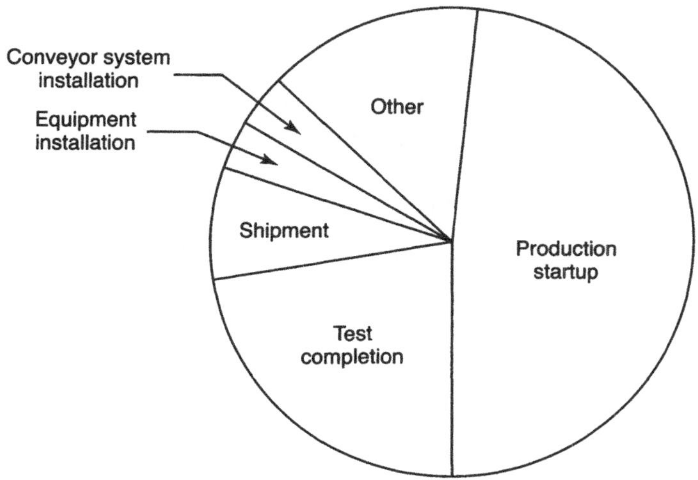

Sixteen percent (44 of 278) of the respondents chose "other" and it included the following:

	Response	Number of responses	Percent of "other" category	Percent of all Q8 responses
1	No DR for manufacturing process	19	43	7
2	Completion of prototype	5	11	2
3	Completion of pilot build	5	11	2
4	Completion of process development	2	5	1
5	Other	13	30	5
	Total	44	100	17

Note: As a rule, DR for manufacturing evaluates the following areas:

- Process specifications (such as for machining or assembly) included in the design of a specific product
- Plant layout and tooling and equipment designs for full production of a specific product
- Manufacturing system designs to support multiple products, such as with an FMS (flexible manufacturing system)

Q9: About how many times is DR conducted per product at your company? (Multiple responses are allowed.)

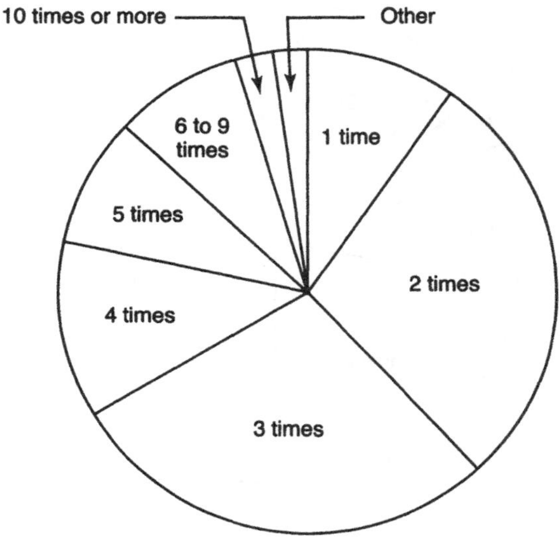

Q10: Does your company establish schedules for DR?

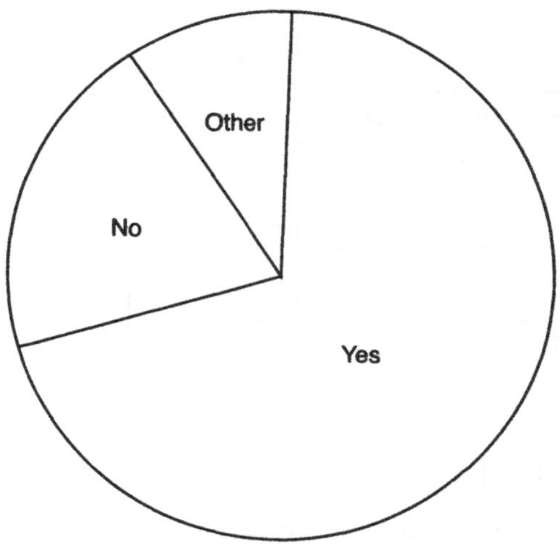

Nine percent (25 of 278) of the respondents gave "other," and it included the following:

	Response	Number of responses	Percent of "other" category	Percent of all Q10 responses
1	Depends on how important the product is	14	56	5
2	Other	11	44	4
	Total	25	100	9

Q11: Who appointed your company's DR committee chairman?

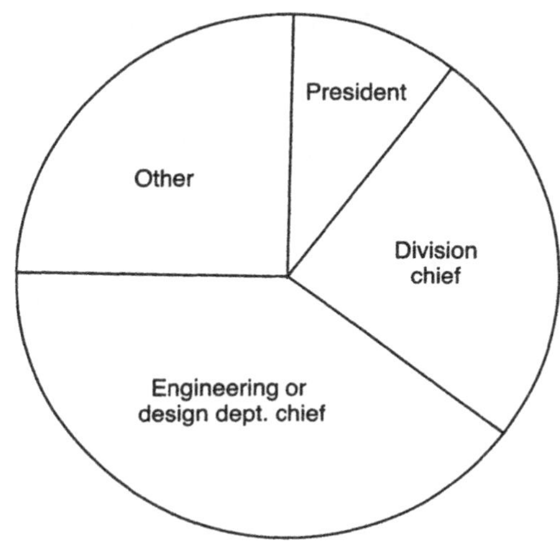

Twenty-two percent (61 of 278) of the respondents gave "other," and it included the following:

	Response	Number of responses	Percent of "other" category	Percent of all Q11 responses
1	Determined by in-house DR regulations	15	25	5
2	Plant manager	5	8	2
3	No appointment system	3	5	1
4	Other	38	62	14
	Total	61	100	22

Other appointing authorities:

- Executive director
- Product development chief
- R&D chief
- Chief engineer
- Production chief
- QC chief

Note: Here is how the results for this question differed between the 1976 and 1987 surveys:

	1976	1987
President	1.4%	9%
Division chief	26 %	25%
Engineering or design chief	33 %	40%

The increase in "president" responses shows growing top management commitment to DR.

Q12: What position does the head of your DR committee normally hold?

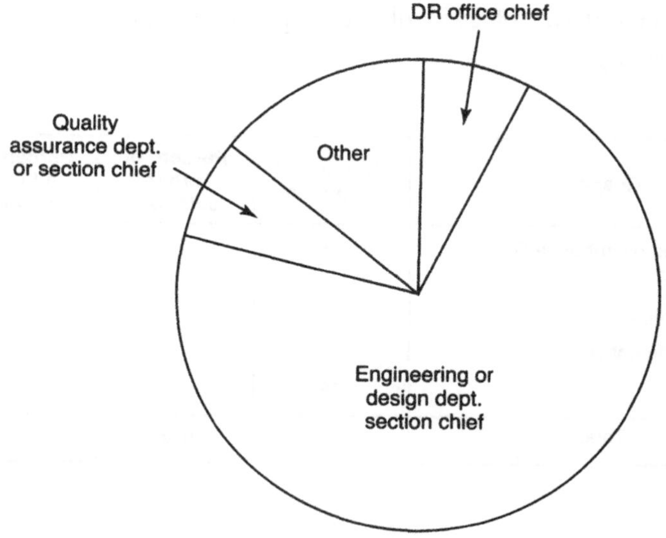

Twelve percent (36 of 278) of the respondents gave “other,” and it included the following:

	Response	Number of responses	Percent of "other" category	Percent of all Q12 responses
1	Engineering or Design middle manager	8	22	3
2	Varies with each development project	4	11	1
3	Rotates according to phase (such as R&D chief for concept phase, QA chief for planning and design phases)	4	11	1
4	Division chief or staff member	3	8	1
5	Other (including 13 not listed here)	17	47	6
	Total	36	99	12

Q13: Which of the following items does your company emphasize during DR? (Multiple responses are allowed.)

Q14: About how many employee-hours per project are devoted to DR? (Multiple responses are allowed.)

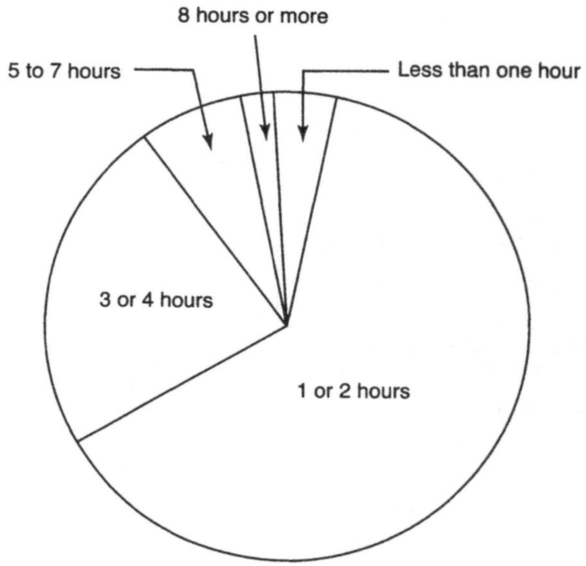

Q15: Please estimate the range of employee-hours that DR committee members devote to DR per project.

Minimum = _______ hours Maximum = _______ hours

TABLE 2-2. DR Hours per Project: Committee Member

Responses by Industry Type	Range of maximum values	Range of minimum values	Range of average values	No. of responses
Process and utilities	30-300	1-3	11-61	17
Machinery	150-300	1-5	17-50	51
Transportation equipment	168-480	1-8	23-75	38
Electrical and electronic	200-400	1-2	18-67	83
Construction	30-60	3-5	9-26	9
Other	70-300	1-2	13-41	19

Responses by Facility Type	Range of maximum values	Range of minimum values	Range of average values	No. of responses
Private use	200-480	1-2	19-71	74
Mixed	30-300	1-2	10-40	21
Industrial use	200-400	1-4	16-55	115
Research or special projects	168-336	1-10	34-84	7

All Responses	Maximum values	Minimum values	Weighted averages	No. of responses
Composite data	30-480	1-10	17-60	217

Q16: Please estimate the range of employee-hours that clerical workers devote to DR per project.

Minimum = _______ hours Maximum = _______ hours

TABLE 2-3. DR Hours per Project: Clerical Worker

Responses by Industry Type	Range of maximum values	Range of minimum values	Range of average values	No. of responses
Process and utilities	40-70	1-3	7-18	14
Machinery	20-80	1-2	6-17	38
Transportation equipment	50-96	1-2	7-17	38
Electrical and electronic	20-60	1-2	4-15	66
Construction	16-60	1-2	6-19	8
Other	30-60	1-2	7-18	13

Responses by Facility Type	Range of maximum values	Range of minimum values	Range of average values	No. of responses
Private use	50-80	1-2	6-16	63
Mixed	16-60	1-3	5-14	18
Industrial use	40-80	1-2	5-17	89
Research or special projects	48-96	1-3	9-21	7

All Responses	Maximum values	Minimum values	Weighted averages	No. of responses
Composite data	50-96	1-2	6-17	177

Q17: Please estimate the range of hours spent in each DR meeting per topic.

Minimum = _______ hours Maximum = _______ hours

TABLE 2-4. DR Meeting Hours per Topic

Responses by Industry Type	Range of maximum values	Range of minimum values	Range of average values	No. of responses
Process and utilities	30-80	1-2	10-28	15
Machinery	45-90	1-3	16-38	53
Transportation equipment	50-88	1-4	15-38	37
Electrical and electronic	50-96	1-2	15-37	77
Construction	25-50	4-8	11-26	13
Other	30-80	2-5	12-36	19

Responses by Facility Type	Range of maximum values	Range of minimum values	Range of average values	No. of responses
Private use	50-96	1-4	15-37	67
Mixed	50-80	1-2	13-32	25
Industrial use	45-90	1-2	14-36	116
Research or special projects	40-70	5-12	19-40	6

All Responses	Maximum values	Minimum values	Weighted averages	No. of responses
Composite data	50-96	1-2	14-36	214

Q18: Who is represented in your company's DR activities? (Multiple responses are allowed.)

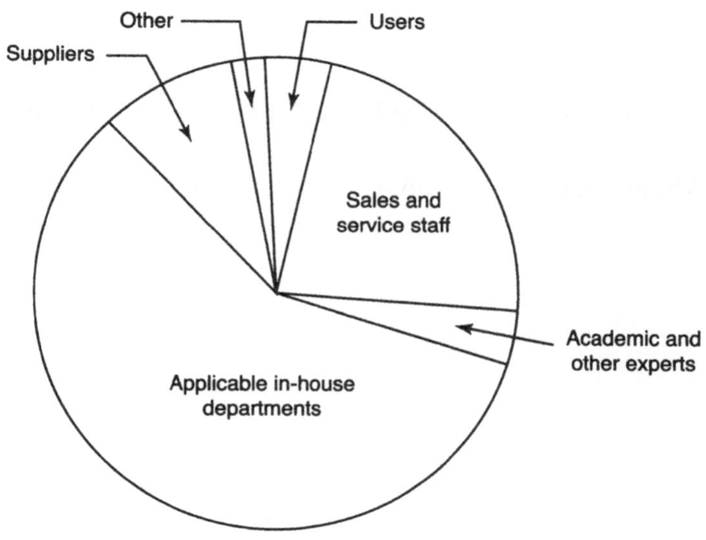

Q19: Does your company use DR checklists?

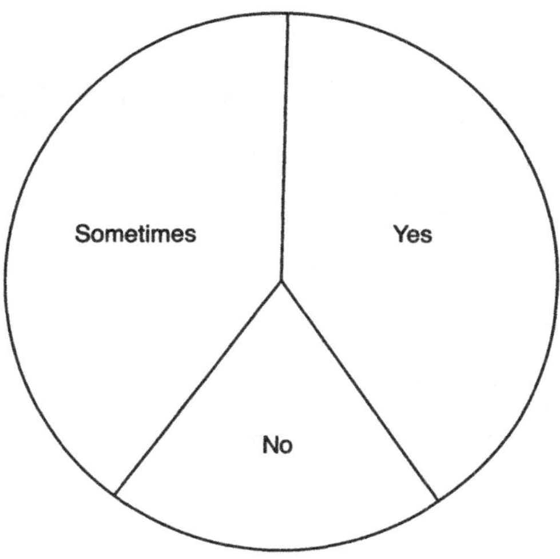

Note: Here is how the results for this question differed between the 1976 and 1987 surveys:

	1976	1987
Yes	69%	41%
No	16%	18%
Sometimes	15%	41%

Q20: Has your company developed (or is it developing) a DR database for any of the following areas? (Multiple responses are allowed.)

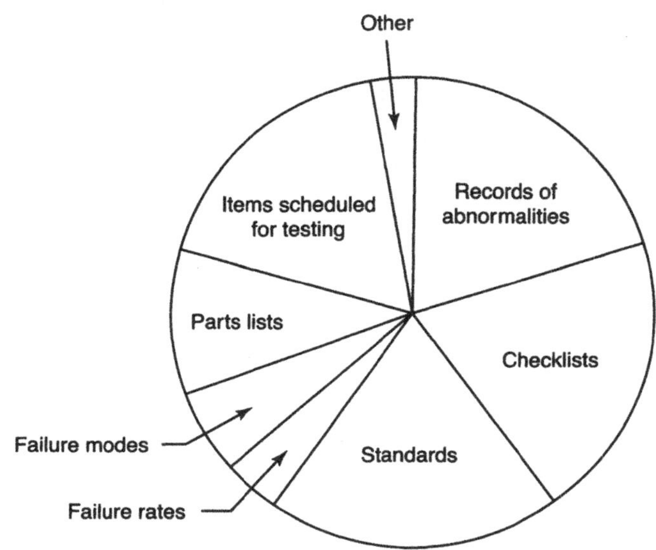

Eight percent (22 of 278) of the respondents gave "other" and it included the following:

	Response	Number of responses	Percent of "other" category	Percent of all Q20 responses
1	Database originally developed for something other than DR	4	18	1
2	QC process charts, quality deployment charts, quality tables	3	14	1
3	Test data	3	14	1
4	Other (such as drawings, specifications, master cost tables, schedule charts)	12	55	4
	Total	22	101	7

Those who gave the first response interpreted the question too narrowly. For their sake, it should have been rephrased as "Has your company developed any databases that can be used for DR?"

Q21: How does your company report its DR results?

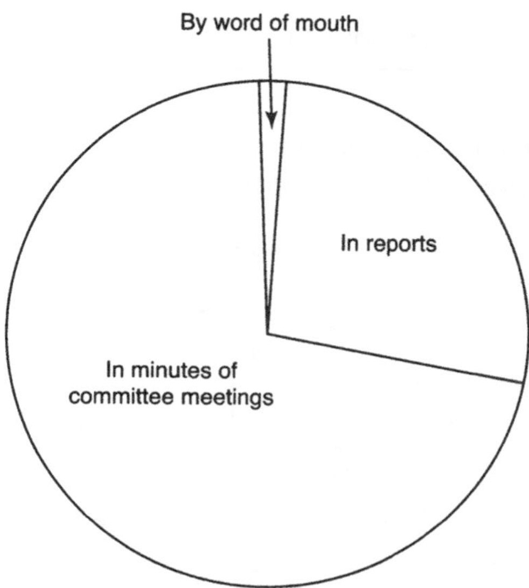

Q22: Which of the following people receive DR reports? (Multiple responses are allowed.)

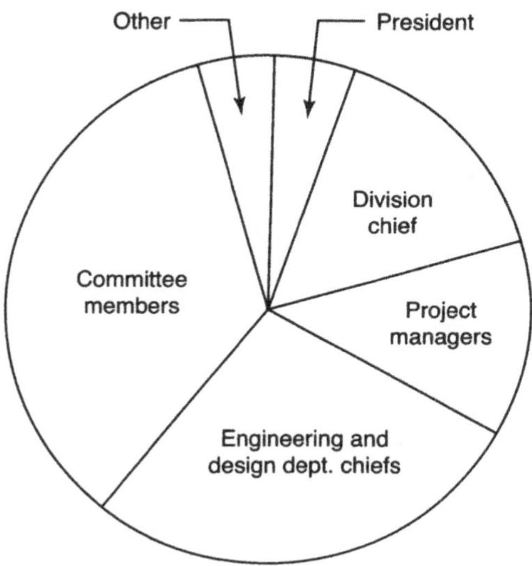

Twelve percent (33 of 278) of the respondents gave "other," and it included the following:

	Response	Number of responses	Percent of "other" category	Percent of all Q22 responses
1	Company officers (directors, executive VP's)	5	16	2
2	Chiefs of appropriate divisions	5	16	2
3	Section chiefs (design, engineering, product development, manufacturing)	4	13	1
4	Plant managers	3	9	1
5	Group leaders in appropriate divisions	3	9	1
6	QC and QA staff	2	6	1
7	Other (including five not listed here)	11	34	4
	Total	33	103	12

Q23: Which department takes responsibility for holding DR meetings?

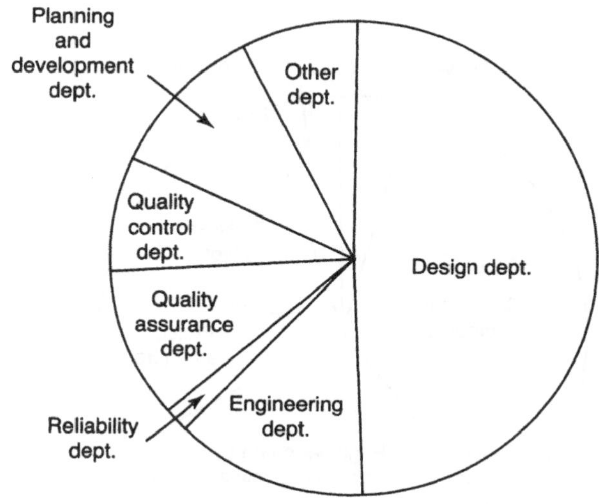

Eight percent (22 of 278) of the respondents gave "other," and it included the following:

	Response	Number of responses	Percent of "other" category	Percent of all Q23 responses
1	Development management department	6	27	2
2	Project planning department	5	23	2
3	Rotates according to phase (such as from R&D to design to quality)	4	18	1
4	Other (final inspection area, or varies with each project or among different parts of the company)	7	32	3
	Total	22	100	8

Q24: Up to what point does the department in Q23 manage DR?

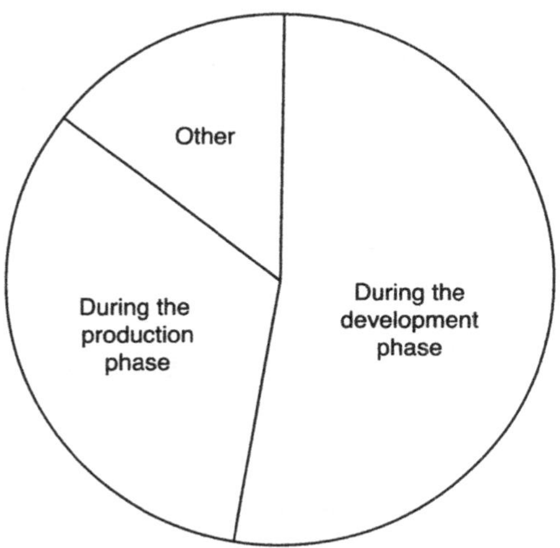

Fourteen percent (39 of 278) of the respondents gave "other," and it included the following:

	Response	Number of responses	Percent of "other" category	Percent of all Q24 responses
1	For each phase	6	15	2
2	Continuously throughout the project	3	8	1
3	Until transfer to full production	3	8	1
4	Other (irregular; through final design approval; until construction starts, 2-3 months after shipment; and 12 other explanations not listed)	27	69	10
	Total	39	100	14

Note: This question (along with Q28 below) follows up on Q7 and Q8, seeking to clarify the degree and extent of DR application.

Q25: How many days before each DR meeting are people notified at your company?

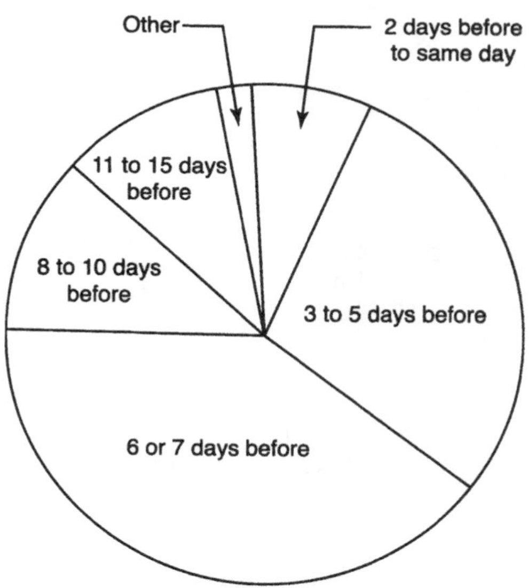

Q26: How many days before each DR meeting are the materials (data packages) distributed at your company?

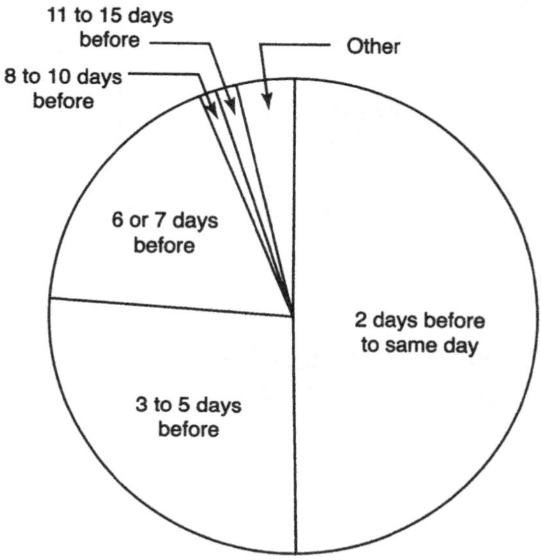

Note: The guidelines relating to Q25 and Q26 are two weeks in advance for meeting notification and one week for distribution of materials, respectively. While all companies are aware of this rule, it appears that few actually follow it.

Q27: *Which of the following items are usually included in your company's DR materials? (Multiple responses are allowed.)*

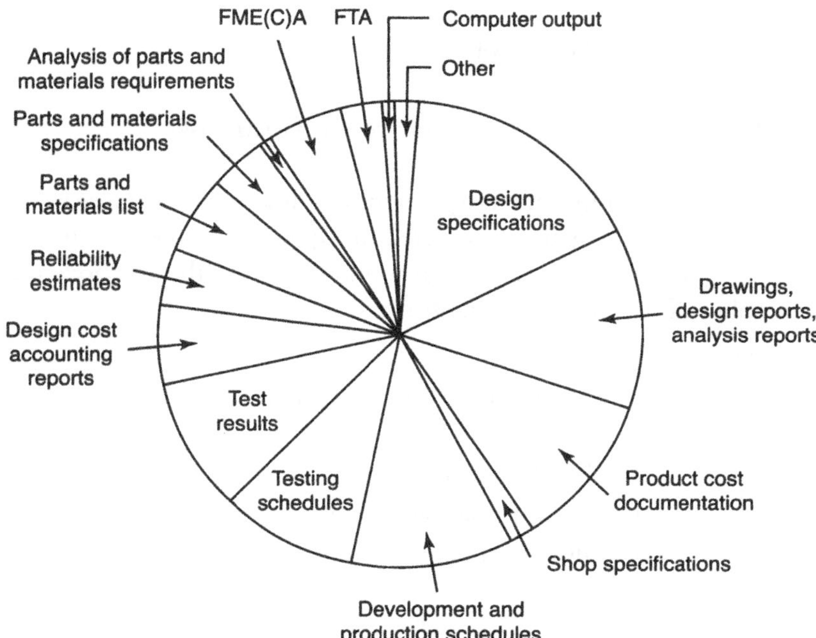

Nine percent (25 of 278) of the respondents gave "other," and it included the following items not already listed:

- Patent specifications or other patent-related documents (mentioned on two responses)
- Evaluation standards (or guidelines) for participants, such as check-sheets, high priority items, development step evaluation tables, and main points related to QCD
- Lists of in-process items or disassembly drawings (not normally included, but still useful in preparing for DR meetings)

It also included these items that fall within the scope of "drawings, design specifications, and analysis reports":

- Comparison charts for similar products, using data either gathered from competitors or developed through joint studies
- Trade-off data
- Quality function deployment charts and quality deployment charts (two responses)
- Comparisons of new and old designs

Q28: What DR follow-up methods does your company use?

This was not a multiple choice question, so a descriptive response was required. Two hundred thirty companies answered this question, some with just one-word descriptions and others in a variety of ways. These are the methods most often cited (number of responses in parentheses):

1. Meetings (125)
    - Monthly meetings, production meetings, project meetings (98)
    - Next DR project (18)
    - Report presentation (7)
    - DR committee meeting (2)
2. Reports (99)
    - Scheduled reports (76)
    - Report papers (17)
    - Meeting minutes (6)
3. Audits (14)
4. Countermeasures, follow-up sheets, management charts, action item lists (12)
5. Routine tasks (9)
6. Part of early warning system (3)
7. Part of approval process for technical documents (1)
8. Reports on specific items as requested (3)

Q29: Where does your company store DR meeting minutes, data packages, and other related documents?

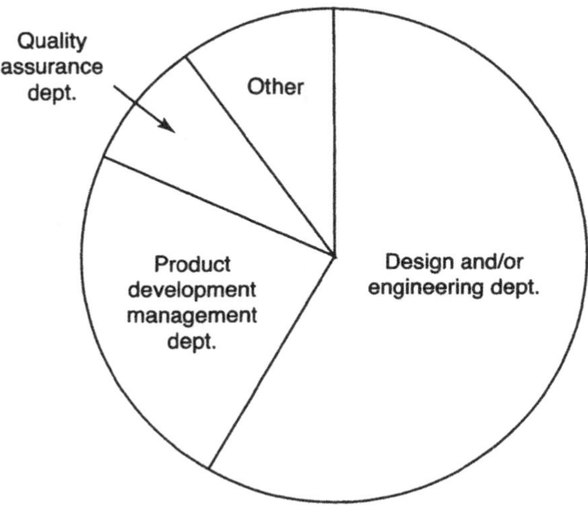

Ten percent (28 of 278) of the respondents gave "other," and it included the following:

	Response	Number of responses	Percent of "other" category	Percent of all Q29 responses
1	QC or QA	7	25	3
2	R&D or product development	4	14	1
3	Production, final inspection, document management, and 8 other responses not listed	17	61	6
	Total	28	100	10

Q30: How highly does your company rate its DR system?

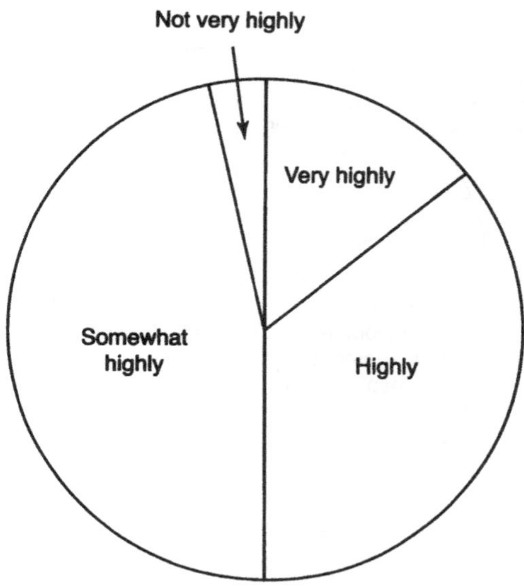

Q31: How effective does your company consider its DR system?

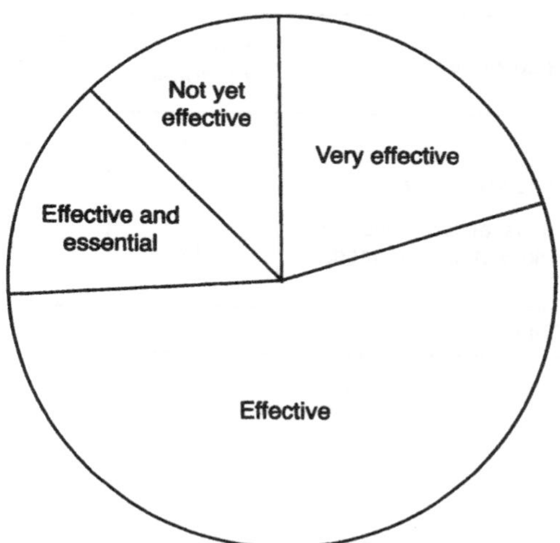

Q32: Does your company's Design group show much initiative?

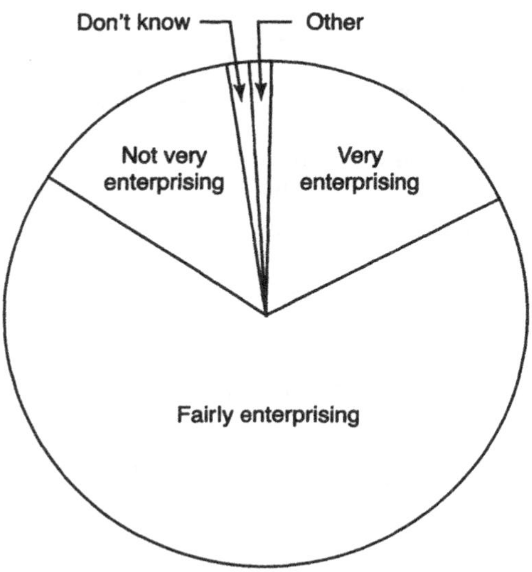

Q33: Has your company defined the DR committee chair's responsibilities and scope of authority in writing?

1. Yes   2. No (please explain how it has been defined)

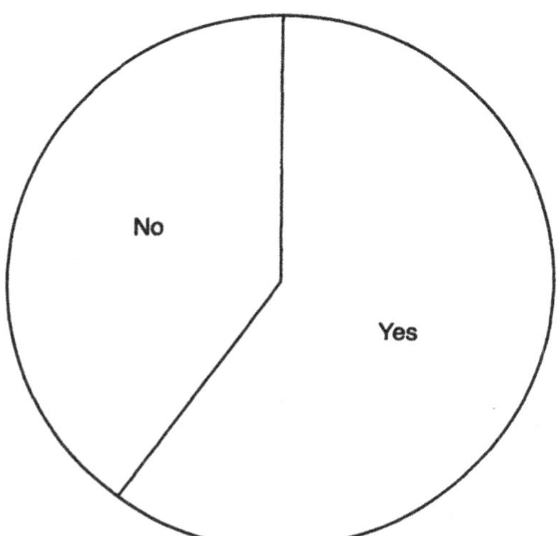

Forty percent (111 of 278) of the respondents gave "no," with the following explanations:

	Response	Number of responses	Percent of "other" category	Percent of all Q33 responses
1	The design (or engineering) division chief is the chair by virtue of position	11	10	4
2	The chair is either a top level manager or is given that authority	8	7	3
3	Decided by internal policy, company tradition, and the chair's personal authority	7	6	3
4	We are now drafting a written policy to address this	7	6	3
5	We address this at DR committee meetings in light of evaluation results	4	4	1
6	Other (decided by the personnel system, plus 63 other explanations not listed)	74	67	27
	Total	111	100	41

Q34: *How much authority is given to your DR committee on design matters?*

1. Final decision-making authority
2. Discuss and advise only
3. Other

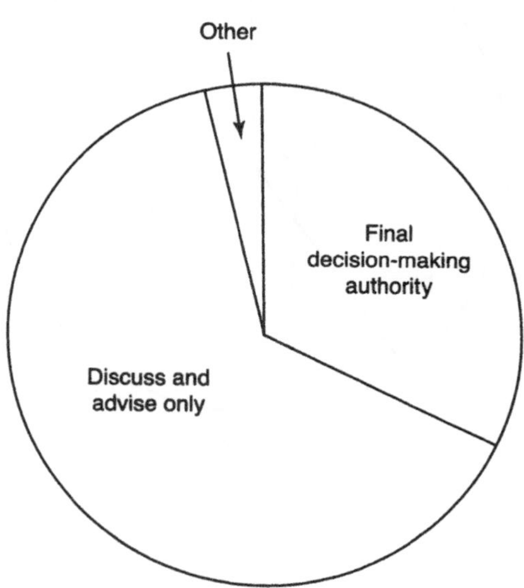

Note: As mentioned in Chapter 1, this issue is fundamental to any company's DR approach.

Q35: Which departments are responsible for DR follow-up? (Multiple responses are allowed.)

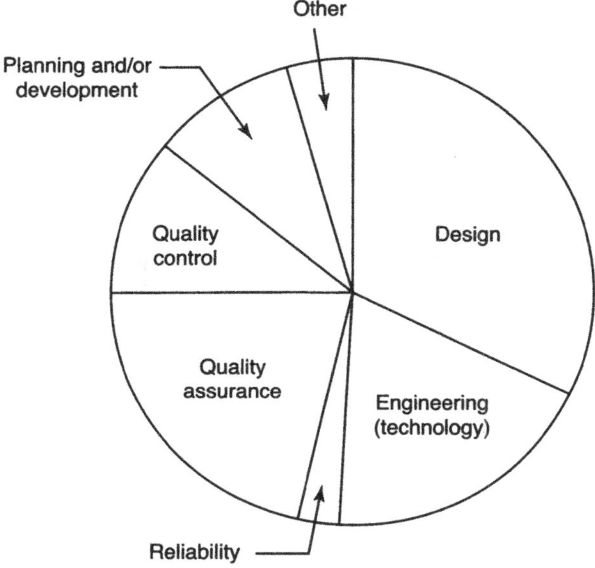

Seven percent (19 of 278) of the respondents gave "other," and it included the following:

	Response	Number of responses	Percent of "other" category	Percent of all Q35 responses
1	R&D, design and product development (DR office)	4	21	1
2	Production management	3	16	1
3	QA, TQC office	2	11	1
4	Other (manufacturing staff, final inspection, sales, and 2 other responses not listed here)	10	53	4
	Total	19	101	7

Q36: To what point do you think the DR office and DR itself have progressed within your company?

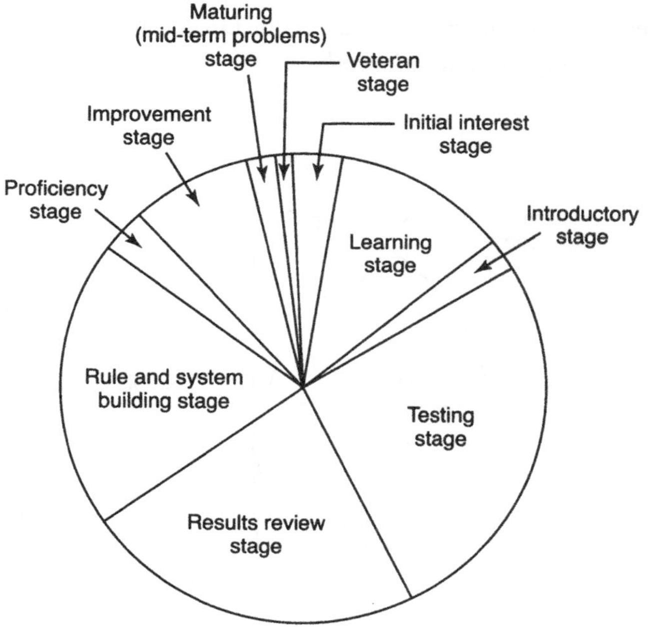

Note: This is one of 16 new questions since the 1976 survey. The responses indicate the vast majority (84 percent) of the companies have advanced to the "prime" stages such as rule and system building. Only three percent had gotten as far as the "facing mid-term problems" or "veteran" stages.

Q37: How widely does your company (or branch) plan to apply DR in the future?

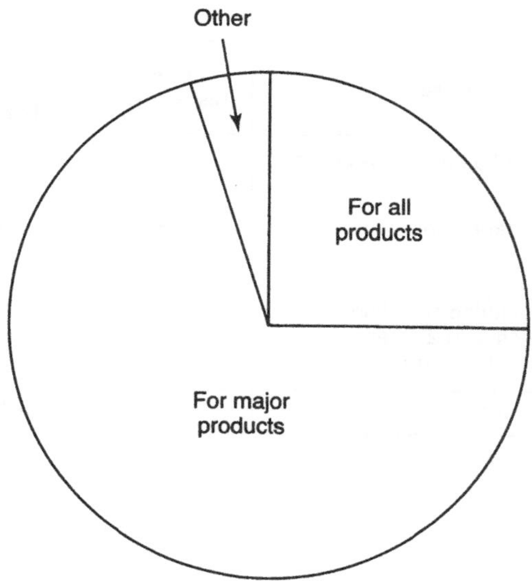

Q38: Will DR be needed at your company's suppliers?

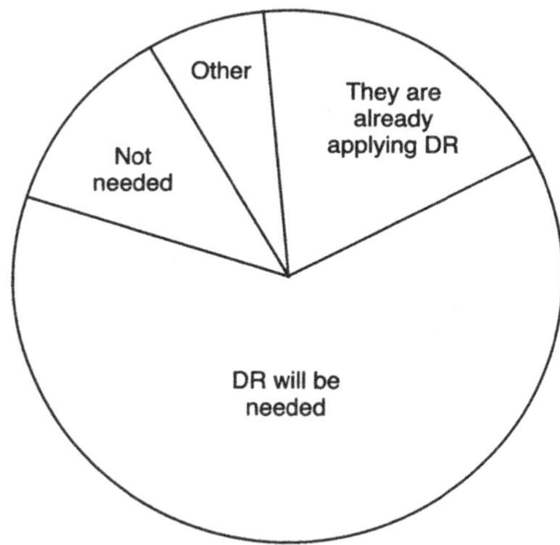

Six percent (18 of 278) of the respondents gave "other," and it included the following:

	Response	Number of responses	Percent of "other" category	Percent of all Q38 responses
1	Our company does not have any suppliers	6	33	2
2	They are currently debating whether or not to adopt DR	6	33	2
3	Some suppliers have already started DR	6	33	2
	Total	18	99	6

Q39: How, if at all, does your company take part in its suppliers' DR activities?

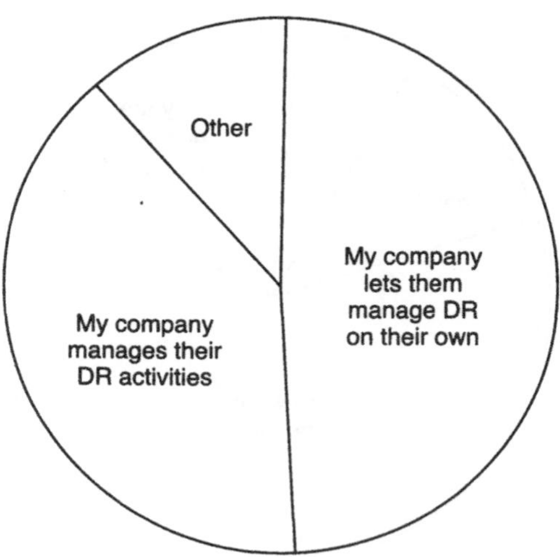

This question was aimed at the 223 respondents who answered Q38 with either "They are already applying DR" or "DR will be needed."

Twelve percent (27 of 223) of the respondents gave "other," and it included the following:

	Response	Number of responses	Percent of "other" category	Percent of all Q39 responses
1	They have not started DR yet, so I don't know	11	41	5
2	Varies with each supplier's needs and capabilities	3	11	1
3	They are doing it on their own terms, but we will still have some involvement	3	11	1
4	They are taking part in our DR activities	2	7	1
5	We are cooperating on DR	2	7	1
6	We will help on an item-by-item basis	2	7	1
7	Other	4	15	2
	Total	27	99	12

Q40: What software applications does your company use for DR? (Multiple responses are allowed.)

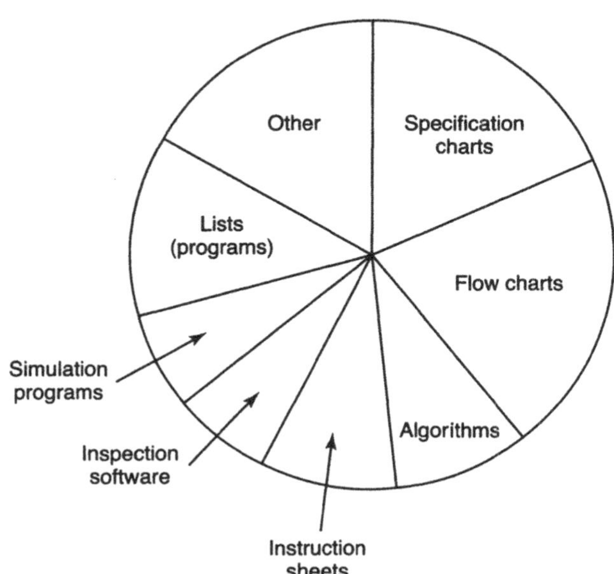

Twenty-three percent (64 of 278) of the respondents gave "other,"and it included the following:

	Response	Number of responses	Percent of "other" category	Percent of all Q39 responses
1	We do not (yet) use any software applications for DR	27	42	10
2	No explanation given	26	41	9
3	Functional specifications	3	5	1
4	Checklists	2	3	1
5	Other (convergence charts, software handled by other division, software not ready yet, still being planned, still at testing stage, based at other facility)	6	9	2
	Total	64	100	23

PART 2

DR CASE STUDIES

All these case studies were contributed by people currently active in DR and representing a wide variety of industries and markets. I asked each author to follow this general outline:

1. Introduction
2. DR Issues and Opportunities
3. Organizing DR Within the Company
4. Example of Application
5. Making DR Effective
6. Benefits of DR and Problematic Aspects
7. Plans for the Future
8. Conclusion

At the same time, I encouraged them to highlight the aspects they deemed most important, and not to worry about giving each part equal emphasis. In fact, you will not see exactly the same outline in any two studies.

Kiyokazu Suzuki
Kajima Corporation

3
DR for building construction
(wide-variety, single-unit production)

This case study concerns DR for the construction industry, specifically building construction, as opposed to civil works.

CHARACTERISTICS OF THE CONSTRUCTION INDUSTRY

Construction differs from manufacturing in many ways. First, there is a wide variety of products (units), and each is made only once. It is also a mobile industry. The project team sets up a job site for each unit it will build, and then moves on to another location upon completion. And unlike most other work environments, construction is affected by weather.

WIDE-VARIETY, SINGLE-UNIT PRODUCTION

Consider the assortment of structures in Table 3-1, which is by no means an exhaustive list. Then realize that for any of these structures, each single unit has unique specifications. For example, even if much of the superstructure can use standard plans, the pilings and foundation must be designed for local soil conditions. In addition, you may not be permitted to use the same equipment in a downtown business district as in a suburban area. In short, it is extremely rare for two identical structures to be erected under identical conditions.

TABLE 3-1. Types of Structures

Business facilities
- Office buildings
- Financial institution branches (banking, insurance, securities, etc.)
- Computer center, etc.

Educational facilities
- Colleges and universities
- High schools, middle schools, and elementary schools
- Other types of schools
- Preschools
- Day care centers
- Lecture halls
- Libraries
- Research centers

Public cultural facilities
- Museums
- Art galleries
- Exhibition facilities
- Memorials and monuments
- Theaters (playhouses)
- Conference facilities
- Religious structures (churches, shrines, temples, synagogues)

Medical facilities
- Hospitals
- Clinics
- Emergency treatment centers
- Convalescent hospitals
- Rehabilitation centers
- Nursing homes
- Medical and nursing schools

Commercial facilities
- Single retail stores
- Department stores
- Shopping centers
- Supermarkets
- Showrooms
- Restaurants
- Studios
- Trade fair facilities

Accommodation facilities
- Hotels
- Inns
- Resorts
- Retirement centers
- Company-owned resort facilities
- Bed-and-breakfasts
- Houseboats

Communications facilities
- Radio and television stations
- Satellite ground stations
- Newspaper publishing facilities
- Wire service facilities
- Teleports

Sports and recreational facilities
- Gymnasiums
- Golf clubhouses
- Stadiums
- Athletic clubs
- Swimming centers
- Fitness centers
- Cinemas
- Leisure centers
- Skating rinks

Housing
- Condominiums
- Single-family residences
- Corporate housing
- Dormitories
- Public housing
- Vacation homes

Distribution facilities
- Distribution centers and warehouses
- Automated storage and retrieval facilities
- Cold-storage facilities
- Port facilities
- Silos
- Storage tanks

Production facilities
- Manufacturing facilities (high tech, continuous process, discrete parts)
- Testing facilities
- Research centers
- Automated factories

Energy-related facilities
- Power plants (hydroelectric, geothermal, nuclear, solar, wind)
- Seawater desalination facilities
- Nuclear fuel treatment facilities

Transportation facilities
- Harbor terminals
- Train and bus stations
- Parking facilities
- Airports and aircraft testing facilities

LOGISTICAL CHALLENGES

Manufacturers bring in materials, process and assemble them at their facilities, and then ship them out to customers. Construction firms must take both their materials and their equipment to the customer's site and do all the processing and assembly there. This is normally accomplished by flatbeds, dump trucks, concrete mixers, and other over-the-road vehicles, but in some remote areas, supplies can be delivered only by helicopter or boat. In any case, precise logistical coordination is always an important factor.

WEATHER CONSIDERATIONS

Even when a construction firm allows for a certain number of rain days, unusually frequent rainfall can increase that number and make it harder to stay on schedule. Many have resorted to measures such as temporary roofs and shelters to help offset these risks.

SEPARATION OF DESIGN AND CONSTRUCTION

Another major difference between the construction industry and most manufacturing industries is the historical separation between design and implementation.

THE TRADITIONAL MODEL

Traditionally, a separate firm or developer has handled each aspect of building design, from the initial conception to the architectural plans and design appraisal. The construction company's job has been to build the structure exactly to specification under the developer's supervision. This approach is still fairly common and remains the norm for government-funded projects.

DESIGN-AND-BUILD CONTRACTORS

Despite this tradition, some builders have been able to use their own detailed design plans with the developer's approval. With experience, they have become increasingly skilled at making competitive design proposals, soliciting feedback both internally and from outside design firms. Others have even established research centers to groom their own design engineers. Over the years these centers have developed proprietary technologies and diversified into project design planning as well as actual design.

In this way, a growing number of builders in our industry have crossed the traditional boundaries to become full service design-and-build contractors. They are thus able to respond to a broader range of business conditions and customer needs.

MANAGING COMPLEX PROJECTS

A proposed project may involve relocating a manufacturing plant away from a group of condominiums to an industrial park, after which the old site can be used for more condos or for athletic fields. Whoever takes on such a project is faced with profit and cost accounting, acquiring an industrial park site, designing and building the new plant, planning the new use for the old site, designing and building new facilities there, and arranging for sales or leasing. There are also local zoning laws and town planning requirements to consider. A design-and-build contractor has an advantage here, if for no other reason than greater ease of coordination.

QUALITY ASSURANCE IN THE CONSTRUCTION INDUSTRY

THE NEED FOR QA

When construction firms vertically integrate their operations to include design, they gain control over the quality of materials presented to the developer. This integration offers additional advantages long familiar to people in manufacturing. The company's design division can use feedback from its construction division to streamline operations at various stages, to eliminate failures and defects, and to shorten overall build time. All this increases the quality, value, and timeliness of construction projects.

If an accident occurs on a project, it is not always clear whether the cause was a design error or a construction method. When two separate firms are involved, the troubleshooting process can be especially time consuming and divisive. Meanwhile, the developer may end up blaming both the designer and the builder. Having a single design-and-build contractor avoids all that.

As mentioned earlier, even when construction and design are separated, a builder with a proven record may propose design changes that the developer and designers accept. But by the same token, when builders make such design proposals, they also assume responsibilities for function and performance that have traditionally rested on the design firm's shoulders alone.

All these issues together demonstrate the need for construction firms to develop effective QA systems.

OUR APPROACH TO QA

At Kajima Corporation, this is the focus of our QA efforts:

Assuring customers of long lasting satisfaction with our products and services, from reliable handling of orders to sales activities and after-sales support.

Our direct customers are usually developers, but for most building developments we also have end users to consider. In addition, we must address the wider social impact that buildings have on the local community.

Kajima Corporation's policy statement mentions "long lasting satisfaction" because structures have very long life cycles and are much less disposable than most manufactured products. Nevertheless, they do deteriorate over the years, so quality assurance in their planning and design should include maintenance requirements and future renovation plans.

DR ISSUES AND OPPORTUNITIES

SOURCE CONTROL

As builders work to assure the quality of their products, they come to see source (design) control as an effective tool against recurring problems.

Most of a structure's quality is built in at the design stage. Feedback from sales and construction operations helps designers be objective and confident in systematically appraising design quality. To minimize the margin of error, they should also examine the design risk from several perspectives, not just one specialized area. This is where builders see DR as critical to raising quality while lowering project cost and duration.

VERTICAL INTEGRATION

As we have already stated, vertical integration makes a construction firm responsible for both design and planning. The design work itself includes a number of administrative tasks. The builder must also satisfy the developer's quality requirements and comply with safety and environmental regulations, not to mention aesthetic and cultural issues. All these come with the designer's job.

BUILDING LIFE EXPECTANCY

The rule of thumb in Japan is a life expectancy of about 20 years for wooden structures and 60 for concrete ones. These figures can vary greatly with maintenance and use, from over 100 years for a well maintained wooden structure to less than five years for a concrete structure with deteriorating equipment and rusty pipes. Of course structures are not easily replaced and must generally be torn down and rebuilt. Use of replaceable components can extend the life of some structures, but high maintenance costs usually rule out that option. Meanwhile, we are beginning to explore the feasibility of maintenance-free structures.

ENVIRONMENTAL FACTORS

Building designs must conform to strict requirements concerning temperature, humidity, dust control, vibration resistance, and noise abatement. The design-and-build contractor usually addresses these issues with the developer as part of the design process.

The climate of Japan varies dramatically between the islands of Hokkaido in the far north and Okinawa in the far south. Construction firms must therefore deal with a variety of site conditions. Thorough preliminary studies are even more critical for Japanese companies bidding on overseas projects.

SOCIAL FACTORS

Social factors are growing in importance. Buildings may function as symbols or landmarks within a certain part of town, as meeting places that can accommodate public events, or as serene, scenic oases where people can rest from their daily activities. More Japanese communities in recent years have been demanding open spaces, leading to the building of sports facilities such as baseball fields and tennis courts.

COST REDUCTION

Construction firms are always seeking to reduce both build times and costs. Developers must also trim their costs to ensure profitability, and we are now seeing more joint effort in this direction. For example, builders may pledge this kind of cooperation to make their bid packages more attractive. This is another way in which construction firms are broadening their perspectives to keep up with a changing market.

Design-and-build contractors have to address all the above factors on top of essential project elements—general design, function, ease of use, structural design, choice of equipment, safety, reliability, maintainability, cost—and consideration of new technologies, materials, and components. This calls for a broad range of skills and expertise. Individual employees cannot effectively confront these myriad responsibilities without strong management support.

These are some of the issues that construction firms in general, and their designers in particular, are seeking to resolve through DR.

ORGANIZING DR WITHIN THE COMPANY

DR AND PROJECT FLOW

During the design stage, where product quality is largely determined, input from experts serves to clarify concepts, promote cost reduction, make technical recommendations, and assess feedback from downstream processes.

Figure 3-1 outlines the work flow for building design and construction.

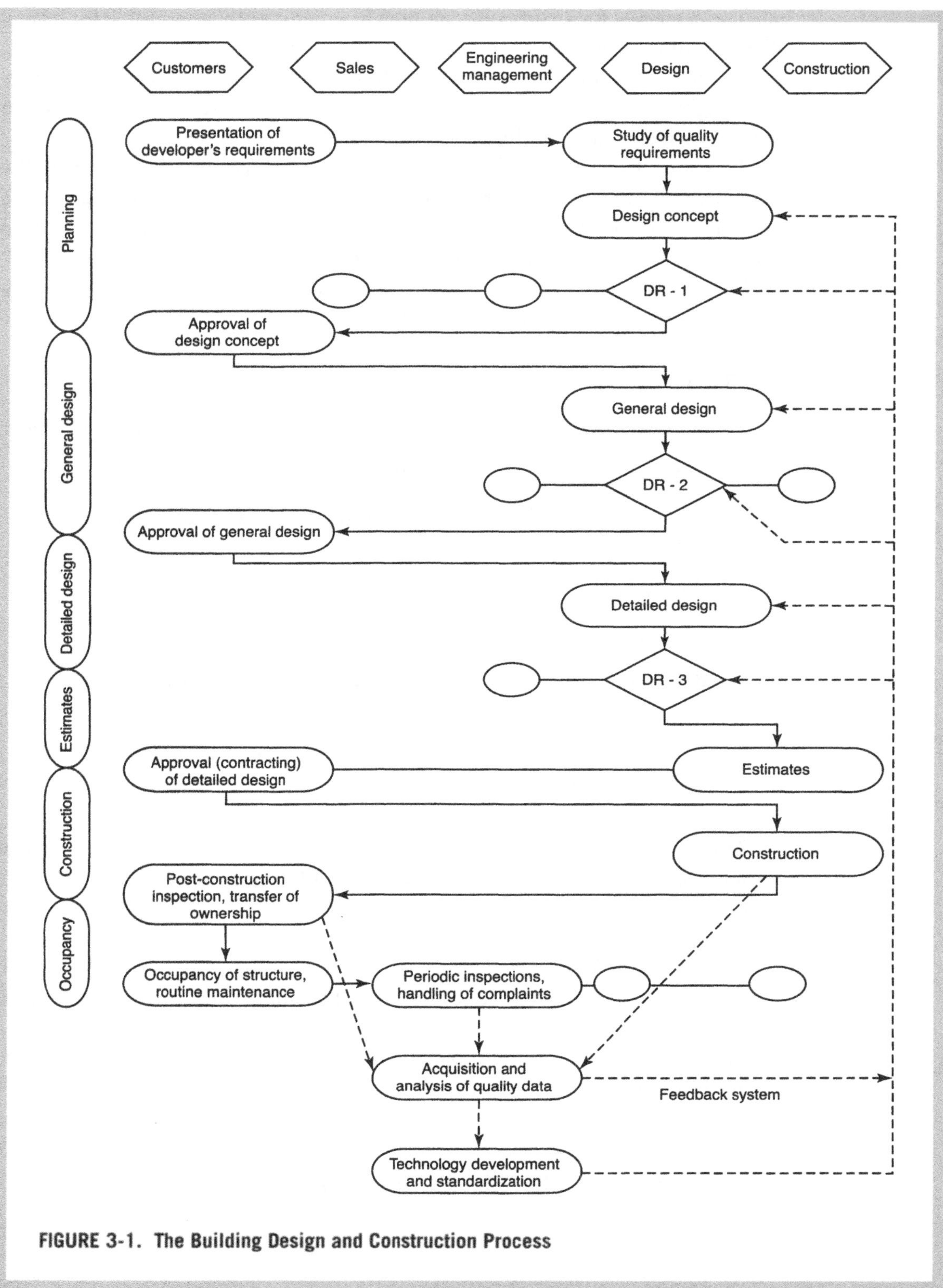

FIGURE 3-1. The Building Design and Construction Process

The designers for a particular job may be concurrently responsible for several others. Within a project there is a separate schedule for each stage: planning, general design, detailed design, and construction. The designers may still be very active right through the construction stage with minor design revisions, color choices, or rechecking of blueprints.

This sort of activity can frustrate DR scheduling. When DR is delayed, the company will often cut it short rather than jeopardize the project budget. As a result, many good suggestions are never heard, let alone used. This is why it is so important for company management to enforce the DR schedule strictly.

Since building construction can involve design of both structures and equipment, there are DR subsystems for each category.

DR SEQUENCE

We have established six DR functions, some associated with specific stages:

1. Reviewing QA policies at the market stage
2. Ensuring that design parameters at the planning stage are based on quality requirements
3. Reviewing the general design
4. Reviewing project reports
5. Reviewing action plans for major design revisions during the design and construction stages
6. Reviewing imported construction materials, new or developing technology, and patents

At Kajima Corporation we use alphanumeric abbreviations for design review at each stage of a project: DR-1 for planning, DR-2 for general design, and DR-3 for detailed design.

DR-1 (PLANNING)

This first review emphasizes overall quality. This means studying and evaluating general design concepts and functional requirements.

Whether or not a project is subject to DR-1 is determined by a group manager, deputy group manager, appropriate department manager, or design coordinator.

Deputy group managers chair the DR-1 committees, which include group managers and division chiefs. Sales department managers and other people also participate as needed. The DR-1 meetings are generally held each Thursday.

DR-2 (GENERAL DESIGN)

DR-2 focuses mainly on solving technical problems. We first evaluate the design in light of the original concept, and then we review the associated design processes. At this stage we also ensure that construction methods and specifications are compatible with the design, identifying any needed changes.

Either a group manager, design engineering reviewer, appropriate department manager, or design coordinator decides which projects need DR-2. Projects that have already been through DR-1 are automatic candidates.

Each DR-2 committee is chaired by the design engineering chief or someone else at the department level. Members include architectural, structural, and mechanical engineering managers, engineering managers from the construction division, and specialists from engineering research centers as needed. DR-2 meetings are generally held each Wednesday.

Both DR-1 and DR-2 may be done more than once for the same job. Either review usually lasts from about 45 minutes to two hours per occurrence, depending on how much is being covered.

DR-3 (DETAILED DESIGN)

DR-3 involves inspecting the detailed designs and guaranteeing their quality before they are released for construction. Most of the committee is staffed by the design engineering department. No particular day of the week is set aside for this stage.

Items raised during each of these reviews are entered on a follow-up sheet and passed along to the appropriate people. Figures 3-2, 3-3 and 3-4 show the follow-up sheets for DR-1, DR-2, and DR-3, respectively.

At every stage, meetings may be held two or three times a week, due to snags in the project. In such cases, the committee includes people ranked at the department chief or assistant department chief level, and special records and follow-up sheets are used.

EVALUATION ITEMS

If quality requirements are not nailed down in the planning stage, they will have to be incorporated later on through time-consuming revisions. The DR committee's job is to obtain these requirements from the developer, along with legal and budgetary constraints, technical requirements, and safety and user satisfaction criteria. In other words, they make sure the company has accurately understood all the developer's requirements and intentions. Of course, they also must address the requirements that apply to any construction project. Once this step is complete, the committee can evaluate the design characteristics against these quality requirements.

DR-1 Follow-Up Sheet (Planning Review)

Project No. Design quality control grade: A B C D (Review No.) Type: a • b • c • d • e • f

Project name:

Dept. chief in charge | Coordinator

Review subjects
- Design coordinator.........
- Architecture ....
- Structure ....
- Equipment ....
- Environment ....
- Interior ....
- Sales ....
- Development ....
- Construction ....

Reviewers

Meeting time
Day:
Hour:
Meeting site: DR room
Office approval:

Problems (Please enter specific DR-related issues)

•5 copies of the design quality follow-up sheet and other reference materials are to be submitted at the DR meeting.

Is an additional DR meeting required? Yes (scheduled for [date]) No	Is a DR-2 meeting required? Yes (scheduled for [date]) No	Confirmation of findings and recommendations: Chair Date: / Coordinator Date: / Manager Date:	Confirmation of follow-up completion: Chair Date: / Coordinator Date: / Manager Date:

No.	Findings	Recommendations	Follow-up record: Action items	Follow-up record: Person responsible Date:

Company standard 206-C 850601 Rev. No. 860501 Rev. No. 870501 Rev. No.

Use the same follow-up sheet for any additional pages required.

Please describe which recommendations were adopted for each finding, when and by whom.

Kajima Corporation, Building Design Headquarters

- Type a:Review of headquarters policies at the market stage (Q2)
- Type b:Review of design parameters at the planning stage (Q3) to ensure they are based on the required quality characteristics
- Type c:Review of the general design (Q4)
- Type d:Review of project reports (Q2 to Q4)
- Type e:Review of plans for major design revisions at the design and construction stages (Q3 to Q10)
- Type f: Review of imported construction materials, research and development, technology development, product development, and patents

	Type		
Q2	a		
Q3		b	
Q4			c

FIGURE 3-2. DR-1 Follow-Up Sheet

DR-2 Follow-Up Sheet (General Design Review)

Project No. Design quality control grade: A B C D (Review No.) Project name:		Coordinator ○
Review subjects: Design coordinator; Architecture; Structure; Equipment; Environment; Interior; Sales; Development; Construction	Reviewers	Meeting time Day: Hour: Meeting site: DR room Office approval: ○

Problems (Please enter specific DR-related issues) •5 copies of the design quality follow-up sheet and other reference materials are to be submitted at the DR meeting.

Is an additional DR meeting required? Yes (scheduled for [date]) No	Send drawings to architectural dept.? Yes (scheduled to be sent on [date]) No	Confirmation of findings and recommendations Chair Date: ○ Coordinator Date: ○ Manager Date: ○	Confirmation of follow-up completion Chair Date: ○ Coordinator Date: ○ Manager Date: ○

No.	Findings	Recommendations	Follow-up record: Action items	Follow-up record: Person responsible Date:
				/
				/
				/
				/
				/
				/
				/
				/
				/
				/
				/
				/
				/
				/
				/
				/

Company standard 207-C 850601 Rev. No. 860501 Rev. No. 870501 Rev. No.

Use the same follow-up sheet for any additional pages required.

Please describe when, where, and how the recommendations were adopted.

Kajima Corporation, Building Design Headquarters

FIGURE 3-3. DR-2 Follow-Up Sheet

Building Design Department Chief's Record of Design Approval ········ Enter application date here

Project No. Design quality control grade: A B C D	First preference: ________ AM.PM Second preference: ________ AM.PM	Coordinator ◯
Project name:		
Review subjects	Reviewers	Meeting time Day: Hour:

Enter notification date here

Confirmation of findings and recommendations	Chair Date: ◯◯	Coordinator Date: ◯	Manager Date: ◯	Confirmation of follow-up completion	Chair Date: ◯◯	Coordinator Date: ◯	Manager Date: ◯

No.	Findings	Recommendations	Follow-up record: Action items	Follow-up record: Person responsible Date:
				/
				/
				/
				/
				/
				/
				/
				/
				/
				/
				/
				/
				/
				/
				/
				/
				/
				/
				/
				/
				/

Building design department standard 010-C

840401 Rev. No.
850601 Rev. No.
860501 Rev. No.
870501 Rev. No.

Use the same follow-up sheet for any additional pages required.

Please describe when, where, and how the reommendations were adopted.

Building Design Department

FIGURE 3-4. DR-3 Follow-Up Sheet

MAKING DR EFFECTIVE

Here are some thoughts on carrying out DR more effectively:

- Before debating DR issues, make sure everyone has the same clear understanding of the goals and review items, so that participants aren't talking past one another.
- Make sure that all materials prepared for a DR meeting are written clearly and simply and that committee members have the opportunity to study them well in advance.
- Make sure that the DR system provides for constant access to expert opinions.
- Solicit feedback on DR materials and findings in order to avoid redundant proposals resulting from lack of communication.

BENEFITS OF DR

BETTER OVERALL BUILDING QUALITY

- DR focuses attention on reliability and quality maintenance over the structure's useful life.
- It also results in cost cutting through supplier reduction, shorter construction periods, fewer delays, and fewer complaints.
- DR promotes safety during both construction and occupancy.

FROM DESIGN BY INDIVIDUALS TO DESIGN BY ORGANIZATIONS

- Bringing people from various departments into DR meetings helps disseminate vital information related to project quality requirements.
- The DR effort consolidates a company's wealth of knowledge from previously segregated domains.
- Group discussions lead to more objective, carefully considered evaluations of product designs.

PLANS FOR THE FUTURE

As you think about our experiences with DR in the building construction sector, please realize that we have by no means "arrived." We are continuously working to apply DR more effectively and efficiently. These are the key ideas for improvement on our agenda:

- Cultivate more experts who can come up with useful DR findings, stated in terms that designers understand.
- Build a database for information on past successes and failures, as well as for technical data. Include keyword search and other user-friendly functions.
- Improve our administration of DR to keep it running smoothly and to ward off quality problems.

Kazuo Kawasaki and Takahisa Hattori
Fuji Electric Company, Ltd.

4 DR for electronic machinery (short lead times)

INTRODUCTION

Japan's vending goods market has grown to over ¥4 trillion (US $40 billion) and continues to expand with an ever-greater variety of merchandise. This has created new challenges in vending machine development. In response, manufacturers are using advanced electronics technologies to build vending machines with more sophisticated mechanisms and controls.

Vending machine development at Fuji Electric is market driven, stressing close and fast-paced teamwork between Production and Sales. We are working as hard as anyone toward new products that address market demands and fully satisfy customers.

DR ISSUES AND OPPORTUNITIES

Our latest models feature mixed hot and cold selections for year-round use, a wider variety of merchandise, updated styling, and larger vending capacity. In the interest of shorter lead times, we depend heavily on the latest technologies for ensuring quality and reliability. We are already working on improvements in our tests for function, durability, refrigeration and heating capacity, motion control, and food hygiene, along with inspections of purchased parts and production line tests.

With this increasing emphasis on quality assurance, Fuji has recently introduced DR for application at the product design and prototype test stages.

ORGANIZING DR WITHIN THE COMPANY

Lead time reduction efforts have led us to clarify department responsibilities for each DR step. Our DR promotion project included participants from Design, Manufacturing, Production Engineering, and QA, who put together a DR schedule plan that has seen good results.

DR SEQUENCE

Our DR program includes five elements: DR-0 (planning), DR-1 (general design), DR-2 (design prototype), DR-3 (pilot build), and DR-4 (customer feedback). In each case the review committee evaluates the design against customer quality requirements (see Figure 4-1).

METHODS AND TECHNIQUES

DEVELOPMENT MANAGEMENT

We use Development Management Charts to highlight current project information, particularly during the prototype build and test. The charts show project schedules, available resources, and DR results. We also display DR committee rosters and schedules for critical components well in advance (see Figure 4-2).

DR MANAGEMENT

After spelling out the review items for each DR meeting, we categorize supporting documents so we can keep track of them. The resulting DR Management Information Diagram (see Figure 4-3) serves as a progress report to the DR committees at the start of each review.

MARKET SURVEYS

To narrow the gap between end users and producers, we travel to our different sales regions to interview customers. Their feedback then plays a key role in planning new products.

QUALITY FUNCTION DEPLOYMENT

We developed a Market-Driven Quality Deployment Matrix to standardize how we handle customer requests and comments. It helps ensure that market considerations drive every step in the product development cycle (see Figure 4-4).

To help speed up quality deployment for key mechanisms, we created a Quality Function Deployment Chart. Design, Production Engineering, Manufacturing, QA, and Sales all use this chart to check the completeness of design drawings at each stage. We also devised and scheduled reliability tests using the FTA (fault tree analysis) and FMEA (failure mode and effects analysis) methods. Finally, we have sped up quality deployment for critical control charts (see Figures 4-5, 4-6, and 4-7).

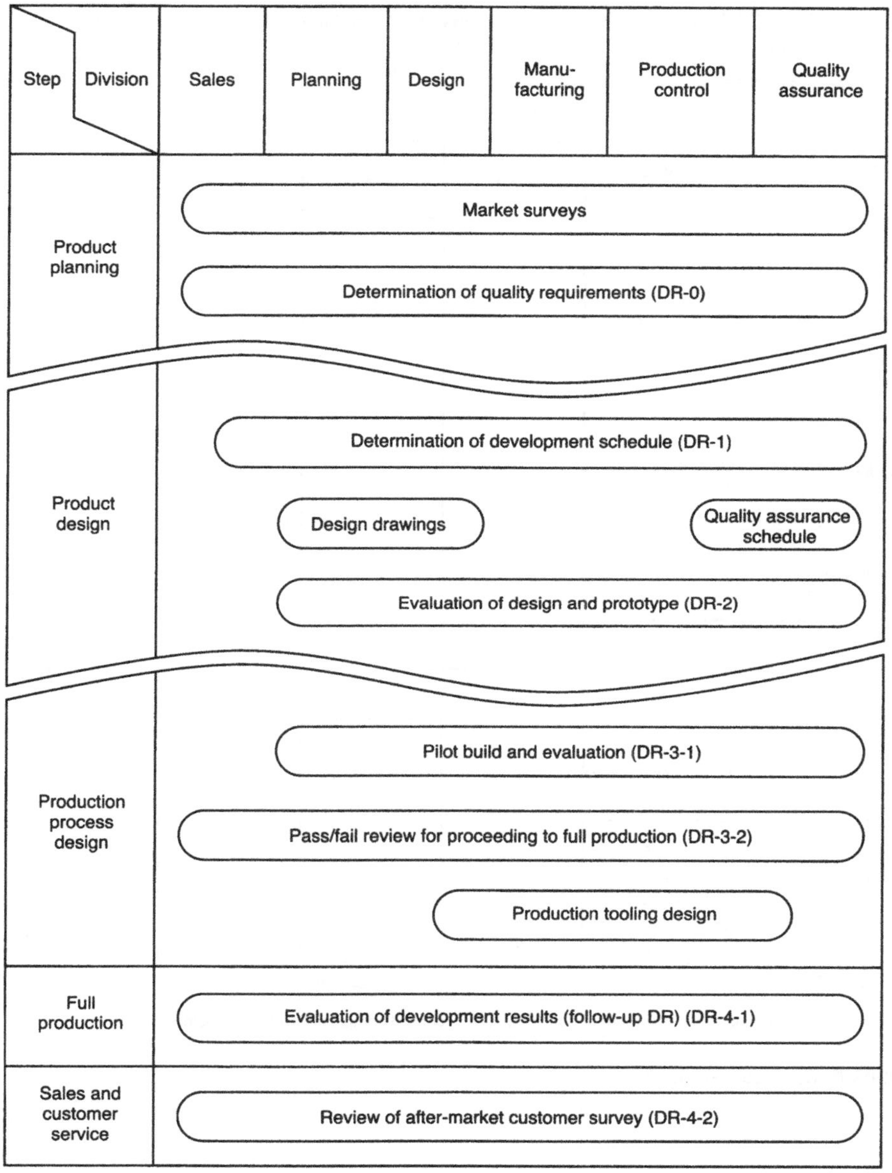

Step / Division	Sales	Planning	Design	Manu-facturing	Production control	Quality assurance
Product planning	Market surveys Determination of quality requirements (DR-0)					
Product design	Determination of development schedule (DR-1) Design drawings Quality assurance schedule Evaluation of design and prototype (DR-2)					
Production process design	Pilot build and evaluation (DR-3-1) Pass/fail review for proceeding to full production (DR-3-2) Production tooling design					
Full production	Evaluation of development results (follow-up DR) (DR-4-1)					
Sales and customer service	Review of after-market customer survey (DR-4-2)					

FIGURE 4-1. Product Quality Assurance System

Development Management Chart	PMS (see note)	Development category	Development project no.	DR registration no.

No.	Item		Schedule	Month	Month	Month	Month
1	Project schedule		Planned				
			Actual				
2	DR schedule (enter document no.)		Planned				
			Actual				
3	Design schedule		Planned				
			Actual				
4	Available resources		Planned				
			Actual				
5	Sales plans						
6	DR results		Actual				
7	Component name:	DR members	Item				
Critical component			Actual				
			Planned				
			Actual				
			Document				

Note:PMS (Program Module System) is a method of development ranking based on technical complexity and other factors.

FIGURE 4-2. Development Management Chart

QUALITY CHECK SHEETS

We created the Quality Check Sheet for DR Items to make sure we do not overlook any past abnormalities or other relevant items for a given mechanism. The QA department also uses these check sheets regularly to confirm the accuracy and completeness of the work at every stage (see Figure 4-8). Furthermore, we confirm these checks at every DR meeting, with the result that the problems in one stage are not carried over to the next stage.

PASS/FAIL EVALUATION STANDARDS

We established a computerized system to compare qualitative factors such as user friendliness and serviceability to market benchmarks (see Figure 4-9).

QUALITY PREDICTION METHODS

Once a prototype has been built, each newly found problem causes considerable delays, since opportunities for improvement are fewer and fewer, so right from the concept stage, we seek to predict such problems before they surface. FTA, FMEA, and simulation exercises all help us identify and carry out needed countermeasures as early in the project as possible.

DR FORMATS

To better align DR activities with the various development phases and steps, we have established both general and mini formats. They differ both in who is involved and in what they evaluate.

GENERAL FORMAT (DR)

Reviews DR-0 through DR-3 fall into this category, which is what we normally refer to as DR. Meetings focus on the conversion of customer requirements into design quality characteristics, in terms of both product and process. Committee members look not only at manufacturing processes, but also at maintenance and services. They propose improvements and check for completeness at each stage, sometimes directing that a process be totally revamped or cut out. All DR decisions must be approved at the project executive level.

MINI FORMAT (MDR)

Like DR, this is a formal review, but more frequent and technically focused. Specialists from appropriate departments run periodic quality checks on design drawings, prototypes and actual products throughout development. Much of the detailed investigation behind DR decisions originates in MDR.

FOLLOW-UP DR

The customer feedback review (DR-4) is essentially a follow-up session. We evaluate both the final product and the development project itself. The committee assesses the project's strengths and weaknesses in light of available marketing information and QCD constraints. It then channels its findings into recommendations for the next generation of products. Supporting documents include product development activity charts and three-dimensional matrices for product/project evaluation (see Figure 4-10).

Vending Machine DR Management Information Diagram

Model year:	Machine model:		
BY	Client:	Type:	

Essential documents

General documents

	New product proposals		Development decision		Development schedule		Design drawings
Stage	Development proposal presentations	Technical studies	Planning review (DR-0)	Development order	Establishment of development policy and schedule	Discussion and final revision of development schedule	Design drawing review (DR-1-2)
Business planning	001 Presentation of marketing proposals		009 Strategic planning committee meeting minutes	101 Marketing proposals and development order			121 Design concept drawings
Engineering, production, logistics		002 Pricing guidelines	010 Minutes of development meeting 011 Minutes of development review meeting	102 List of development items	104 Development schedule chart 105 Minutes of cost review meeting		122 Development management chart, PMS in ranks A and B only
		003 Customer feedback 004 Design concept drawings	012 Minutes of concept presentation meeting	103 Planning manual B 103-I Development (design) policy manual	106 Development project index 107 Product design planning manual	116 Minutes of DR-1-1 meeting 117 Quality deployment table	123 Design drawings 124 Design know-how check sheet (one-point check sheet) 201 D 202

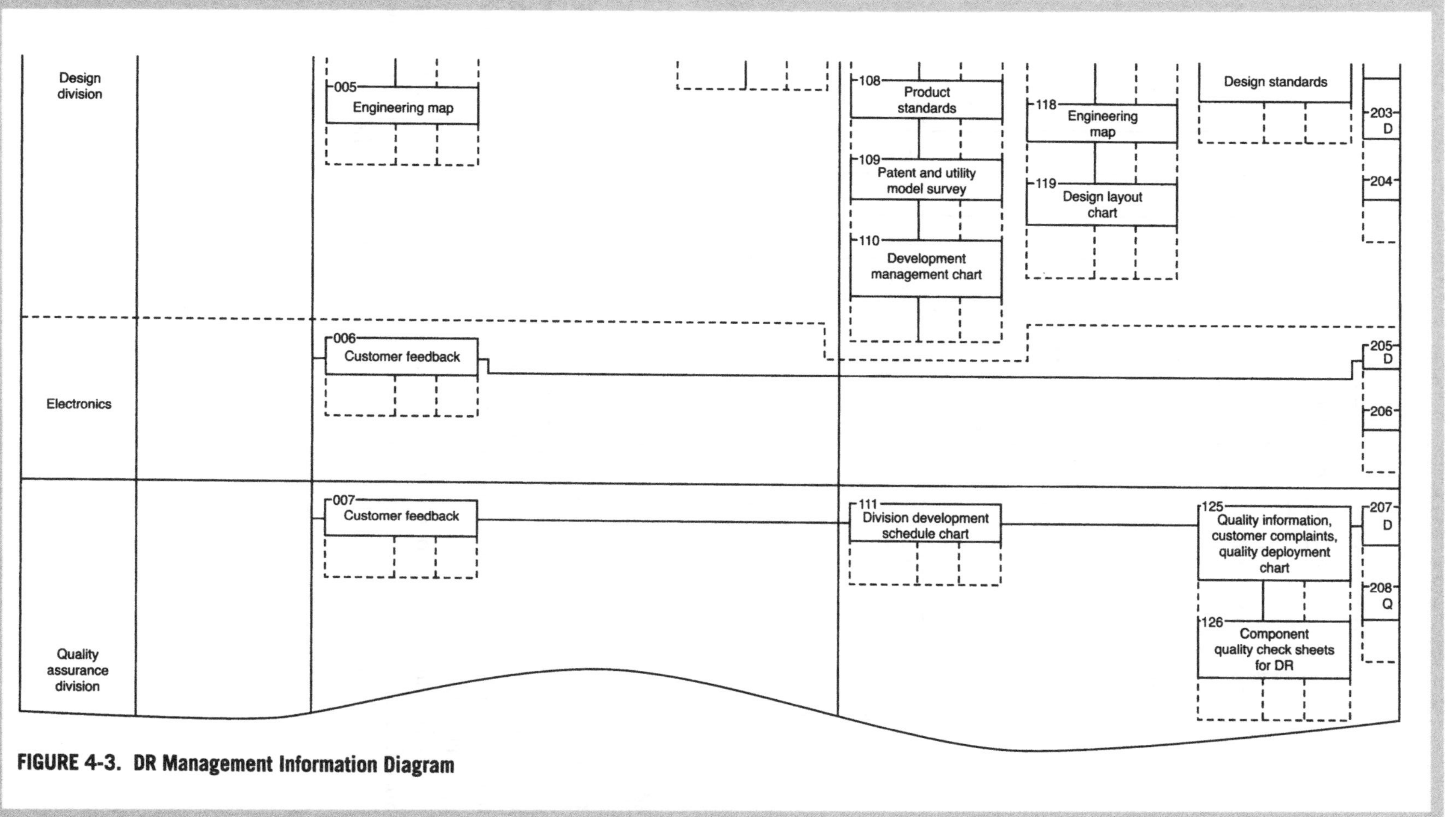

FIGURE 4-3. DR Management Information Diagram

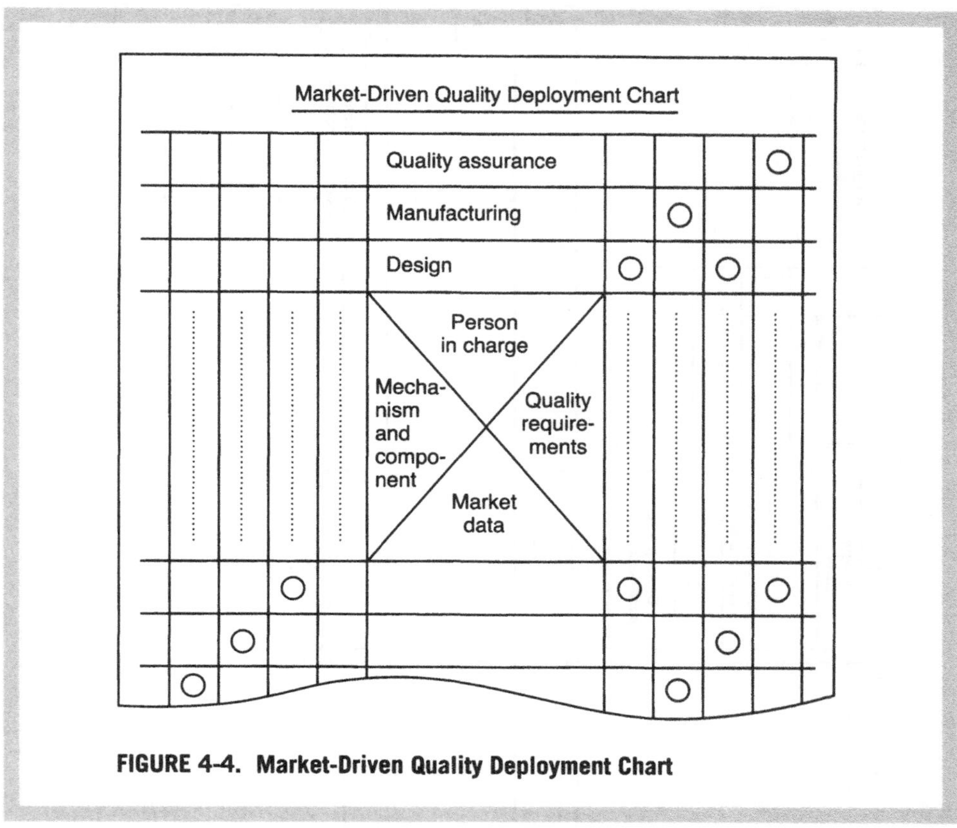

FIGURE 4-4. Market-Driven Quality Deployment Chart

MAKING DR EFFECTIVE

The DR committee has drawn up a standards manual for vending machine quality characteristics and key functions. It accounts for environmental conditions such as temperature, humidity, rain, vibration, wear and tear, sunlight, dust, and noise. The committee has also been verifying DR results and conducting follow-up reliability tests.

Each year we look to improve reliability testing with better equipment. Specific areas of interest are automated evaluation of certain parts, mechanisms, and whole units, and a centralized monitoring system for DR verification.

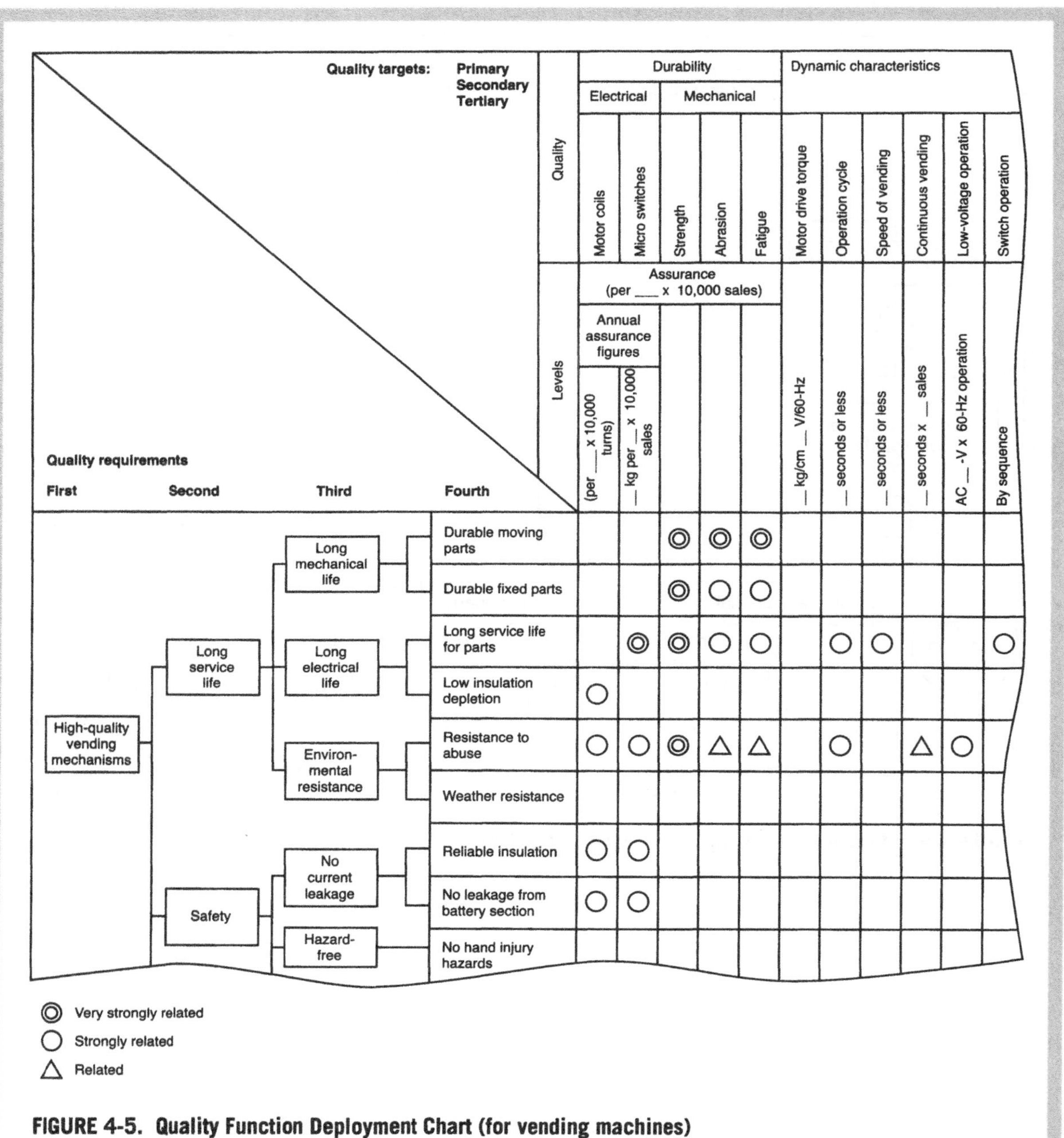

FIGURE 4-5. Quality Function Deployment Chart (for vending machines)

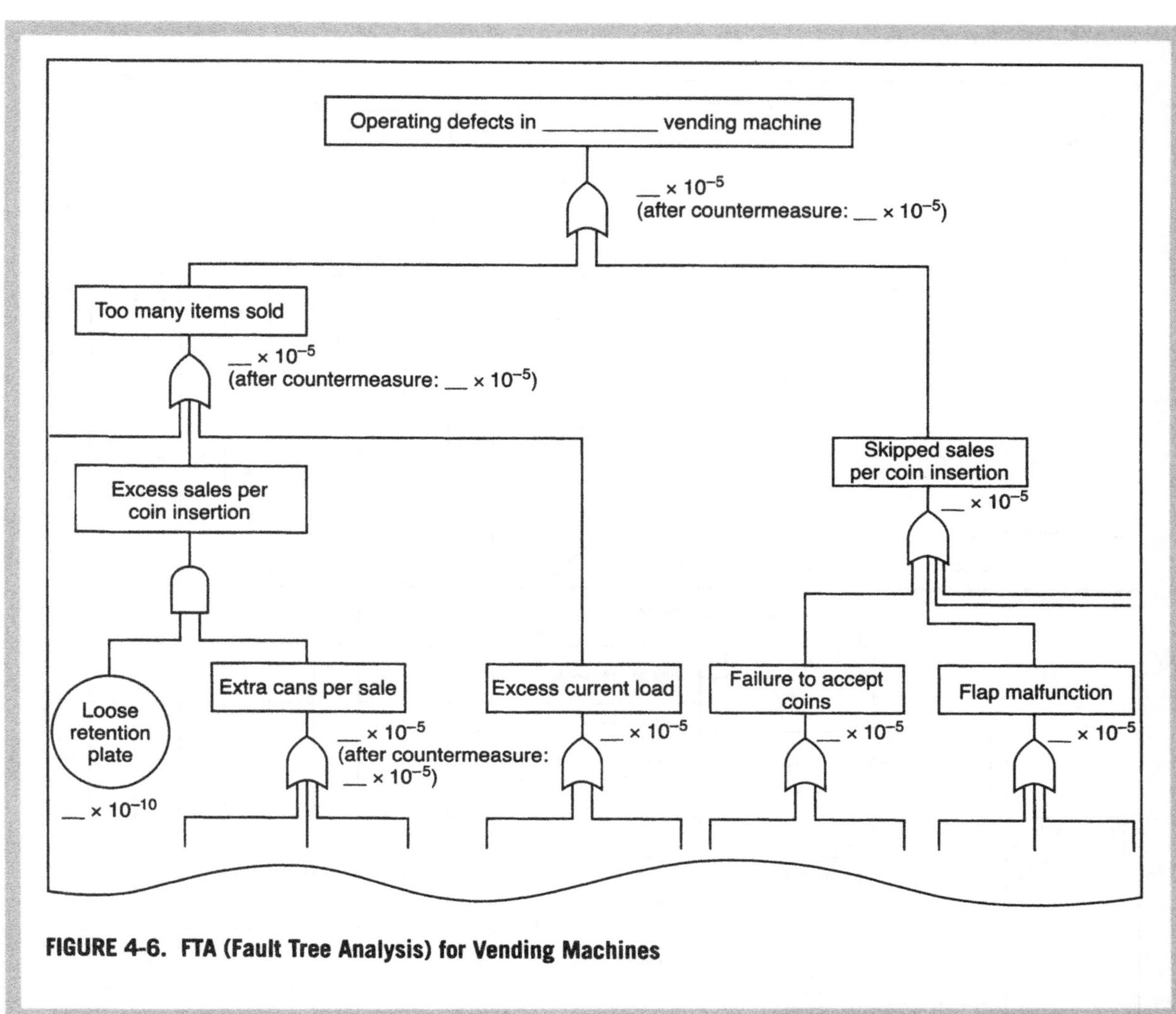

FIGURE 4-6. FTA (Fault Tree Analysis) for Vending Machines

BENEFITS OF DR

Our emphasis on starting DR for new products as early as possible has enabled us to identify and solve problems at the source. In turn, the company is taking on ever larger and more complex projects without falling into disarray and confusion.

Two of the more tangible benefits are fewer abnormalities during pilot build (Figure 4-11) and fewer employee-hours lost during production startup (Figure 4-12).

DR has increased our collective quality awareness while helping us better exploit emerging technologies. Both these trends have been key ingredients in our company's growth.

PLANS FOR THE FUTURE

Looking forward, we plan to apply DR even more thoroughly at the front end of product development. Our goal is always to bring each phase—planning, design, prototype and pilot build, production, and marketing—into alignment with customer needs, delivering quality products in a timely manner.

FMEA for _______ conveyor-type vending machines

No.	Part	Function	Failure mode	Possible causes
1	Door switch	1. Prevents conveyor from operating when loading door is open (safety cover, restricted loading position)	1-1. Switch does not operate	1-1-1. Incorrect switch position 1-1-2. Switch turned by actuator 1-1-3. Defective switch 1-1-4. Warped actuator
2	Conveyor motor	1. Rotates product shelf	1-1. Unable to rotate	1-1-1. Broken coil 1-1-2. Layer short circuit 1-1-3. Brake malfunction 1-1-4. Mechanical lock
		2. Stops conveyor at specified positions	2-1. Defective brake (overrun)	2-1-1. Broken coil (for brake) 2-1-2. Clearance from contact surface 2-1-3. Open diode
3	Shelf sensor switch	1. Detects shelf position 2. Stops shelf at specified position 3. Executes read timing for shelf codes and sold-out switches	Device condition 1-1. Remains on	1-1-1. Defective switch 1-1-2. Loose shelf card 1-1-3. Sensor lever does not reach
			1-2. Remains off	1-2-1. Defective switch 1-2-2. Loose spring 1-2-3. Defective lever return
			1-3. Chattering	1-3-1. Warped shelf 1-3-2. Defective card setting 1-3-3. Shelf is too loose 1-3-4. Defective adjustment a. Pushed in too far b. Incorrect gap setting for lever
4	Shelf code switch	1. Shelf selection no. memory	1-1. Remains on 1-2. Remains off 1-3. Chattering	Same as above
5	Sold out switch	1. Detects presence/absence of products on shelf	1-1. ON (product is on shelf)	1-1-1. Warped actuator 1-1-2. Incorrect switch setting 1-1-3. Defective switch
			1-2. OFF (no product on shelf)	1-2-1. Loose spring 1-2-2. Lever malfunction (defective lever return) 1-2-3. Defective switch

FIGURE 4-7. FMEA (Failure Mode and Effects Analysis) for Conveyor-Type Vending Machines

Effects		Failure detection method	Response	Failure severity	Comments
Parts	System				
	Unable to operate (cannot rotate)		1-1-1. Adjust switch 1-1-2. Replace switch 1-1-3. Change switch position	III	
1-1-1. 1-1-2. Weld relay contacts 1-1-3.	1-1. Unable to operate (all sold out) Same as above	1-1. 75 73	Replace motor	II →	Check motor compatibility (operability)
		1-1. 75 1-2. 75	Replace switch	II →	Difficult replacement
None	Same as above	1-3. 77	Adjust	III	
Same as above	Incorrect selection (door opens to wrong product)	Set remaining number Diagnose problem by comparing shelf sensor cards	Replace switch	II →	Difficult replacement
	1-1. Door opens to empty shelf compartment 1-2. Unable to operate (reads as empty)	(Check confirmation technique) Push setting switch and recheck	Replace (switch actuator) Adjust	III	

FIGURE 4-7. (cont'd.)

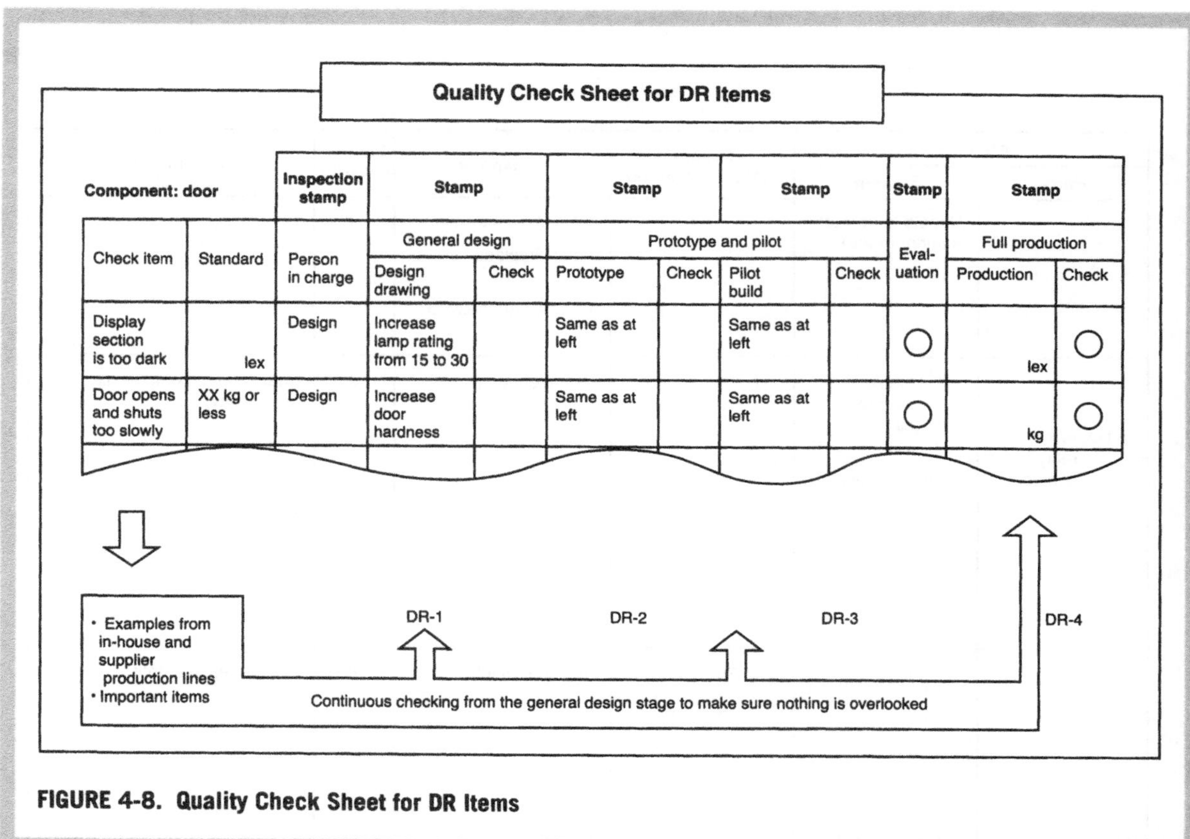

Quality Check Sheet for DR Items

Component: door		Inspection stamp	Stamp		Stamp		Stamp		Stamp	Stamp	
			General design		Prototype and pilot					Full production	
Check item	Standard	Person in charge	Design drawing	Check	Prototype	Check	Pilot build	Check	Eval-uation	Production	Check
Display section is too dark	lex	Design	Increase lamp rating from 15 to 30		Same as at left		Same as at left		○	lex	○
Door opens and shuts too slowly	XX kg or less	Design	Increase door hardness		Same as at left		Same as at left		○	kg	○

FIGURE 4-8. Quality Check Sheet for DR Items

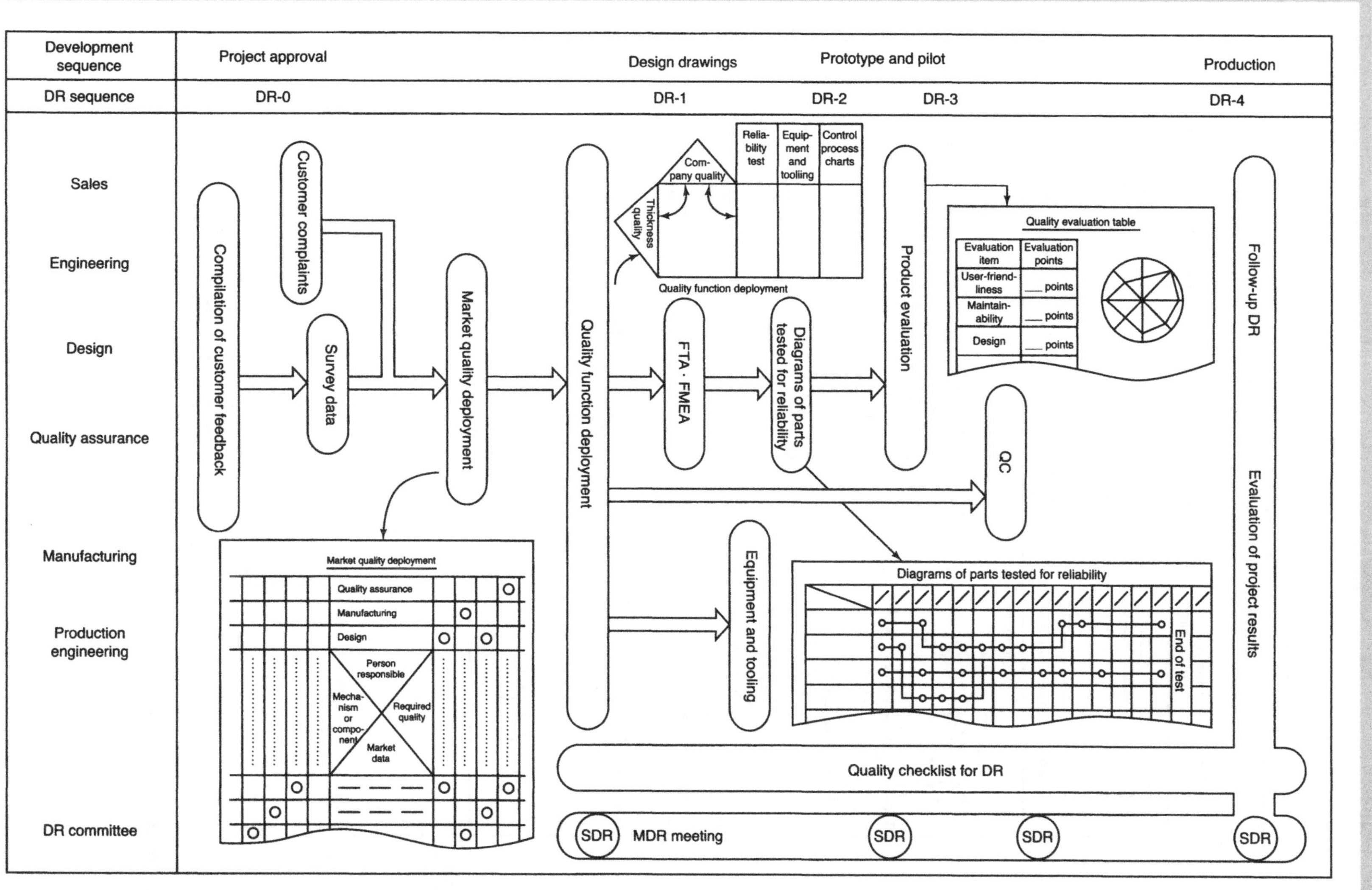

FIGURE 4-9. Design and Prototype Evaluation System

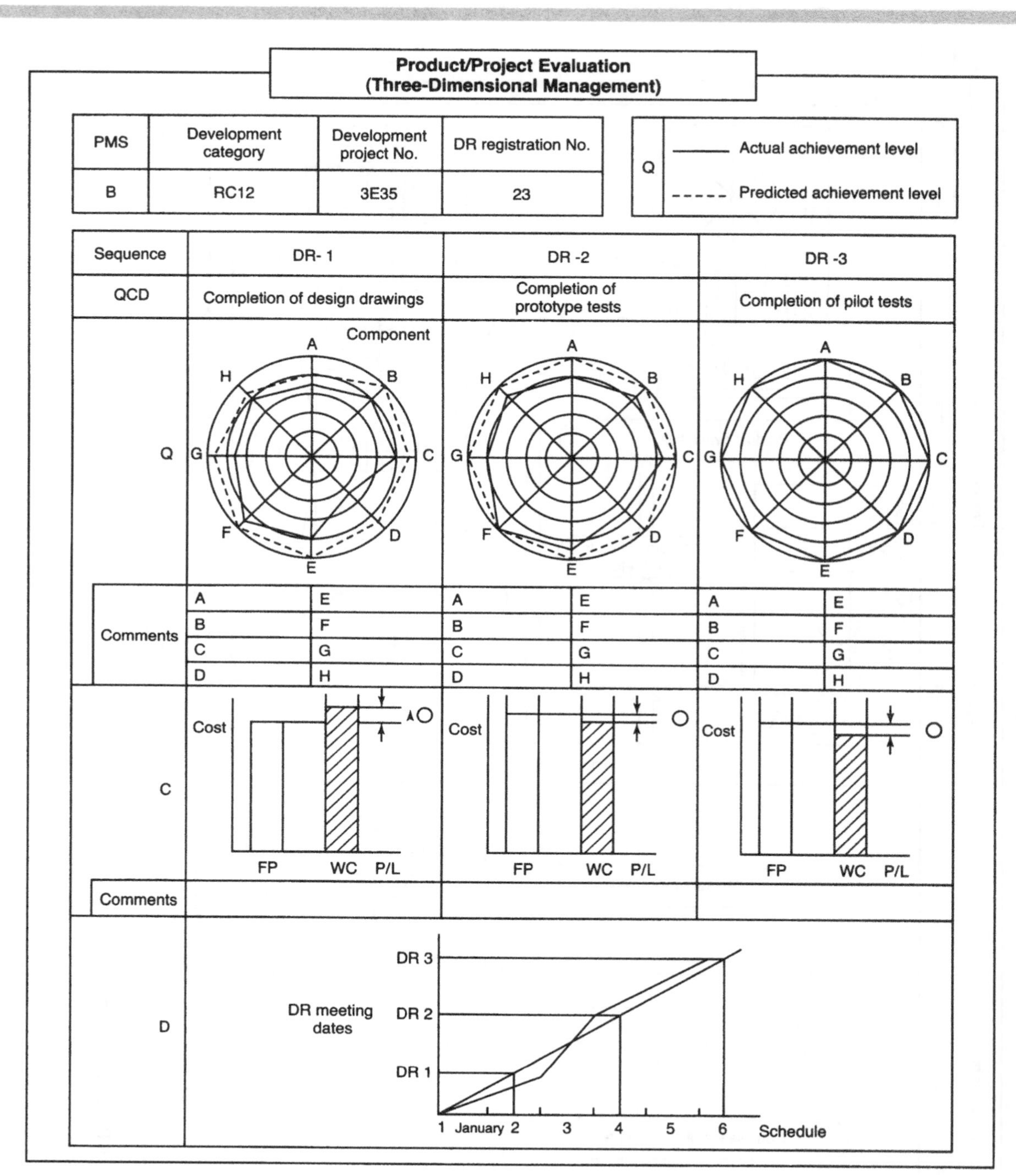

FIGURE 4-10. Product/Project Evaluation (Three-Dimensional Management)

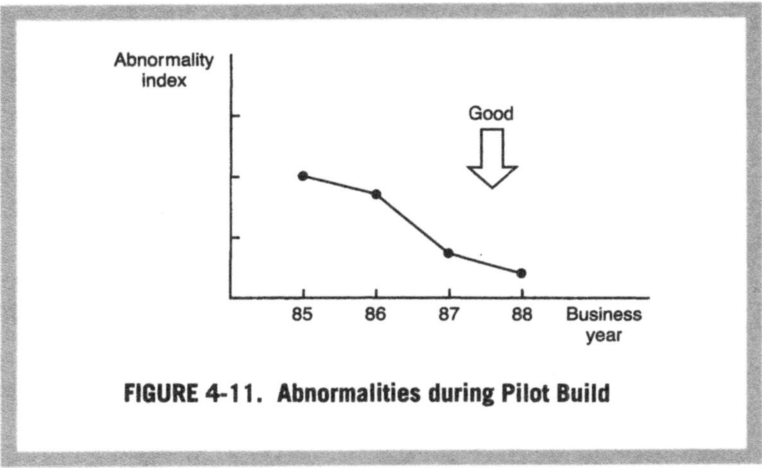

FIGURE 4-11. Abnormalities during Pilot Build

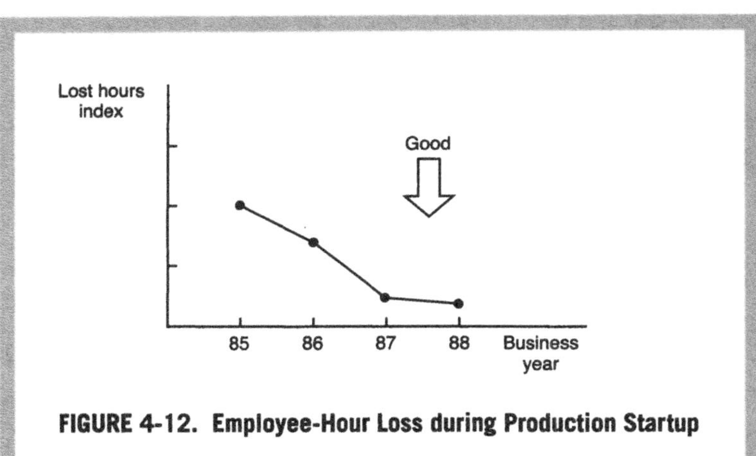

FIGURE 4-12. Employee-Hour Loss during Production Startup

Hiroshi Wada
Matsushita Electric Industrial Company, Ltd.

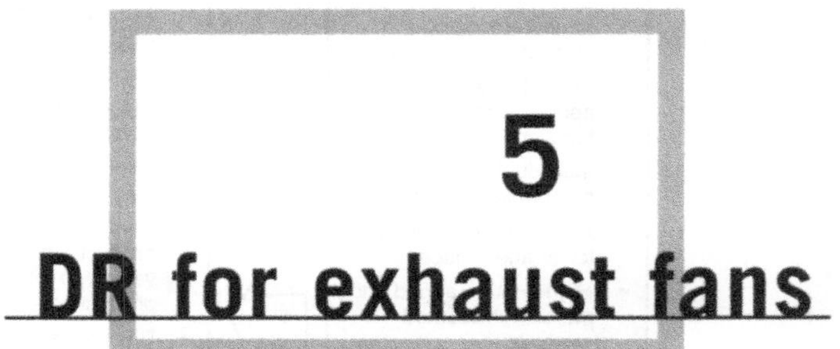

5 DR for exhaust fans

(consumer products)

INTRODUCTION

To keep up with diversifying market needs, our company must create appealing products with high reliability. Today's customers demand nothing less than products they can count on *all the time*.

We believe that the foundation of quality assurance is summed up in the motto "Customer satisfaction comes first." TQC activities begin at the earliest stages of product development, where we base design quality characteristics on customer requirements. As can be seen in Figure 5-1, design quality covers a wide range of subjects at Matsushita.

DR ISSUES AND OPPORTUNITIES

Market surveys indicate that about 70 percent of product quality problems are design related. That figure increases to 90 percent if you include problems that could have been avoided during the product design phase through stricter quality control. A comprehensive DR program, using experts from a broad knowledge base, can help companies minimize these problems. Predictive techniques spot potential failure modes, and thorough testing verifies that any such weaknesses have been designed out.

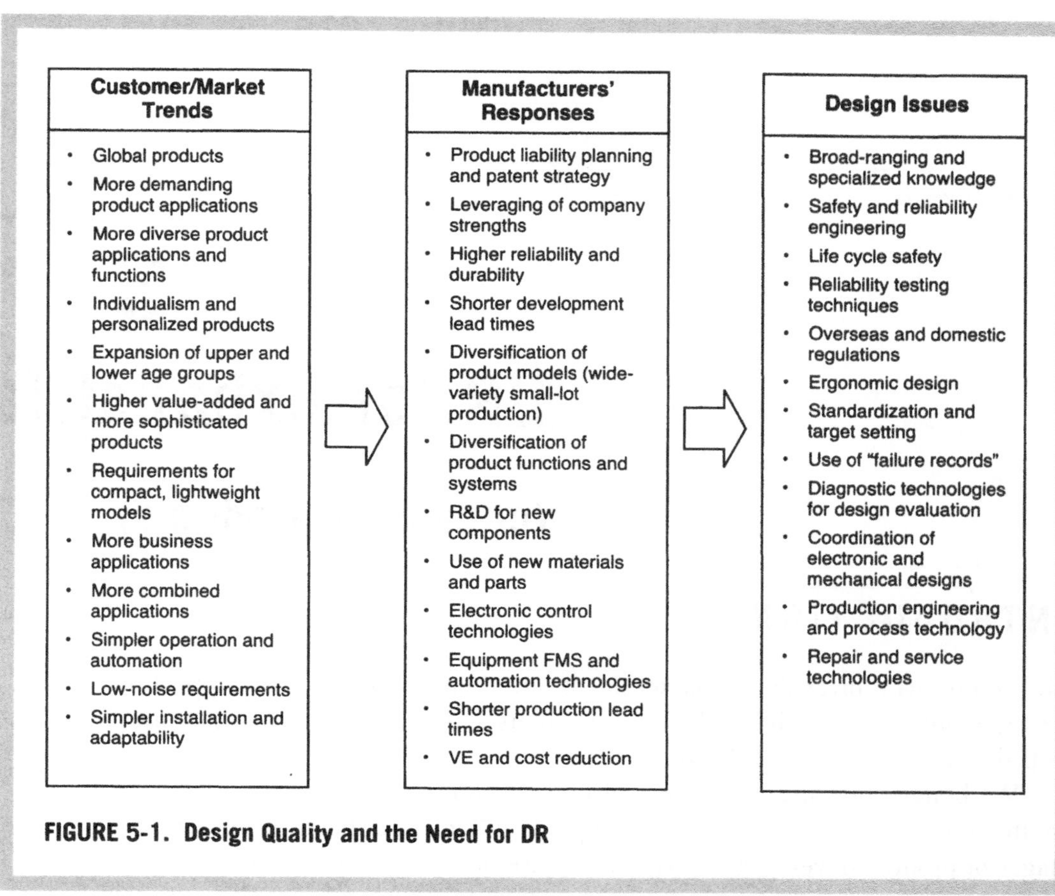

Customer/Market Trends
Global products
More demanding product applications
More diverse product applications and functions
Individualism and personalized products
Expansion of upper and lower age groups
Higher value-added and more sophisticated products
Requirements for compact, lightweight models
More business applications
More combined applications
Simpler operation and automation
Low-noise requirements
Simpler installation and adaptability
Manufacturers' Responses
Product liability planning and patent strategy
Leveraging of company strengths
Higher reliability and durability
Shorter development lead times
Diversification of product models (wide-variety small-lot production)
Diversification of product functions and systems
R&D for new components
Use of new materials and parts
Electronic control technologies
Equipment FMS and automation technologies
Shorter production lead times
VE and cost reduction
Design Issues
Broad-ranging and specialized knowledge
Safety and reliability engineering
Life cycle safety
Reliability testing techniques
Overseas and domestic regulations
Ergonomic design
Standardization and target setting
Use of "failure records"
Diagnostic technologies for design evaluation
Coordination of electronic and mechanical designs
Production engineering and process technology
Repair and service technologies

FIGURE 5-1. Design Quality and the Need for DR

ORGANIZING DR WITHIN THE COMPANY

Our product line runs from consumer electronics items such as VCRs, TVs, and air conditioners to fax machines and industrial robots. We thus have organized DR into independent subprograms by product line, allowing subsidiaries to address their own development needs and capabilities.

Nevertheless, all the subprograms have certain things in common:

- Use of compiled quality data to keep problems from recurring
- Effective use of FMEA, FTA, and other predictive techniques
- Thorough product review system (checking from the user's perspective)
- Linkage of DR with the AQ (action quality) system, whereby division chiefs must confirm product quality at each stage of development.

The product in this case study is an exhaust fan used in both homes and businesses. You will see how DR was applied and what impact it made.

INTRODUCING DR

We did not start DR in a vacuum. Engineering had already instituted meetings during prototype build to check drawings, study prototype proposals, perform FMEA, and even conduct design reviews. However, we lacked a system for tying together the various management and engineering tasks between finalizing the design and issuing the official drawings. These are the improvements we made:

- Identified and applied the best DR methods for reviewing prototypes
- Required follow-up on each problem to prevent recurrence
- Kept all DR source documents and findings on file to accumulate technical data
- Built in more preparation time ahead of DR activities to increase their efficiency
- Emphasized verification through testing and review of test results
- Established strict design approval standards for proceeding to pilot build

K-DR

Recognizing DR's importance in ensuring quality and reliability, department staff instituted the K-DR System. "K" is the first letter in both the Japanese word for "exhaust fan" and the name of the manufacturing facility (the Kasugai plant). The sense of ownership in this system has boosted interest in making DR work, as well as department morale.

K-DR is not a specific type of review, but rather an umbrella term covering all our DR activities for exhaust fan development.

DR SEQUENCE

Figure 5-2 shows where DR fits in. The development project begins with Marketing's final design decisions and specifications. K-DR includes S-H review, design FMEA, review of test results, the first product review, and the drawing review before the product is approved for transfer to production. After production process design and pilot build, there are then two more product reviews before the full production stage.

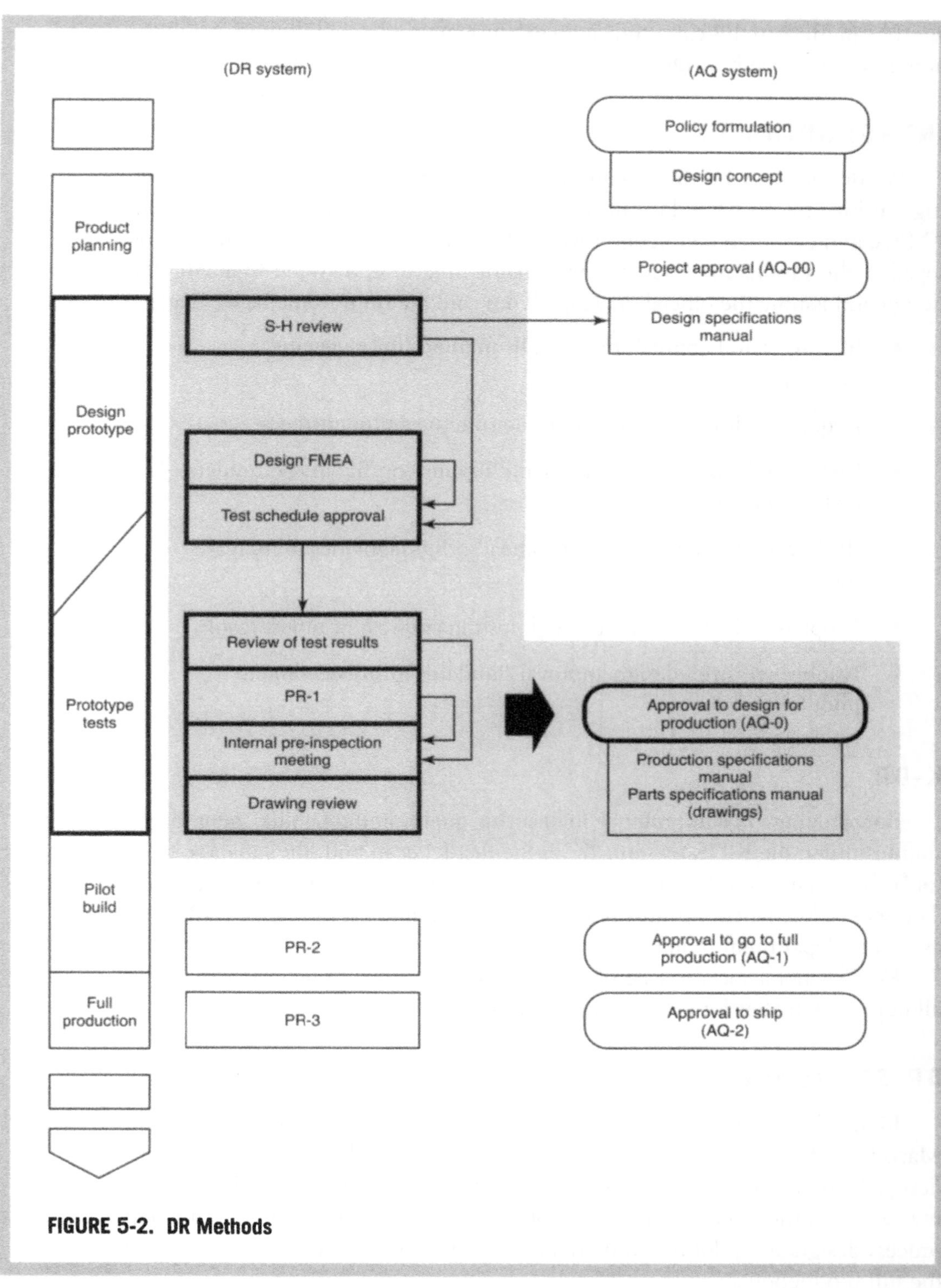

FIGURE 5-2. DR Methods

USE OF QUALITY DATA

Information from market studies and surveys, manufacturing processes, and various experiments and simulations can be used to uncover problems and prevent their recurrence. That is why the exhaust fan department keeps all this information on file for ready access.

In fact, case study records from all departments are stored on our computer network for companywide access as technical and quality-related data. People can retrieve and print data using search keywords connected with parts, materials, failure modes, or stress factors. This QUICS (quality information control system) database is oriented primarily toward design, testing, and DR applications (Figure 5-3).

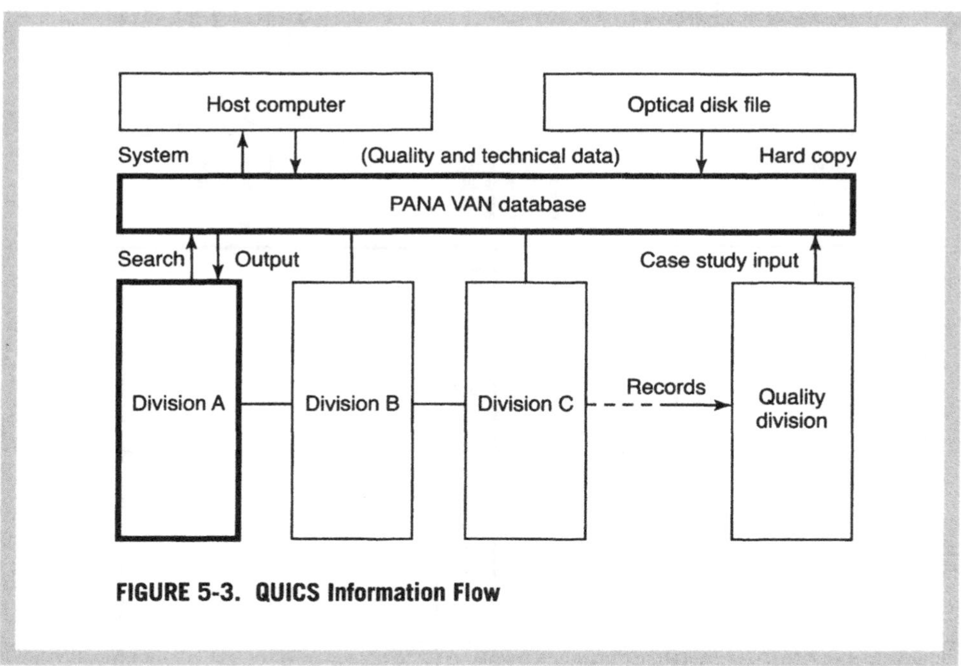

FIGURE 5-3. QUICS Information Flow

We put QUICS to work at the front end of new product planning. Field experience and production statistics for previous exhaust fan models help us set quality targets for a well-defined project. The database also allows us to review completed projects from other parts of the company, looking for design precedents and avoiding duplicate effort. Figure 5-4 shows the form we use for incorporating QUICS data into new product design.

New Product Planning Form (Quality Targets)	Name: (Part No.:)	Rank	. .	. .	. .

	Results	Pareto chart	Defects	Preventive measures
Quality of previous and similar models	Market Sales volume No. of defects % 			
	Process Production yield Defects %			
QUICS data	Item	Failure mode	Stress factor	Preventive measures for new products

	Model series	Market	Process	
Quality targets				
	Target	Improvement		
Improvements needed to achieve targets				

Applicable standards and regulations			Item	Regulated value	Standard value
	Technical standards for parts used				
	Technical standards for electrical equipment				
	Technical standards for construction equipment				
	Fire hazard assessments				

FIGURE 5-4. Use of QUICS Data

S-H REVIEW

This method was originally developed to evaluate product safety at the concept stage. S-H stands for "soft-hard," contrasting a product's actual uses with its physical structure and functions. It forces us to design for safety (or any other property) in terms of real-world conditions.

HOW IT WORKS

The S-H method has enhanced our DR efforts. It not only allows designers to check for safety, but also brings in other departments (such as Customer Service and QA) for evaluation in depth. We use two-dimensional charts to list the various "soft" and "hard" factors, as well as quality matrixes and diagrams and another FMEA-related chart.

The S-H Review is our first K-DR meeting, where we begin drafting exhaust fan design specifications. Starting with the "S" half of the study, we take the perspective of potential users and look into possibilities for careless misuse beyond normal wear and tear.

For "H" we make a detailed list of component safety functions. We investigate the potential for function loss due to malfunction or deterioration over each component's estimated service life, then apply the results to product structural safety design.

When S and H factors overlap (which shows up on the matrix), that warns us that someone may get hurt by doing the wrong thing to the wrong part of the product. We conduct special studies to evaluate the risk associated with such overlaps, the effect on overall product safety, and the degree of difficulty in recognizing abnormal conditions.

HOW IT HELPS

Using the S-H method prior to detailed design offers these advantages.

- Categorizing the different ways a product has been used in the field makes it easier to identify quality requirements and to compile resource data.
- Even when general safety regulations or standards exist, they may not adequately address every product use situation (S factors). The S-H review helps fill in those gaps.
- Studying component safety functions enables us to find out in advance whether backup systems will be necessary and/or feasible as a safety measure for potential breakdowns.

In short, we gain a clear and detailed understanding of applicable safety requirements well in advance, which serves our ultimate goal of guaranteeing a safe product by building it that way. For the same reason, we also use S-H in product evaluation after the design is complete. Figure 5-5 shows an example of S-H applied to exhaust fan design.

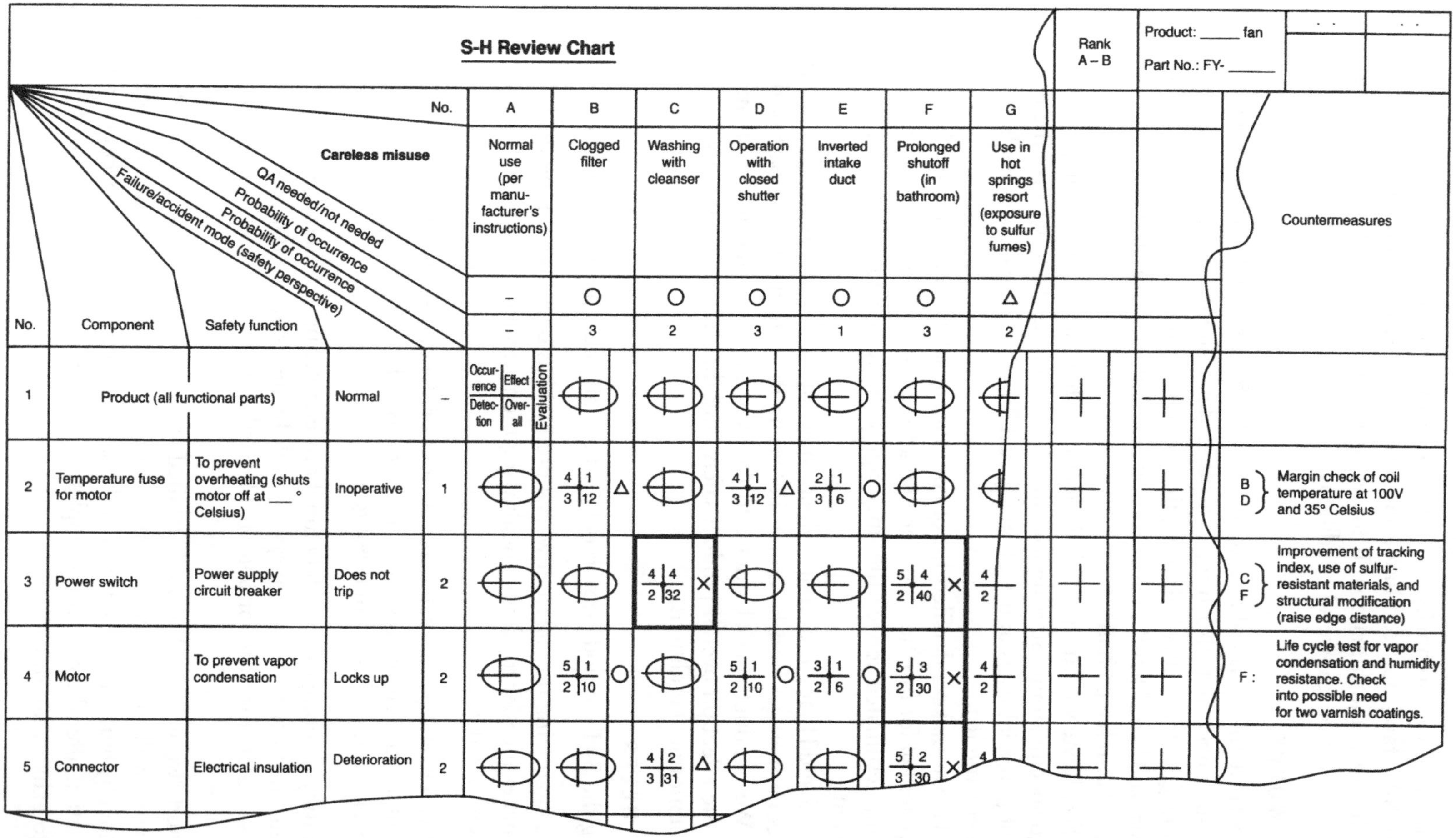

S-H Review Chart

Product: _____ fan
Part No.: FY- ______

No.	Component	Safety function	Failure/accident mode (safety perspective)	No.	A	B	C	D	E	F	G	Rank A – B		Countermeasures
			Careless misuse		Normal use (per manu-facturer's instructions)	Clogged filter	Washing with cleanser	Operation with closed shutter	Inverted intake duct	Prolonged shutoff (in bathroom)	Use in hot springs resort (exposure to sulfur fumes)			
			QA needed/not needed		–	○	○	○	○	○	△			
			Probability of occurrence		–	3	2	3	1	3	2			
1	Product (all functional parts)		Normal	–	Occur-rence, Effect / Detec-tion, Over-all; Evaluation	⊕	⊕	⊕	⊕	⊕	⊕	+	+	
2	Temperature fuse for motor	To prevent overheating (shuts motor off at ___ ° Celsius)	Inoperative	1	⊕	4, 1 / 3, 12 △	⊕	4, 1 / 3, 12 △	2, 1 / 3, 6 ○	⊕	⊕	+	+	B, D } Margin check of coil temperature at 100V and 35° Celsius
3	Power switch	Power supply circuit breaker	Does not trip	2	⊕	⊕	4, 4 / 2, 32 ×	⊕	⊕	5, 4 / 2, 40 ×	4 / 2	+	+	C, F } Improvement of tracking index, use of sulfur-resistant materials, and structural modification (raise edge distance)
4	Motor	To prevent vapor condensation	Locks up	2	⊕	5, 1 / 2, 10 ○	⊕	5, 1 / 2, 10 ○	3, 1 / 2, 6 ○	5, 3 / 2, 30 ×	4 / 2	+	+	F : Life cycle test for vapor condensation and humidity resistance. Check into possible need for two varnish coatings.
5	Connector	Electrical insulation	Deterioration	2	⊕	⊕	4, 2 / 3, 31 △	⊕	⊕	5, 2 / 3, 30 ×	4	+	+	

FIGURE 5-5. S-H Method Example

S-H ANALYSIS TOOLS

We use a checklist (as in Figure 5-6) and other means to make sure that our lists of S and H factors are complete and well organized. This checklist is also useful for planning the collection of documents.

S Factor Analysis Table (for careless misuse)		Rank A – B	Product: ________ fan Part no.: FY- ________		. .	. .
Careless misuse checklist		Description		Pass/fail	Reason for rejection	
Category	Item					
Per-formance-related	• Overload • Idle operation • Insufficient power • Continuous operation (switch left on)	Filter 100% clogged Left in bathroom for a long time with the fan shut off		○ ○		
User-related	• Instructions not followed in the correct order • Lid or door left open (or closed) • Use of nonstandard model (or material) • Deviation from design environmental conditions • Air inlet chamber installed wrong • Installed in reverse direction	Operation with shutter closed Operation in hot, humid environment Exhaust duct installed backwards		○ × ○	Environment test (45° Celsius, 95% humidity)	

H Factor Analysis Table (product safety function)		Rank A – B	Product: ________ fan Part No.: FY- ________	. .	. .
No.	Component	Safety function		Comments • Display for user • Recovery method	
		Hazardous condition	Automatic response		
1 2 3	Motor temperature fuse Power switch Motor	When coil starts over-heating (improper operation) (due to user operation)	Motor shuts off Power supply circuit breaker	Replace motor	

FIGURE 5-6. S-H Documents

Of course all of these DR tools are only as effective as we make them. The checklists had been fairly generic, requiring revision of some terms to apply to product development. We thus developed the Careless Misuse Checklist shown in Figure 5-6.

FMEA APPLIED TO DESIGN

FMEA (failure mode and effects analysis) is an effective DR tool for reliability studies during the design phase. We use it to examine the intended function of new mechanisms, parts, and materials, and to plan improvements where needed. In development, we use design FMEA to plan operational countermeasures. Figure 5-7 shows an example of FMEA for exhaust fan design.

RANKING PRODUCT DEVELOPMENT PROJECTS

Product rankings of A, B, or C were once based solely on certain technical criteria, but we now factor in a market perspective:

- A = Completely new application
- B = Innovative variation on an existing application
- C = No change in application

Examples of "A" products are cordless irons and the world's first automatic breadmakers for household use.

To avoid confusion, we append subscripts to these rankings to indicate whether they are technology-based (subscript T) or application-based (subscript A). In the case of exhaust fans, the S-H review focuses mainly on products ranked B_T or above, while during design FMEA we are concerned with those at or above B_A.

REVIEW OF TEST RESULTS

The central objects of DR evaluation are drawings, prototypes, and test results. Reviewers look particularly for design quality and for related factors such as performance, reliability, durability, and safety.

TEST PREPARATION

When it comes to prototype tests, we must define a number of things in advance: items to be evaluated, testing methods, evaluation criteria, number and duration of tests, people in charge, and equipment needed. Then once tests are complete, the appropriate DR committee reviews the results and proposes countermeasures as required.

Part name: _______ fan (FY - XXX)		Rank B – A	Failure Mode and Effects Analysis Chart		Analysis period: from _______ to _______ / Committee member						／	／	／	Page 3/7
Component		Function	Failure mode	Effect on product	Probable cause	No. of occurrences	Effect rating	Detection rating	Failure rating	Countermeasures		Department in charge	Due date
8	Frame	Holds fan motor	Rust	Motor may fall from frame	Zinc coating is unsatisfactory for rustproofing	2	5	2	20	Change zinc coating thickness from _______ to _______		Engr. Dept. 1	10/18
					Vapor condensation due to inadequate exhaust	3	5	2	30	Confirm with condensation tests		QC	10/21
					Electrical spot corrosion	2	5	2	20	Confirm using saline steam test		"	10/28
			Distortion	Product not attached	Vibration not absorbed by packing material during shipment	3	3	1	9	Check by raising vibration 30% from MIS- _______ level		Engr. Dept. 1	10/12
					Inadequate hardness in motor mounting fixture	3	3	1	9	Add ribs in two places		"	10/18
		Determines path of air flow	Gap	Loss of air flow (insufficient volume)	Spot welding defect	3	3	2	18	Change spot pitch from _______ to _______		"	"

FIGURE 5-7. Design FMEA Example

NEW PRODUCT VALIDATION TABLE

We use a standardized test evaluation sheet called a New Product Validation Table for exhaust fans, like the example shown in Figure 5-8. A department chief, usually one from Engineering, QA, or Manufacturing, must approve every line item before testing can begin. Some of information listed is as follows:

- Test items generated by the S-H review and design FMEA.
- Target quality levels for prototypes. Because only a few are made, these targets must be conservative to allow for greater variability in full production.
- Indication of which test items may or may not be omitted (indicated by circles or X's in the execution column). These decisions are based both on product rank and on cost reduction guidelines.

Similarly, those responsible in each department also review the test results for these same items to clear the product for advancement to the next stage (see Figure 5-8).

Because this New Product Validation Table provides space for three runs of test results (prototype, pilot, initial production), we can compare successive quality levels. This serves as useful historical data concerning product development.

PRODUCT REVIEW

Matsushita has maintained a product review system since 1959 to bolster quality assurance from the customer's perspective. Within each division, an independent office reporting directly to the division chief handles product review activities. The head of this office also chairs the actual meetings.

As the terms imply, product review considers the product as a whole, while design review is internal and technical, looking at the product as the sum of its mechanisms, components, parts, and materials.

The typical exhaust fan customer is a retail store, so the product review office evaluates a prototype for ease of use, versatility, function and performance, ease of installation, serviceability, simplicity, and clarity of user documentation. The more subjective elements are confirmed by market study and survey data from actual users and by competitive comparisons.

PASS/FAIL RATING SYSTEM

Product review items are evaluated as Failed (X), Needs Further Study (triangle), or Passed (square). An "X" is a definite call for countermeasures. All review findings, recommendations, and subsequent actions are reported to the division chief.

PR-1 (the first product review) is held at the prototype stage and PR-2 and PR-3 at the end of pilot build and initial production, respectively (see Figure 5-2). Later meetings follow up on the results of the measures for improvement.

New Product Validation Table	Product: ________ fan	Rank	Environmental conditions	Operating temperature and humidity ranges: From ___ to ___ °C From ___ to ___ % RH	Test schedule approval			Test schedule generation			Page
		B-B			. .	. .	. .	. .	. .	. .	7/15
				Storage temperature and humidity ranges: From ___ to ___ °C From ___ to ___ % RH	Quality dept.	Manu-facturing dept.	Engineer-ing dept.	Section chief	Super-visor	Person respon-sible	

Category	No.	Test items	Test methods (main points)	Evaluation criteria (main points)	Execution	Quality target	Design prototype results	Estimated and measured values / Pass/fail	Pilot build results	Estimated and measured values / Pass/fail	Initial production results	Estimated and measured values / Pass/fail
Reliability	3–1	Storage at high temperature	• ___ ± 3°C ___ % RH T-2302	• Check for cracks or distortion in plastic and coated parts • Insulation resistance > ____ MΩ D-0304-4	●	• Insulation resistance > ___ MΩ	• ___, ___, ___ MΩ					
	3–2	Operation at high temperature	• ___ °C ___ % RH Rated voltage T-2201	• Insulation resistance > ___ MΩ • Check for Tf operation A-0704-2	●	• Coil surface temperature = ___ °C or less	• Insulation resistance > ___ MΩ • Coil surface temperature ___, ___, ___ MΩ					
	3–3	High temperature, high humidity	• ___ ±3°C 95% ±2% RH T-2106	• Insulation resistance > ___ MΩ Voltage resistance 1000V for one minute A-0605-3	○	• Insulation resistance > ___ MΩ						
	3–6	Heat cycle	• ___ °C, ___ °C, XX Cy switchover for up to five minutes T-2202	• Check for cracks or distortion in plastic and coated parts • Insulation resistance > ____ MΩ A-0507-1	●	• Insulation resistance > ___ MΩ	• ___, ___, ___ MΩ • Check for solder cracks					

Revised on: . .	Revised on: . .	Revised on: . .	Quality dept. chief	Manu-facturing dept. chief	Engineer-ing dept. chief	Section chief	Super-visor	Person respon-sible	Section chief	Super-visor	Person respon-sible	Section chief	Super-visor	Person respon-sible
Reason:	Reason:	Reason:	. .	. .	. .	. .	. .	. .	. .	. .	. .	. .	. .	. .

FIGURE 5-8. New Product Validation Table

DRAWING REVIEW

After evaluating design principles, functions, and performance at the prototype stage, we are ready to issue drawings for production. The committees that review these drawings include members from each appropriate department. They use the sequence listed below to make DR as effective as possible.

INTERNAL PRE-INSPECTION MEETING

Before each department begins studying the drawings, specialists from Engineering hold an internal pre-inspection meeting. The agenda is built around these tasks:

- Careful examination of results from past S-H, design FMEA, and product reviews
- Review of the New Product Validation Table and various test data
- Incorporation of quality data, design standards, records of failed experiments, and other valuable information from QUICS
- Particular attention to the experiences of each person involved in order to learn from mistakes as well as successes

DRAWING INSPECTION

This is the final K-DR review before the development project is transferred to production. It proceeds as follows:

1. Designers explain the new product's design principles, selling points, new functions and parts, and other related matters. The design drawings are distributed to DR committee members at this point.
2. The meeting adjourns. Assuming the role of a product specialist, each member takes the drawings back to study them with other people from his/her own department.
3. They study the drawings alongside a prototype, one of which is circulated within each department for inspection.
4. Within a set period (usually five days), each department must report its findings and recommendations on a Drawing Improvement Suggestion Sheet (see example in Figure 5-9).
5. In addition to their pre-inspection duties, Engineering representatives visit the various department work areas to check progress and plan their input to the DR committee's final decisions.
6. Once those final decisions have been worked out, committee members meet to identify and report on their recommendations. Engineering has final authority over the committee's decisions.

Drawing Improvement Suggestion Sheet	Product: ______ fan Part No.: FY- ______	Rank	Distribu-tion	Period	Suggestion date	Submitted	. .	. .	Engineer-ing	. .	. .
		—	. . ( )	. . ( )	. . ( )						

No.	Problems	Suggested improvements	Engineering input	DR committee input	Adopted/ rejected

FIGURE 5-9. Drawing Improvement Suggestion Sheet

Figure 5-10 illustrates this DR decision-making flow for drawing inspections.

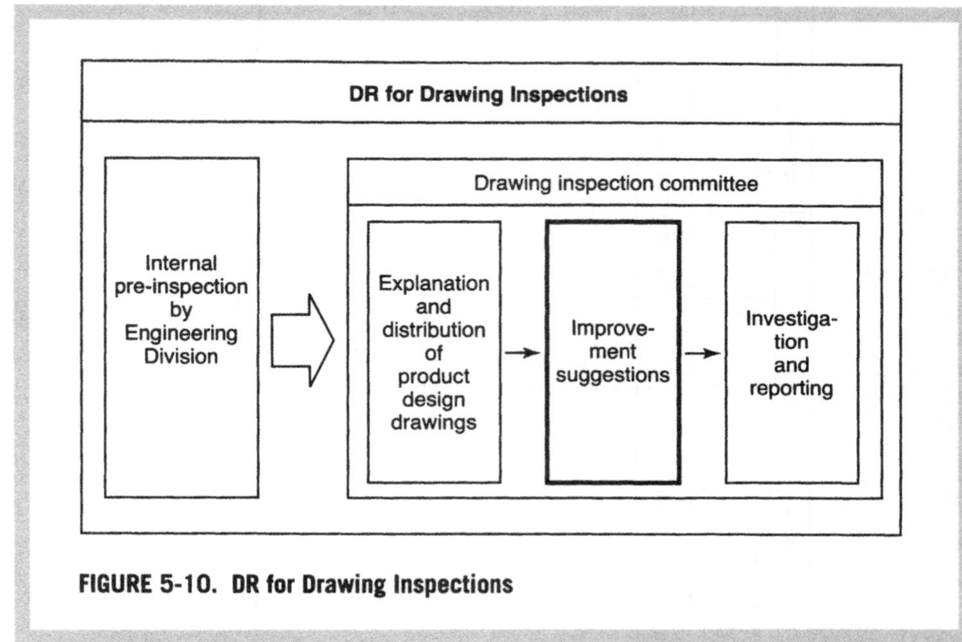

FIGURE 5-10. DR for Drawing Inspections

Although the drawing review process is time consuming, it ensures that designers pay close attention to design quality in areas often overlooked, such as processing, manufacturing, installation, and customer service. By recommending improvements while they are still easy to make (on paper, before the dies have literally been cast), we avoid more expensive design changes that will drive up costs and drive away revenues at later stages.

An added benefit of this process is better communication and cooperation across departmental boundaries.

TRANSFER TO PRODUCTION (AQ-0)

The pass/fail decisions for each stage—from planning to prototype, pilot build, and initial production (and shipment)—rest with a division chief. The approval criteria are based on QCD factors, including those from the AQ system mentioned earlier in this chapter: AQ-00 for concept approval, AQ-0 for the design prototype, AQ-1 for pilot build, and AQ-2 for initial production. AQ is essentially a shorter version of K-DR at a higher level.

After they have completed their AQ-0 evaluation, Engineering hands the project over to Manufacturing by officially issuing the production drawings (refer back to Figure 5-4).

During the AQ-0 meeting, the engineering chief goes over test results for performance, reliability, durability, and safety, and reports on overall K-DR progress to date. One of the review documents is the Design Quality Check Sheet (see example in Figure 5-11).

Because the product must clear AQ-0 to reach the next development stage, participants ask questions like these:

- Does the product meet initial quality and reliability targets?
- Are there any major items that require further consideration?
- Are there any items that will require checking later on and, if so, under what conditions?

Summarizing the approval process on one sheet of paper, the Design Quality Check Sheet is not only a decision record, but also a useful inventory of DR methods. For example, the DR committee for the next project can refer to this check sheet to confirm which improvements were identified and carried out.

MAKING DR EFFECTIVE

Since DR has now been introduced in one form or another throughout our division, everyone is aware of its importance. However, we want it to play a much larger and more effective role. One thing we need to do differently is to make sure that all K-DR participants also have a say in evaluating its success. The greater the results, the more critical it is to evaluate them right away, while the information is still current.

Rejecting a wait-and-see attitude, DR takes the initiative in preventing defects. We collect and analyze market quality data as soon as possible for the next product development cycle. By addressing problems that reached the customer despite our best efforts, we learn what we have overlooked and how we can improve our evaluation criteria. Prompt access to market data thus provides a valuable feedback mechanism.

However, most of this data is not available immediately, so we use the DR Summary Report Form (Figure 5-12) for an interim assessment of K-DR.

Quantifying DR effectiveness on any project is always somewhat difficult, but we write down our best estimates for information purposes. For the division chief, who receives the report, these estimates indicate whether the K-DR committee had enough members and whether certain tasks should be done in advance to reduce meeting time.

(K-DR Kasugai Design Review System)

Design Quality Check Sheet

Approval	Division chief	Quality dept. chief	Engineer-ing dept. chief

Product	____________ fan	Part number	FY- ____________	Rank	B – A	Related models	FY- ______, ______, ______	
Stage	S-H review	Design FMEA	Test Schedule approval	Test review	PR-1	Internal pre-inspection	Drawing inspection	AQ-0
Meeting date	. .	. .	. .	. .	. .	. .	. .	. .
Participants	Supervising engineering section chief	Supervising engineering section chief	Supervising engineering dept. chief	Supervising engineering dept. chief	DR office chief	Supervising engineering section chief	Supervising engineering section chief	Chaired by: Division chief Presentation by: Engineering dept. chief
	Engineering dept. chief QC dept. chief DR office chief Safety manager Service dept. chief	Engineer-ing dept. chief QA dept. chief DR Office chief Safety manager Production dept. chief Union rep. Manu-facturing dept. chief Purchasing dept. chief Service dept. chief	QA dept. chief Manufacturing dept. chief	Quality assurance dept. chief Manufacturing dept. chief	(DR members)	Other dept. chiefs	Engineering dept. chief QA dept. chief DR office chief Production dept. chief Union rep. Manufac-turing dept. chief Purchasing dept. chief Service dept. chief	QA dept. chief Service dept. chief Manufac-turing dept. chief DR office chief Safety manager Sales dept. chief
Main improvements	1. 2. 3.	1. 2. 3.	1. 2. 3.	1. 2. 3.	1. 2. 3.	1. 2. 3.	1. 2. 3.	Conditions for approval 1. 2. 3. 4.

FIGURE 5-11. Design Quality Check Sheet

<table>
<tr><td colspan="7">FMEA,
S-H Investigation Results</td></tr>
<tr><td rowspan="3">Product:</td><td rowspan="3">(FY-)</td><td rowspan="2">Rank</td><td>Dept. chief</td><td>Section chief</td><td>Person responsible</td></tr>
<tr><td>. .</td><td>. .</td><td>. .</td></tr>
<tr><td>–</td><td></td><td></td><td></td></tr>
<tr><td>Date and time</td><td colspan="4"></td><td rowspan="2">(Employee-hours)</td></tr>
<tr><td>Members</td><td colspan="4"></td></tr>
<tr><td>No.</td><td colspan="2">Problems and uncertainties</td><td colspan="2">Countermeasures</td><td>Evaluation points</td></tr>
<tr><td></td><td colspan="2"></td><td colspan="2"></td><td></td></tr>
<tr><td>Pilot build results</td><td colspan="4"></td><td>DR efficiency (%)</td></tr>
<tr><td>Market results</td><td colspan="5"></td></tr>
</table>

Evaluation points : ◉New and critical (50) ○New (30) △Critical (10)
DR efficiency : (Total evaluation points/employee-hours) × 100%

FIGURE 5-12. DR Summary Report Form

This is how we calculate DR efficiency:

$$\frac{\text{(Total evaluation points)}}{\text{(Number of persons} \times \text{Hours per person)}} \times 100\%$$

The number of evaluation points varies with each item's significance (see point ratings in Figure 5-12).

BENEFITS OF DR

The effects of DR show up in the marketplace. Figure 5-13 is a line graph showing total product defects reported from the field, which is one measure of DR's impact on quality.

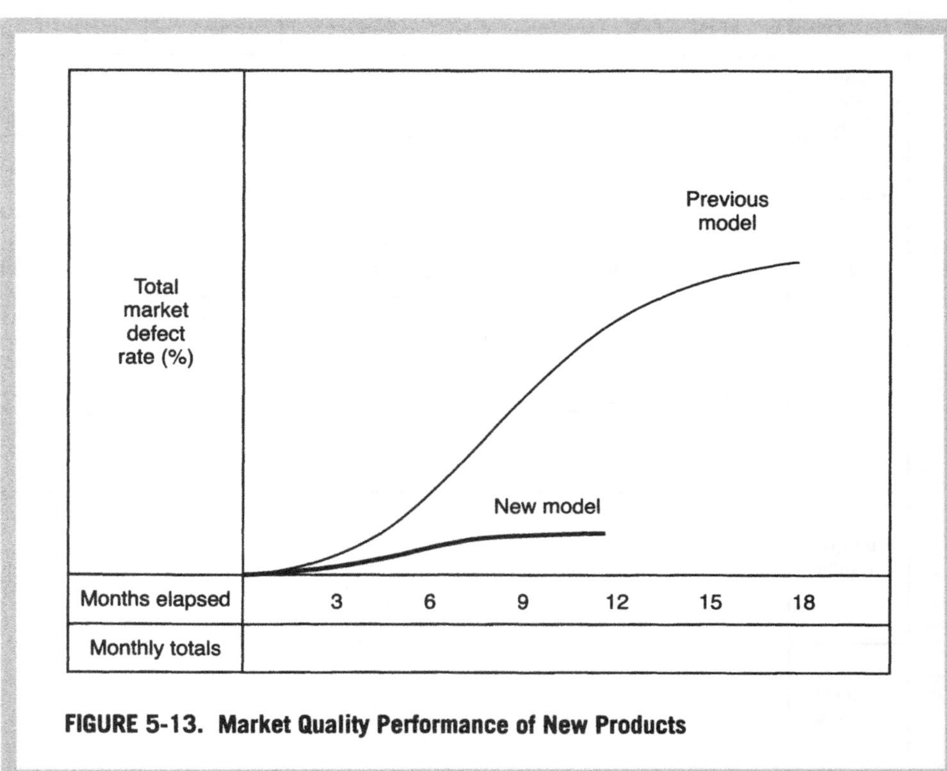

FIGURE 5-13. Market Quality Performance of New Products

PLANS FOR THE FUTURE

The more you apply DR, the better you understand how much it contributes to product quality. And there are still many ways we can improve the K-DR system. Our experience has borne out these lessons learned:

- DR does not design products directly. It is a review and evaluation process in support of design, and its participants include non-designers. DR organizes and assigns various tasks that apply market and case study data, test results, and QC techniques to prevent oversights in quality assurance. Yet DR alone cannot make a good product.

- Techniques such as S-H and FMEA make it easier to predict and prevent quality problems and are therefore essential to DR. However, in the early days of DR at Matsushita, mastering these techniques became a goal in itself. Too many people lost sight of the ultimate goal: ensuring a quality product.
- DR can thrive only within a culture of continuous improvement, as opposed to a rubber stamp mentality that looks only at whether certain items pass inspection.
- While the DR process helps us lay out all aspects of product design and spot the problems, we still must apply our own expertise and resourcefulness to come up with effective solutions. DR provides the form, not the substance.
- The results of DR depend greatly on who is involved. Levels of technical skill and expertise can vary considerably, as can priorities and methods.
- Most important are the standards of the person in charge of DR. Product quality and reliability levels ultimately reflect what the division chief is willing to accept. Similarly, committee members and other participants are not likely to invest much in DR unless they are given challenging goals.
- DR also requires clear operating guidelines so that it will help and not hinder new product development (see Figure 5-14). Again, even with well-defined procedures, a lot depends on the people and organizations involved. With each new development project we should look for ways to improve the DR system and revise these guidelines accordingly.

This case study has used exhaust fan development to illustrate how DR is applied in our division. We will continue to promote K-DR, developing methods best suited to Matsushita and its products and to all related quality issues. We hope thus not only to satisfy our customers, but also to cultivate trust among divisions and to sharpen one another's capabilities.

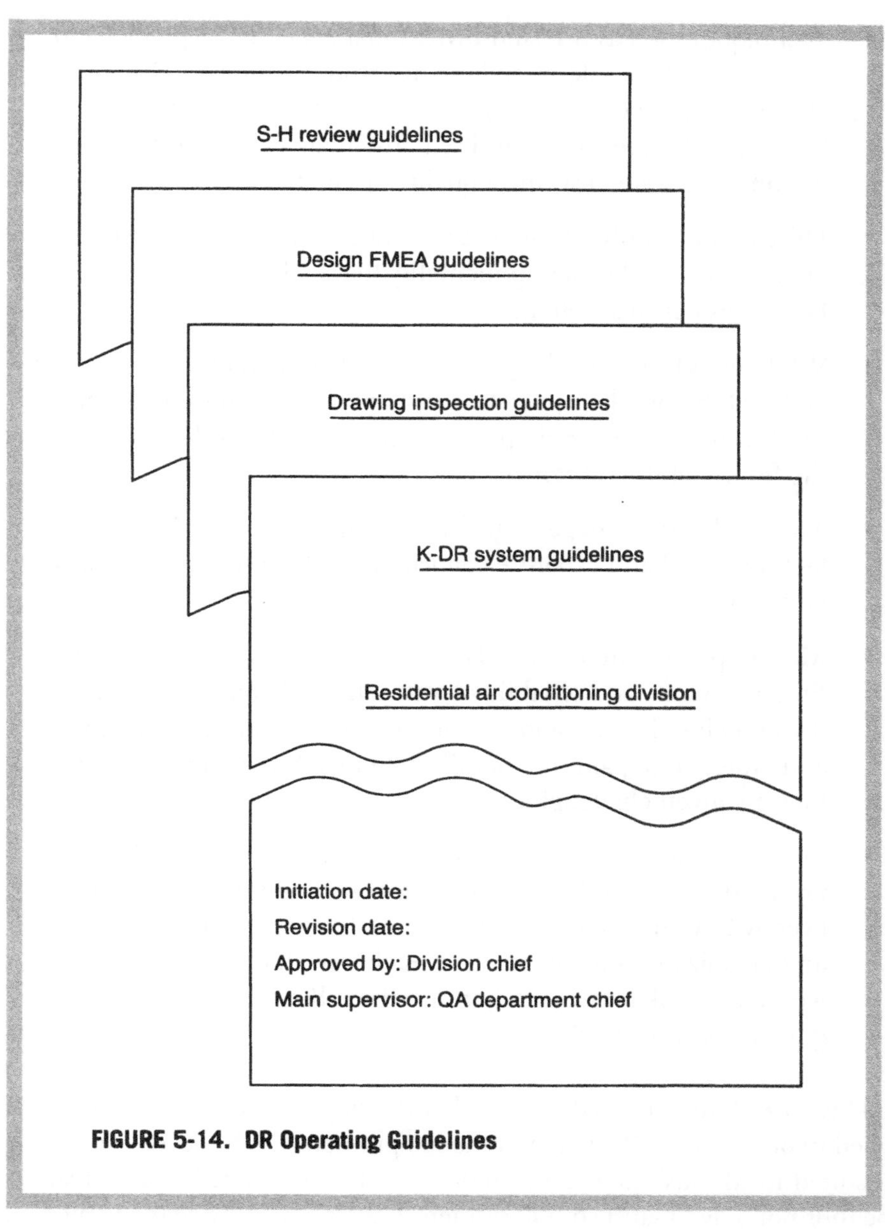

FIGURE 5-14. DR Operating Guidelines

Shin'ichi Takahashi, Research Center for Development of Resource Exploration and Surveying Systems
Takao Takahashi, NEC

6 DR for electronics and telecommunications

(complex systems)

INTRODUCTION

DR has evolved as a product development tool that helps connect customer requirements to company design capabilities. It is now widely recognized as a means of improving design quality. In surprisingly many cases, however, DR projects have yielded few tangible benefits for all the time and hard work invested.

Such disappointing results can often be traced to lack of planning and preparation. Companies charge headlong into DR without first addressing various existing problems. This chapter is about avoiding such mistakes. You will see how DR can build on work that has already been done to improve product design. This case study looks at how one company experienced initial setbacks, analyzed its methods and processes, solved the underlying problems, and saw measurable improvement.

The products involved are satellite telecommunication devices. These are quite complex systems, even within the sophisticated world of electronics and telecommunications. You will learn how designers took the initiative in preparing for DR, working closely with the DR staff and with outside resources, and also how the staff handled different problems during DR execution.

DR ISSUES AND OPPORTUNITIES

DR can fail for any number of reasons. It may be a matter of inappropriate goals or inept management. On the technical side, you may have unclear customer requirements, confusion over design standards, or a poorly organized approach to troubleshooting. Perhaps the most critical factor is human cooperation. Even if you fall short in some of these other areas, DR can be highly effective if people are willing to help each other work through the obstacles.

These are some of the key principles of successful DR:

- If you simply try to duplicate another DR case study, your goals will not match your specific needs.
- If you do not first analyze the product's operating environment, your design targets will be off the mark.
- If you establish a vague design baseline, your DR schedule will have to be revised later.
- If those in charge of design overlook or ignore the findings of the DR committee, your rate of improvement will be limited.
- If your plan for improvement is inadequate, you will not be able to execute it efficiently.

ORGANIZING DR WITHIN THE COMPANY

GENERAL STRUCTURE

Back when we were still fairly new to DR, our development process for space satellites started with various preliminary designs. It then proceeded to prototype models (PM) and extensive tests, resulting in flight models (FM) for production.

Better techniques have since enabled us to greatly reduce development costs and lead times. For example, we may run stress tests on an existing product to identify the weak points, then replace just those components with more stress-resistant counterparts. The resulting "proto-flight model" (PFM) is sort of a hybrid between old and new, allowing for more thorough quality evaluation. DR at this stage now includes detailed analysis of accumulated stress conditions and causes.

Both PFMs and new products must be able to endure transportation to the launch pad, the launch itself, and then the harsh conditions of outer space, all without any malfunction. Hence the need for meticulous reviews of product life expectancy and system durability right up to the very last design step.

So while the systems themselves are complex, their development process is now well defined. Figure 6-1 illustrates the basic flow of DR. When formulating review items we consider both component and system complexity, as well as reliability and safety requirements. For any given project, however, we will modify the standard DR process when circumstances warrant.

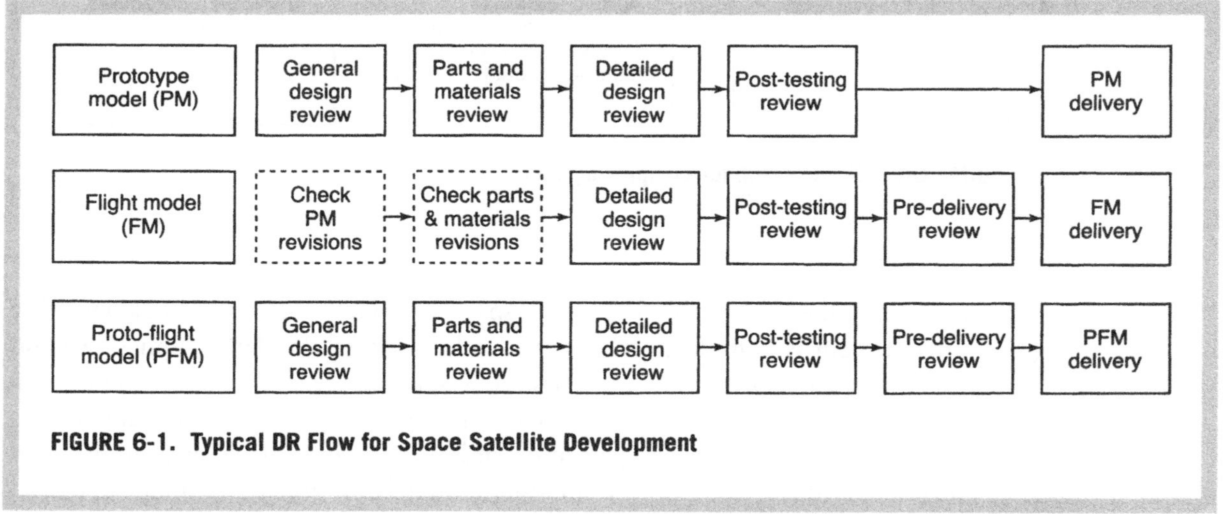

FIGURE 6-1. Typical DR Flow for Space Satellite Development

TYPICAL DR FLOW

When system operating conditions, general functions, standards, and specifications are relatively simple, whether for new or existing products, the approach shown in Figure 6-2 is usually suitable.

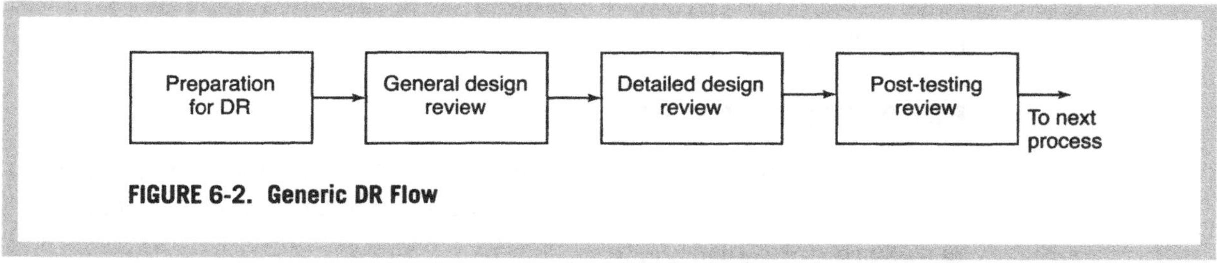

FIGURE 6-2. Generic DR Flow

THREE-PART DR FOR COMPLEX SYSTEMS

Otherwise or when in doubt, it is better to break DR into the three elements shown in Figure 6-3, still keeping the same overall development flow.

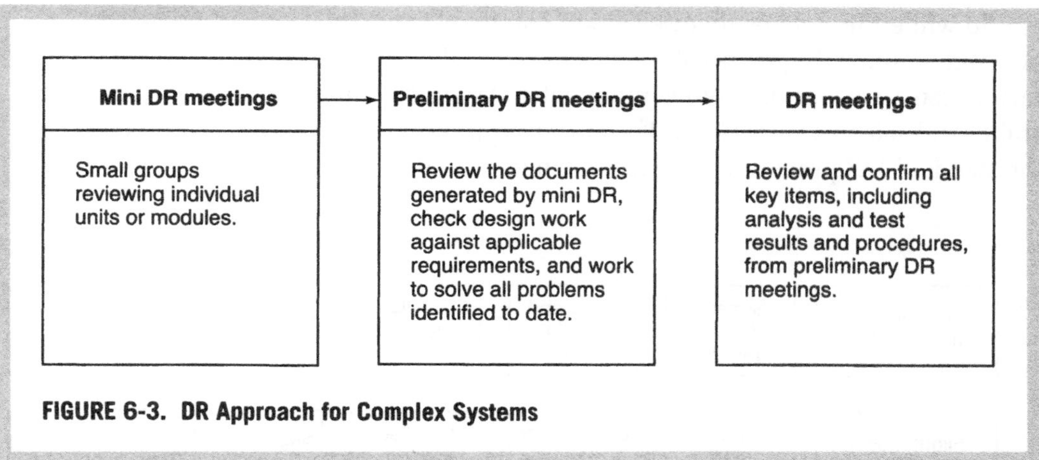

FIGURE 6-3. DR Approach for Complex Systems

When the relationship between a space satellite's functions and its operating environment is complex, and when a wide range of standards applies (weight, thermal balance, electricity), the basic DR approach is likely to miss some problems along the way. As these problems are passed along to each succeeding phase, they become that much bigger and harder to resolve. MDR and preliminary reviews minimize this risk by evaluating design from more than one perspective.

ESTABLISHING DR BASELINES

Before any DR activities begin, we list the system's main functions and then organize them into components. Often using function trees as a visual aid, we then apply DR starting with the highest priority (most critical) components. From there we establish the baseline for design specifications. A clearly defined baseline is essential to DR for complex systems. Figure 6-4 summarizes these preparatory steps.

PREPARING FOR DR

As systems become more complex, so does the DR process itself. Without adequate preparation, DR becomes chaotic and falls far short of expectations.

MANAGING COMPLEXITY

The accelerating pace of technology no longer allows us to rely on hardware alone and ignore the software side, and as the market grows more diverse, product reliability and safety requirements are stricter than ever. Meanwhile, manufacturers are moving ahead with rapid, high-precision component mounting systems and other cost saving measures. Getting the most out of these advances means a shift toward complex divisions of labor, a high degree of standardization,

Example of key review items	Review and reorganize (priority blocks) →	Establish baseline (for next process)
Categorize system functions	Review tolerances, thermal design, and weight	Establish system specifications
Check suitability of individual functions	Conduct FMECA (failure mode, effects, and criticality analysis)	Establish subsystem designs
Check environmental resistance features	Confirm operational safety	Establish environmental specifications
Check integration functions	Check suitability of interfaces	Establish interface specifications
Check suitability of parts and materials	Replace unsuitable parts and materials and check for quality conformance	Check suitability of recommended parts

FIGURE 6-4. Tasks Necessary for Smooth DR Execution

and interface technologies. Other factors to consider are production automation, advanced materials, regulatory restrictions, and manufacturing liability.

All this means more inputs to the DR process, so we try to sort out as much as possible in advance. As just one example, Figure 6-5 outlines the preliminary work we do on parts and materials selection.

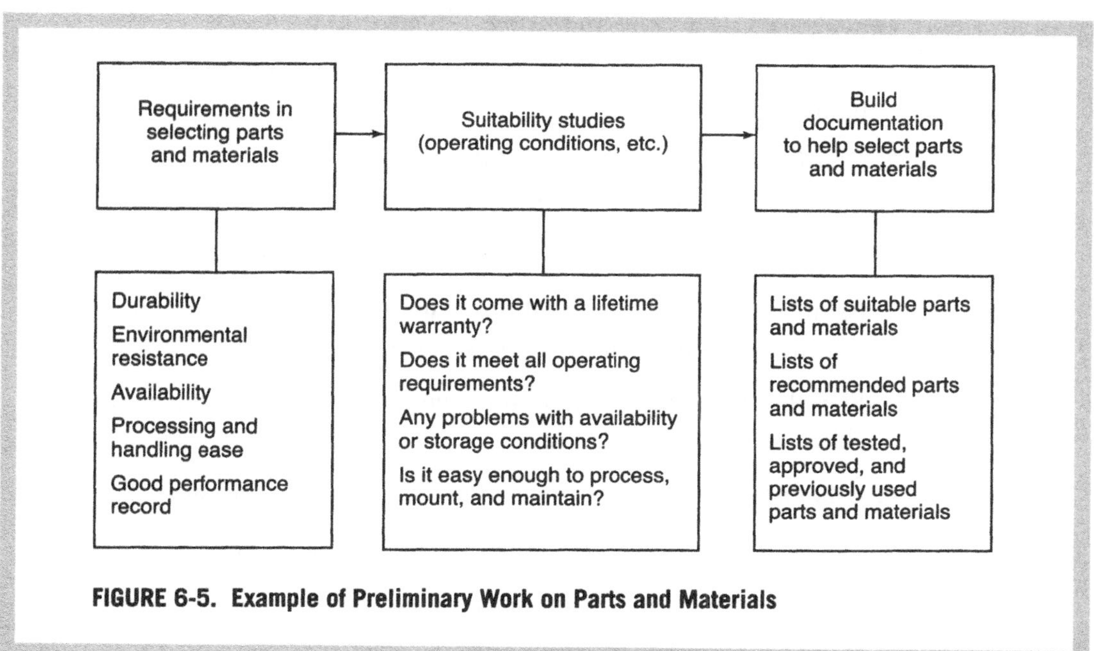

FIGURE 6-5. Example of Preliminary Work on Parts and Materials

CLARIFYING DR OBJECTIVES

In satellites, where many precision devices are crammed into limited space, electronic interference can easily cause system failures. Thus DR must look both at individual components and at the system as a whole. Here are other important points to consider as you approach DR:

- Benefits to be realized from new technologies and QA methods to go with them
- Warranty terms for new parts and materials
- Environmental test results for special operating conditions
- Test conditions and methods of execution
- QA conditions for off-standard designs

GENERATING DR MATERIALS

Those on support staff who draft DR documentation and other materials are far less visible than the designers and managers, but no less vital to the program. They compile lists of customer concerns and design needs after consulting with design specialists, quality engineers, and/or designated customer contacts. The value of such information for DR depends largely on how well it is researched and organized. Consequently, staff members need many of the same skills as system engineers. The input they provide is in fact incorporated into the system design at that point.

The following steps precede the compiling and editing of DR documentation, although not necessarily in the order listed:

1. Form the DR support staff and seek cooperation from designers and managers.
2. Clarify the range and types of DR review items in order to keep the scope of future discussions manageable.
3. Clarify key functions and draft a quality function deployment map.
4. Estimate the scope of the DR program. Can the documentation be prepared within a matter of hours or will it take days?
5. Plan the size and makeup of the review committees, using applicable case studies as a guide.
6. Establish close liaison between the DR office and the support staff.
7. Establish a DR schedule and begin tying in required documentation.
8. Assign specific compilation tasks with guidelines that encourage clear, concise writing.

9. Specify documentation format, style, and volume to facilitate editing.
10. Thoroughly apply the 5W2H (who, what, when, where, why, how, and how much) approach to weed out extraneous data.
11. Establish guidelines for visual presentation of data.
12. Prepare documentation lists for each DR meeting, including the name of the person who will explain the documentation.

ASSIGNING PREPARATORY TASKS

The DR office should coordinate the details of the schedule in close cooperation with the technical departments, making sure everyone concerned receives a copy once it is complete. You can reinforce this process by explaining the schedule at a presentation for those same people. Figure 6-6 shows a typical DR schedule configuration.

<table>
<tr><th colspan="7">Design Review Schedule</th></tr>
<tr><td>Review topic</td><td colspan="4"></td><td>Review site</td><td></td></tr>
<tr><td>Design stages</td><td>Concept</td><td>Definition</td><td>General</td><td>Detailed</td><td>Start date</td><td></td></tr>
<tr><td>Contract report</td><td colspan="3"></td><td colspan="2">Management report</td><td></td></tr>
<tr><td>Baseline report</td><td colspan="3"></td><td colspan="2">Restrictions</td><td></td></tr>
<tr><td rowspan="2">Review committee members</td><td>Chair</td><td>Reviewers</td><td>Designers</td><td>DR office</td><td colspan="2">Support staff</td></tr>
<tr><td></td><td></td><td></td><td></td><td colspan="2"></td></tr>
<tr><td>No.</td><td>Task assignments</td><td>Time frame</td><td>Person in charge</td><td>Task description</td><td>Documentation</td><td>Confirmation</td></tr>
<tr><td>1</td><td>Clarification of DR scope and objectives</td><td>Two months before start date</td><td>Supervisor</td><td>Clear up uncertainties and compile design specifications</td><td></td><td></td></tr>
<tr><td>2</td><td>Draft DR list</td><td>Two months before start date</td><td>DR office</td><td>Compile list of review items based on DR scope and objectives</td><td>DR outline</td><td></td></tr>
<tr><td>3</td><td>Issue list of applicable reports</td><td>Two months before start date</td><td>Management and engineering departments</td><td>Draft baseline report and documentation source list</td><td>Materials for configuration control, DR source documents</td><td></td></tr>
<tr><td>4</td><td>Compile and edit DR documentation</td><td>One month before start date</td><td>DR office</td><td>Further consideration of DR objectives, problems, and technical issues</td><td>DR input package</td><td></td></tr>
<tr><td></td><td></td><td></td><td></td><td></td><td></td><td></td></tr>
</table>

FIGURE 6-6. DR Schedule with Task Assignments

IDENTIFYING DR PRIORITIES

In view of the complex systems being developed, we try to keep DR as simple as possible. Preparatory work to spell out design requirements (or even development stages) helps considerably. System designers must work closely with people in other departments to set priorities, or else key organizational elements may be left out while design hours increase due to lack of proper planning.

Figure 6-7 shows an example of items that system and subsystem designers have identified as critical. Going through this process at the outset of each stage helps narrow the focus of DR in checking against functional requirements and tolerances before the next stage.

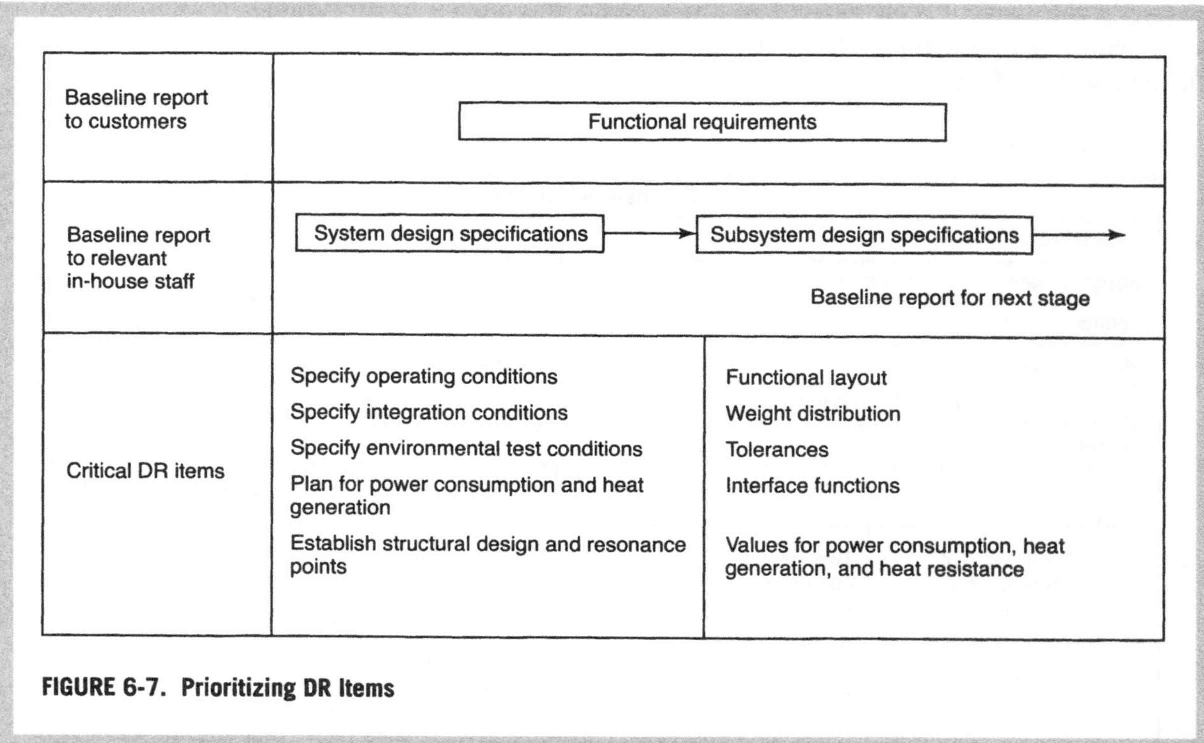

FIGURE 6-7. Prioritizing DR Items

Prioritization in this case involved portable satellite components. To avoid making their review list too short, designers observed the following guidelines:

- Be able to verify system requirements for reliability, safety, and operability
- Make sure the system design addresses items requested by the customer

- Check for estimates of all environmental changes that could affect system operation
- Use FMEA to minimize critical defects and devise effective countermeasures
- Work out countermeasures to deal with development restrictions and risks
- Establish the design baseline before planning the review

MAKING DR EFFECTIVE

As you apply DR to succeeding development cycles, it naturally grows more efficient with continuous improvement. For any product, satellites included, DR initially confronts a wide array of issues. The most effective methods are those that consider both the customer's needs and the wide spectrum of things that can go wrong with any design. Below is an example of such an approach.

1. Establish cooperation between the DR office and support staff.
2. Prepare and display materials that make the DR presentation interesting and relevant to the audience.
3. Establish DR documentation policy to include the following:
    - Keep explanations of review items clear and simple.
    - Make a list of values for each design requirement and a list of design results.
    - Draw correlations between individual items and DR as a whole.
    - Clearly explain the indexing method for DR items, support data, articles, and other reference materials.
    - Establish style guidelines for documentation text and graphics.
    - Make sure all follow-up reports on problem investigations and countermeasures are practical and to the point.
4. Establish procedures for printing, distributing and editing documentation prior to DR.
5. Set up a system for confirming recommendations and actual improvements resulting from each review.

CONFIRMING IMPROVEMENTS

Along with adequate preparation and active management support, thorough follow-up of recommended action items is a key DR ingredient. These results should be incorporated into DR documentation as quickly as possible.

When our DR committees start deliberating at length over complex systems, a few helpful words from the chair can often help them reach a decision. They also need staff support for recording the minutes and for checking up on action taken. Described below are some of the methods used at our company.

COMPILING THE MAIN DR AGENDA

DR committees must address matters ranging from use of new technologies and components to safety planning for extremely tough operating environments. We have found several ways to resolve difficult issues and come to a successful conclusion:

- Hold separate ad hoc meetings to deal specifically with one problem until a decision is reached.
- Record high-priority unresolved action items in the minutes and assign each an action proposal deadline.
- Recommend redesign work for problems related to the design baseline.
- Set up task assignments, follow-up procedures and reporting deadlines for unresolved problems.
- If deliberations are not completed within the allotted time, set up an additional DR meeting to finish them.

ACTION ITEM TRACKING

The 3-W (what, who, when) sheet shown in Figure 6-8 helps track review items, questions, or problems under deliberation. The completed sheets are attached to the DR meeting minutes for future reference.

This form is valuable because it can highlight hot development issues and provide an ongoing update of their status.

COMPILING DR RECORDS

It is important to compile the results of DR committee deliberations, along with any pertinent 3-W sheets. Upon DR completion we submit them to the designer(s), the committee chair, and selected members for confirmation. Copies of the approved and signed minutes are then distributed to everyone involved.

Delays of even just a few days can make it more difficult to obtain all the required signatures. That in turn delays the prescribed action items and, in the

No.	Item description	Responses	Action	Person in charge	Due date

FIGURE 6-8. 3-W Sheet

end, the whole development process; so in the space systems industry, we emphasize prompt distribution of DR meeting minutes.

Meeting minutes typically cover the following:

1. DR item(s) and scope
2. Baseline and other relevant reports
3. Negotiated and preexisting restrictions
4. Items under deliberation and proposed actions (from 3-W sheet)
5. Overall evaluation of results
6. DR participants
7. Main technical documentation
8. List of documentation used in the review
9. List of items to be checked during DR at the next process (as required)

The 3-W sheets encourage timely response and also facilitate document revisions for design changes.

POST-DR ACTION ITEMS

We have already pointed out why action items arising from DR need to be wrapped up quickly. Anything involving design revisions takes top priority, followed by development management issues.

The example in Figure 6-9 shows plans for three important action items.

Item/category	Action item flow chart and summary		Administrative follow-up
Action item management	Revision procedure →	Confirmation →	Reporting and checking items
Revision of customer requirements	• Obtain customer approval and carry out technical revisions	• Handle via in-house measures • Check output from designers and QC engineers • Check again at next stage DR	• Update specification manuals
Revision of in-house baseline report	• Obtain customer approval and carry out technical revisions • Inform customer of action item results via technical revision report	• Handle via in-house measures • Check output from designers and QC engineers • Submit action item records to QC supervisor for checking • Check again at next stage DR	• Update in-house technical manuals
Revision of other related documentation	• Follow in-house management procedures	• Submit action item records to QC supervisor for checking • Check again at next stage DR	• Update other applicable reports and data

FIGURE 6-9. Action Item Plans

FOLLOWING UP KEY ACTION ITEMS

High-priority action items require the QC supervisor's confirmation and are also followed up at the next stage DR. One thing we make sure of is that no action taken creates unforeseen problems elsewhere. Figure 6-10 shows the action item follow-up form.

DR SUPPORT

We have been describing the most important aspects of our DR program. But DR for complex systems includes many other tasks that designers alone cannot manage. This is where the support staff performs an essential service.

System design managers, not the DR office, usually sort out staff duties. We believe those responsible for the final outcome should decide who does what.

No.	Device name	Prescribed action	Result	Documentation

FIGURE 6-10. Action Item Check Sheet for Next Stage DR

Incidentally, this division of tasks has proven efficient even on small-scale development projects with far fewer participants. DR support staff generally handle the following:

- DR schedule management in line with the design process
- DR cost estimating and tracking
- Effective use of AV equipment (VCRs, overhead projectors) for DR presentations
- Selection, preparation and distribution of reference materials
- Coordination with customer representatives to communicate their needs and concerns to in-house staff
- Establishment of regular DR meeting location and room layout
- Organization for timely completion of DR tasks
- Establishment of DR follow-up measures after project completion

CONCLUSION

This case study bears out two keys to effective DR for complex systems: setting clear design/development goals and making detailed plans right from the start. If you experience disappointing results, resist the temptation to discard DR altogether. Look first for mistakes or omissions at the planning stage, the most likely source of problems that surface in the final product.

We hope this case study will help others learn from initial setbacks and make DR work at their own companies.

Ayatomo Kanno
Science University of Tokyo

7 DR for software packages (information systems)

INTRODUCTION

Computer software is born almost exclusively of human creativity and intellectual labor. Tables 7-1 and 7-2 and Figure 7-1 lay out the applicable quality characteristics.

All groups with a hand in software production must work together on a firm grasp of these quality characteristics. Because of the strong emphasis on teamwork in Japanese culture, this kind of collaborative effort is basic to our QC and DR activities.

On the other hand, Western countries have always gravitated toward a more individualistic outlook. While the spirit of cooperation has given Japan the edge in traditional manufacturing, the reverse has been true for software development, where the individual's creativity is a key element. This chapter reports how Japanese-style DR is helping to close the gap.

DR ISSUES AND OPPORTUNITIES

Application of DR at each stage can greatly enhance software development. It can bring to light peculiarities of software relative to hardware, clarifying essential design points.

TABLE 7-1. Software Quality Characteristics

No.	Quality characteristic	Description	
1	Functionality	• Suitability	: meets functional requirements
		• Validity	: meets minimum technical specifications
		• Security	: allows no unauthorized access to internal system data
		• Compatibility	: works on existing hardware without modifications
		• Connectivity	: links up readily with other systems
2	Reliability	• Defect-free operation	: (self-explanatory)
		• Error detection	: responds to input or operation errors
		• Availability	: recovers quickly from faults and keeps downtime to a minimum
3	User-Friendliness	• Comprehensibility	: operating concepts are easy to understand
		• Learnability	: easy to learn
		• Operability	: easy to operate
		• Interactivity	: interacts with user to resolve problems and answer questions
4	Productivity	• Speed	: responds quickly to input
		• Capacity	: can process a lot at once
		• Efficiency	: conserves system resources
		• Resource utilization	: gets the most out of system resources
5	Maintainability	• Repairability	: can be easily fixed
		• Expandability	: functions can be easily changed or expanded
		• Testability	: can be easily tested
6	Portability	• Machine independence	: can run on more than one machine
		• System independence	: can run on more than one system
		• Installability	: components can be easily installed
		• Modifiability	: can be easily reconfigured for another machine/system

AUTOMATION

Automation is making rapid inroads into the software industry, just as it is in many others. It is now commonplace in document editing, updating, and appending, as well as in coding, testing, and verifying. In addition, software production relies increasingly on CIM (computer integrated manufacturing). This trend has been very positive for Japan's high tech industries, and we can only expect it to accelerate.

But automation does not replace quality assurance. Otherwise, what good is a faster, more efficient way of turning out bad products? If you wait until defects materialize before sounding the alarm, too much defective software will have

TABLE 7-2. Software Quality Characteristics

Category	Quality characteristic	Description
Operation	Suitability	Software meets the particular needs of the user.
	Operability	Software is easy to learn and use.
	Performance	The computer has enough memory and processing speed to execute the specified functions.
Functionality	Reliability	Operates as specified without faults.
	Availability	Recovers quickly from faults and keeps downtime to a minimum.
	Security	The system protects itself against damage to internal data by denying access to anyone who lacks proper authorization.
Convenience	Maintainability	Causes of software defects are easy to identify and repair.
	Expandability	Functions can be easily changed or expanded.
	Compatibility	Can be used on existing platform without changes.
Versatility	Portability	Can easily run on other machines and operating systems.
	Modifiability	Can be easily reconfigured for other systems.
	Connectivity	Can easily be connected to other systems.

already reached the customer. The preventive approach is essential, which points up the importance of wide participation in DR as a prerequisite for automation.

INDIVIDUAL VS. TEAM APPROACH

Software quality and productivity depend greatly on the developers' abilities. In a cottage industry environment, disparate skill levels will inevitably yield inconsistent quality. And while it is true that "two heads are better than one," we should also remember the principle of the least common denominator. In other words, you can negate the benefits of teamwork by adding too many unqualified people to a small group of qualified people.

Thus leaving a great deal of power in the hands of a few is not an ideal approach, but it is often the most sensible approach for day-to-day work. However, at some point there is much to gain from fresh perspectives. People not immersed in a given process are often better at recognizing problems. This is where the cross-functional aspect of DR fits in, provided you have an effective supervisory organization.

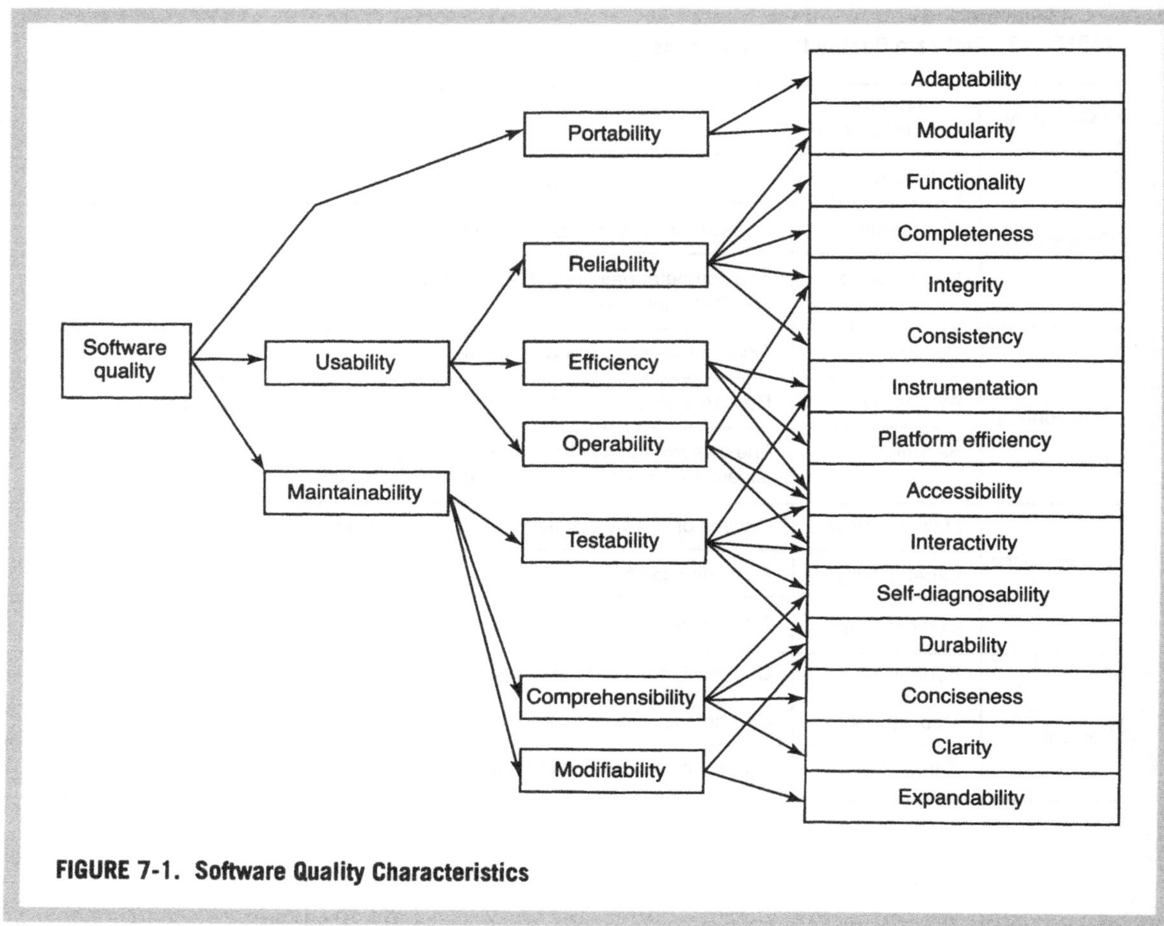

FIGURE 7-1. Software Quality Characteristics

SOFTWARE PACKAGES FROM THE DESIGN PERSPECTIVE

For any product, the proper starting point is identifying what the customer needs. In the case of software, this is a complex process. Perhaps the greatest challenge is determining the "value added" by specifying customer requirements. Many software packages have failed to provide the functions and features that users really want. As a result, production people have had second thoughts about the traditional approach of locking in specifications as early possible.

The paradox is that we are never fully aware what a software package *should* do until we know what it *can* do—until we use it. Unfortunately, this also means that it rarely can do all the user expects it to do. In any event, software design entails many vague elements from the start. Throughout the development process we must strive to reduce uncertainty, or at least to manage it, using DR as a framework.

Although user requirements are ever changing, there is much we can still learn from existing software packages. In addition, we must recognize that quality characteristics address not only function and performance, but also such intangibles as how users feel about the software. This forces us to think in terms of basic human psychology. So DR should address such human frailties as inconsistency, laziness, inattentiveness, impatience, dullness, illogic, panic, and confusion. Needless to say, relating these to software design is not easy.

It is precisely these human factors that require so much input from as many perspectives as possible. But for all the work involved, DR can mean the difference between success and failure in the software market.

SOFTWARE DOCUMENTATION

Documentation is a prime target for DR scrutiny, especially in light of the many descriptive terms for software characteristics. The tables above are a classic example. There is even a maze of terminology associated with evaluating software, so it is easy to get confused. The best solution here is first to decide which characteristics are critical, and then to agree on a common "language" for describing and discussing them.

Of course there is more to software documentation than text. We must decide what graphics—tables, figures, charts—to use based on content, usefulness, and presentation style. Figure 7-2 gives a general categorization of software programs and documentation. This outline helps us determine the appropriate descriptive format as we proceed from general to specific.

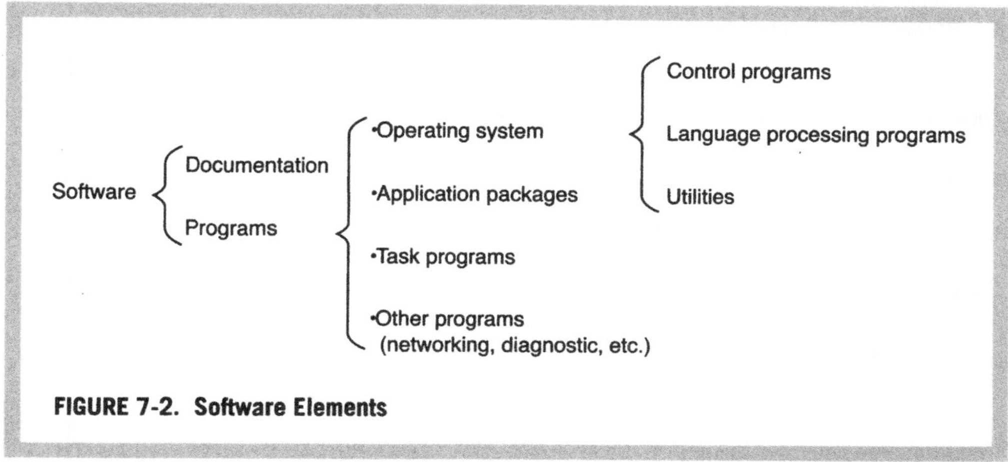

FIGURE 7-2. Software Elements

Figure 7-3 lists software documentation categories. Good documentation is always easy to understand, easy to learn, easy to update and expand, and above all accurate. This is the appropriate standard for DR evaluation.

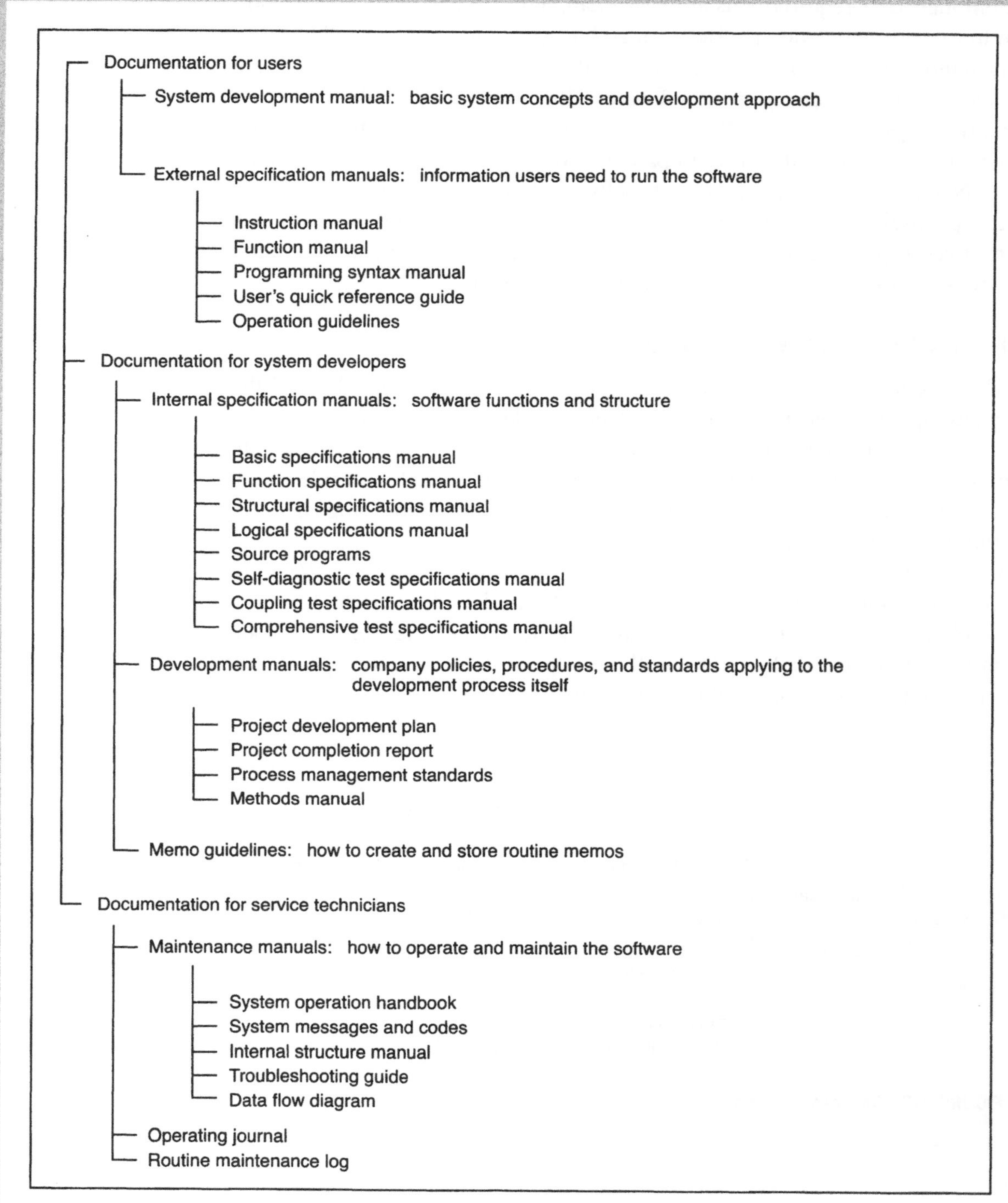

FIGURE 7-3. Documentation Categories

ORGANIZING DR WITHIN THE COMPANY

Each market, company, or culture has its own unique personality, which DR helps impart to quality designs and successful products. In the fiercely competitive, fast-paced software industry, we cannot afford to regard DR as an option. Nor can we expect it to work without good planning and organization. Even for existing products, we should bring in DR upon any change in design conditions. This may include changes in the market, in company organization, or simply in the individuals involved.

DESIGN-DRIVEN APPROACH

DR both leads and is lead by design activities. When it identifies needed revisions, designers should carry them out as soon as possible. On the other hand, when designers do an adequate job of preparation, DR goes a lot more smoothly and quickly. Over the long haul, design division managers bear chief responsibility for growing and refining the DR program.

CRITICAL DR ITEMS

Table 7-3 highlights certain questions to ask during DR. These are critical in light of DR's very high upstream position in the flow of product development.

TABLE 7-3. Critical DR Items

Traceability	Does the software design incorporate all requirement specifications? Are all software elements traceable to corresponding requirements?
Risk	Does this design entail any high risks? In other words, can it be developed without having to clear any difficult technical hurdles?
Utility	Does the design actually solve problems identified within the list of requirements?
Maintainability	Does the design foster an easy-to-maintain system?
Quality	Does the design incorporate quality characteristics that make for "good" software?
Interface	Are the external and internal interfaces properly defined?
Technical clarity	Has the design been expressed in language that can be easily converted into code?
Alternatives	Was an alternative design proposed? What determined the final design choice?
Limitations	Do any of the software's limitations conflict with its requirements?
Special items	Does the software score high on ergonomics? Is it easy to diagnose? Is it compatible with other system elements? Do the software and documentation agree?

TECHNOLOGY REVIEW

DR also provides a base from which to review all production technologies related to the target product. It should address the following:

- Quality function deployment studies
- Functional modularization
- Prototyping studies
- Investigation of modifiability
- Prevention of product liability problems
- Expert analysis of intellectual property rights
- Proper identification and application of development tools
- Differences in equipment, environment, or tasks
- Close monitoring of quality and productivity
- Skills improvement training

Establishing such a base requires real effort, not just an administrative exercise. Best of all, improvements from each DR application improve this base for the next stage.

SOFTWARE QUALITY INDICES

One challenge in software DR is selecting meaningful quality characteristics. Table 7-4 lists some common choices, but many of these are too general to quantify. The substitute characteristics shown in Table 7-5, however, are measurable evaluation indices. By combining the two into a matrix (Table 7-6), we can overlay a qualitative, user-oriented perspective on top of one familiar to manufacturers.

MAKING DR EFFECTIVE

We all acknowledge the contribution of DR to product quality, whether the product is software or something else. Accordingly, we should try to evaluate DR effectiveness upon completion, instead of waiting until after the product has reached the customer. In doing so, however, we should weigh the availability of staff resources.

TABLE 7-4. Software Quality Characteristics

Quality characteristic	Description
1. Functionality	Conformance to functional requirements
2. Reliability	Performance of target functions at specified precision
3. Efficiency	Minimum use of system resources to perform target functions under a given set of conditions
4. Security	Control of system access to prevent unauthorized users from causing failures
5. User-Friendliness	Ease with which users can learn and operate the software, prepare input, and understand output
6. Maintainability	Ease with which users can discover and eliminate errors and add or revise functions as necessary
7. Flexibility	Ease with which users can modify programs to improve performance, reliability, efficiency, security, user-friendliness, and maintainability
8. Portability	Ease with which users can transfer the software from one operating environment to another without impeding operation
9. Testability	Ease with which users can run diagnostic tests to verify their target functions
10. Interoperability	Ease with which users can transfer data and perform operations after establishing a logical link between two different systems
11. Installability	Ease with which users can introduce the software to a given enviornment without impeding other programs
12. Reusability	Ease with which users can reconfigure all or part of the software into another program or an expanded version of the same program

SIMPLIFICATION

Many DR staff members have been pulled away from already busy schedules to work on product development. Naturally, this means they want to wrap it up cleanly and promptly, leaving no loose ends that they will have to deal with later. The example in Table 7-7 saves time for reviewers by laying out documentation problems in a logical, easy-to-follow arrangement. They can start with an even simpler list like the one in Table 7-8. In either case, the list needs to reflect the review items and recommendations covered during DR.

TABLE 7-5. Software Quality Evaluation Indices

Substitute characteristic	Description
1. Completeness	Incorporation of all target functions
2. Consistency	Agreement between software and documentation, and between one manual and another
3. Traceability	Access to (1) documented steps in the software development process, (2) performance records, (3) test data, (4) various review reports, and other reference information
4. Failure resistance	Continued performance of target functions at specified precision under abnormal conditions
5. Availability	Availability of target functions when they are needed
6. Accuracy	Conformance of actual to expected results under specified precision
7. Complexity	Public perception of the software as difficult to understand
8. Storage efficiency	Minimum use of virtual and real storage during execution
9. Execution efficiency	Minimum CPU time during execution
10. Access control	Control of access for reading or updating data
11. Access audit	Tracking of read/update transactions
12. Operability	Ease with which users can run the software
13. Learnability	Ease with which users (including beginners) can learn the software
14. Communicability	Ease with which users can input data and output results

When the responses to either list reveal a large number of problems, they point to a need for better DR preparation. For example, the design department should pick up items such as those in Table 7-7 during a pre-DR review. One common solution is a documentation checklist to ensure that all key aspects are covered (see Table 7-9).

Post-DR evaluation should also verify that the recommended improvements actually reduced defects. In our experience, DR has had the greatest impact on interface problems.

TOOLS FOR SOFTWARE DR

There is a growing assortment of software tools that make DR more effective and efficient. Most are commercially available, removing the burden of developing them in-house:

TABLE 7-5. (cont'd)

Substitute characteristic	Description
15. Conciseness	Extent to which source code enables target functions clearly and concisely
16. Modularity	Extent to which product modules are closely linked with each other and with specified data
17. Self-descriptiveness	Extent to which source code describes sfotware functions, input and output modes, processing algorithms, and other elements
18. Generality	Independence of function algorithms from specific operating environments
19. Expandability	Capacity for additional memory, data storage, and processing or other functions
20. Instrumentation	Provisions for measuring and displaying operating parameters, error conditions, and other items
21.Machine independence	Independence from specific hardware functions and specifications
22.System independence	Independence from specific operating system functions and specifications
23.Connectivity	Use of standard protocols and interfaces for communications with other systems
24. Data compatibility	Use of standard data expressions and I/O routines
25.Language independence	Independence from specific user languages (such as English or Japanese) for menus and messages
26. Code independence	Independence from specific character codes (such as ASCII or ANSI)

- Automated documentation writing
- Utilities that generate FTA graphics and calculate probability
- Various utility programs for compiling performance statistics

The rapid advancement of computer systems is causing integration of information, control technologies, and communications. Networks of all sizes and configurations are making decentralized processing and software production simpler than ever. Software designers can now access systems at almost any time and place, with some working odd hours or operating out of their homes. All this just helps DR run more smoothly.

As technology allows software designers to work very much as individuals while staying in constant communication, we see more creative, integrated, practical, and, at the same time, efficient results. DR works to raise the value of this collective asset we call "creative intellectual labor."

Naturally, every tool has limits on its usefulness. The most effective are usually also the most application-specific. Thus we take care not to use them indiscriminately, but rather to apply each one for its own most suitable purpose.

TABLE 7-6. Quality Characteristics and Evaluation Indices

Substitute characteristic (index) \ Quality characteristic	Functionality	Reliability	Efficiency	Security	User-friendliness	Maintainability	Flexibility	Testability	Portability	Modifiability	Interactivity	Installability
Completeness	O	O		O	O							
Consistency	O					O						
Traceability	O	O				O						
Failure resistance		O		O	O							
Availability		O	O		O							
Accuracy		O		(O)								
Complexity		O	O	O		O		O				O
Storage efficiency			O									
Execution efficiency			O		O							
Access control				O								
Access audit				O								
Operability					O							
Learnability					O							
Communicability					O							
Conciseness			O			O	O	O		O		
Modularity						O	O	O		O		
Self-descriptiveness						O				O		
Generality									O	O		
Expandability						O	O			O		
Instrumentation		O		O				O				
Machine independence									O	O	O	O
System independence							O		O	O	O	O
Connectivity									O		O	O
Data compatibility											O	
Language independence							O			O		
Code independence							O			O		

TABLE 7-7. Recommendations for Text Review

Item No.	Category	Item Description
1 2	General	Not up to text format standards Inconsistent terminology
3 4	Terminology	Word errors Vague sentences
5 6 7	Accuracy	Words misspelled or omitted Typographical errors Inadequate description
8 9	Technical Content	Omissions Incorrect descriptions

TABLE 7-8. Software Review Items

Item No.	Category	Item Description
1 2	Memory	Vague or unclear Inappropriate (better expressions are available)
3 4 5 6	Specifications	Omitted function Basic conflict with system Inappropriate specifications Inadequate study of essential operating conditions
7 8 9 10	Interface	Poor interface with hardware Poor interface with other program Poor interface within same program Conflict between documentation files
11	Other	General

TABLE 7-9. Standard Documentation Checklist

Check item	Check date
1.Are terminology and graphic styles consistent?	
2.Are the descriptions structured into sections?	
3.Are abbreviations overused?	
4.Are there any misspelled or missing words?	
5.Is the descriptive style too vague?	
6.Are there standards for documentation format?	
7.Are there standards for documentation content?	
8.Are two or more terms used to refer to the same thing?	

DR AND THE INFORMATION CULTURE

The Information Age is moving us steadily toward a common global culture. One of our greatest challenges for the future is realizing the benefits of this trend without wiping out the unique traditions that individual regions and nations hold dear.

For all their good points, vast and complicated information systems are also bringing new levels of stress into social activities. The more powerful these systems become, the less know-how their users require. People are getting so accustomed to instant feedback and gratification that their senses are growing dull. All this adds up to a new kind of pollution for modern civilization. This pollution is invisible and intangible, but its effects are very real.

CHANNELING CREATIVITY

One of these effects is computer crime. Analysts of this phenomenon are predicting unprecedented monetary losses, more sophisticated techniques, less guilt over corporate theft, more "hacker clubs," greater participation by the youngest (and most inquisitive) age groups, longer intervals before crimes are discovered, and globalization of computer crime. Most legal action is after the fact, and as such has little deterrent value. Physical security measures, while they do much to prevent crime, tend to be prohibitive in cost.

The basic problem is on the demand side. Too many computer-literate people turn to illegal activities as outlets for their curiosity and creativity. While no method or technique will change the human psyche, we can offer alternatives that will at least make crime less appealing. From the DR perspective, this means making software packages more "transparent" to the user.

Giving the user as much flexibility as possible amounts to a transfer of control. When we allow computer enthusiasts to customize programs as they see fit, we have given them a healthy alternative for self-expression. This is the exact opposite of placing tighter controls on computer use, and it brings the shadow activity of computer hacking into the open.

CHANGING ATTITUDES TOWARD DR

Most software engineers are well-educated people whose lives have been fairly comfortable. They are often very conscious of their status as intellectual workers. Strongly influenced by Western traditions of individual achievement, their focus is primarily on their own work and day-to-day existence.

Not surprisingly, motivating this group to take DR seriously is no small challenge. DR calls for a willingness to receive constructive criticism, to glean wisdom from others outside one's own field, and above all to help others as well as oneself. Even if a DR project starts well in this environment, it typically breaks down at the first significant obstacle.

LEARNING FROM FAILURE

There is no substitute for overcoming adversity. All over the world and throughout history, people emerge from hardship with a new resolve to meet future challenges. Think of how often the threat of bankruptcy has brought out the best in companies. Such situations engender teamwork and a sense of common purpose.

On a smaller scale, initial failures can actually serve to advance DR. I can easily think of several case studies that fit this description, each resulting in a single-minded determination to make DR work.

The surest approach is a radical one. If adverse circumstances do not materialize on their own, then create them. In other words, intentionally direct people down a path to failure. The experience will teach them at least what *not* to do. It takes a skillful manager to understand this and pull it off convincingly, but the benefits are undeniable. Here are some possibilities:

- ***Conduct DR without documentation.*** This approach rarely succeeds. It becomes quickly and painfully obvious that a lack of documentation invites careless mistakes and confusion.

- ***Conduct DR with sloppy documentation.*** The effect is virtually the same as having no documentation at all, and it is sure to leave a bad taste in the mouths of the participants.

- ***Approach DR meetings spontaneously.*** Start everyone with a clear idea of what the project is all about, but then make no further arrangements before each DR meeting. During the actual meetings, have people make spontaneous presentations. It will not take them long to see the value of adequate preparation.
- ***Discourage plain talk and frank opinions.*** Embrace form over substance until plain speaking is a relief that demonstrates the futility of a superficial approach.
- ***Hold DR meetings at inappropriate places and times.*** Hold DR meetings in the hallway or shortly before people have to leave for other appointments, or at other times and places with plenty of distractions. When DR suffers, everyone will understand why.
- ***Choose an incompetent DR group.*** DR carried out by unqualified participants is a sure bet for substandard results, no matter how much discussion occurs.
- ***Ignore the lessons of past failures.*** Launch the DR group into a project that failed miserably in the past, but withhold any evidence that such a project even took place, let alone with bad results. By the time they find out, they will truly appreciate the importance of case study research.

I recommend that managers expose new DR participants to at least one of these approaches. Firefighting brigades in Japan receive similar training. They first learn various techniques that *fail* to get water onto the fire. By the time they arrive at the correct method, their first-hand knowledge of accompanying hazards makes them far more likely to remember it. Conversely, when people are aware only of what can go right, complacency lies just around the corner.

CHOOSING THE RIGHT PEOPLE

The DR manager's most important task is selecting the right people. Some individuals just need time and experience to sharpen their skills. On the other hand, you are just wasting your time with those who are clearly unmotivated or unqualified. Taking one of the failure-prone approaches described above is a good way to separate these two groups.

Kiyotaka Otsuka
Matsushita Electronic Components Company, Ltd.

8

DR for electronic components

(multilevel DR)

INTRODUCTION

These are some of the challenges facing the electronic components industry:

1. Rapid technological advances ensure very short product life cycles.
2. The variety of components is immense.
3. Any one device or machine tends to use many of these components.
4. Components must meet high standards of reliability.
5. Competition and market pressure keep prices low.

What we have is a fast changing field that is also getting more and more competitive. Each year, electronic components offer higher performance in increasingly smaller packages. A 20 to 30 percent annual turnover rate of components replaced by new models is not uncommon.

The range of component types is snowballing as customer demands broaden. Product standardization efforts have helped somewhat, but the overall trend is still upward. At Matsushita Electronic Components Company (MEC), we now sell about 10,000 different types of electrolytic capacitors each month, with some 15,000 on our overall product list. We also turn out a wide variety of ceramic capacitors, fixed and variable resistors, coils, transformers, and switches.

COMPONENT RELIABILITY

Countless televisions, VCRs, camcorders, and other consumer electronics products use large numbers of electronic components, sometimes more than 20,000. For such products we calculate breakdown risk based on the reliability of individual components. Consider this example:

(a)	(b)	(c)	(c^b)
Component	Quantity	Reliability	Factor
X	5	95%	77%
Y	2	80%	64%
Z	1	98%	98%

$$\text{Product reliability} = 77\% \times 64\% \times 98\% = 49\%$$

In this case, the product has a better than 50 percent chance of breaking down, even though all the components are at least 80 percent reliable. The bottom line is that every single component must comply with product quality requirements.

COMPONENT PRICING

Most resistors and capacitors are priced below ¥10 (10¢) each, with some less than ¥1. Yet failure of just one of these inexpensive parts can mean several hundred thousand yen (thousands of dollars) in repair or replacement costs, especially on high-priced equipment. It is important to realize that a breakdown rate of 0.1 parts per million and monthly sales of a billion components equates to 100 defective components. Of course, if the equipment is capable of detecting them, the breakdowns can be prevented. Unfortunately, most of these defects do not surface before the product reaches the final customer.

We thus have to make a wide variety of extremely reliable electronic components at very low cost, while updating or replacing 20 to 30 percent of them each year.

DR ISSUES AND OPPORTUNITIES

One of the major difficulties in quality assurance is accurately understanding user needs up front. Several decades ago, I worked as a section chief in the QC department. At that time we were so flooded with quality problems that we hardly knew where to begin. But realizing that giving up would get us nowhere, we proceeded to take a good, hard look at these problems. After initial investigation pointed us to the design stage, we started carrying out thorough design quality checks. We got the plant manager to stipulate that no new products would be allowed out of Design without the QC department's approval.

Within six months to a year we saw positive results as our workload began to slack off. Next we worked to overhaul the quality management system for manufacturing, inspection, and other areas, and this also led to improvement. This is how I first learned that quality assurance starts with DR. Meanwhile, newly calculated quality statistics revealed that 60 percent of our major problems were design related. We could only marvel at how many years we had been ignorant of this connection.

There is no overstating the usefulness of quality checks at the design stage. Truly effective DR looks at not just quality and reliability factors, but also cost, parts and materials selection, manufacturing methods, safety and environmental measures, related patents, laws and regulations, and sales and customer service. Any problems not addressed at this point will be far more complicated and expensive later on. Consequently, at MEC we have been pouring a lot of time and attention into DR for new products.

ORGANIZING DR WITHIN THE COMPANY

Table 8-1 illustrates the flow of new product development within MEC.

Let us now examine some of the key elements of DR at different organizational levels and then within our capacitor division.

MATSUSHITA QUALITY REVIEW

The parent firm, Matsushita Electric Industrial Company, supports subsidiaries in new product review and quality control through its so-called Quality Headquarters. Matsushita has always strongly emphasized DR as an effective QA tool. They long ago instituted a product inspection station, where products are closely evaluated in terms of function, safety, design, user documentation, packaging, patent issues, and competitiveness. Almost all the items covered under today's DR program were first targeted by the product inspection station.

Although MEC grants a great deal of autonomy to its divisions, all major quality-related decisions must pass through Quality Headquarters. No products can be shipped without their approval. They have proven particularly strict in the area of safety compliance.

As a general rule, the Matsushita quality review system does not involve regular DR meetings. Instead, Matsushita sends representatives to its suppliers' meetings. However, DR is applied in-house for mass market consumer products or others of strategic importance.

TABLE 8-1. Flow of New Product Development

Basic Steps		Purpose
Product planning	(Planning meetings)	Identify product and determine development policy
Project definition	(Development meetings)	Determine product and project targets
Product design and prototype		Develop design drawings, build and test prototype, evaluate results
Production process design	(Process design meetings)	Determine manufacturing methods
Production planning	(Production planning meetings)	Arrange for materials, parts, equipment, and tooling for pilot build
Design qualification	(Design qualification meetings)	Give final approval of design quality
	Design quality review	Evaluate design quality from a third-party perspective
Pilot build		Evaluate and arrange for materials, parts, equipment, and tooling for full production
Transfer to production	(Handover meetings)	Hand over the development project to Production
Product launch		Start full production according to schedule
	First-run inspection	Conduct a quality check on the first production run
	Development management review	Evaluate the development project once the product is in full production
Market survey		Follow up on production and sales by gathering and analyzing data on quality, price, and other market factors

AQ SYSTEM

Several years ago, Quality Headquarters inaugurated the AQ (action quality) system for the entire Matsushita Group. In the AQ check system, division chiefs personally take charge of evaluating performance, cost, quality, and reliability at major stages of product development. For capacitor division projects there are three such checks:

- AQ-0 (design prototype)
- AQ-1 (pilot build)
- AQ-2 (initial production)

Each of these AQ checks serves to reinforce DR as the division chiefs responsible compare the new product with corresponding products from other companies in terms of quality and reliability.

MEC QUALITY ASSURANCE CENTER

In addition, MEC's home office features a quality assurance center. This center provides a double check of critical products (categories A and B described below) that have already been reviewed at the division level.

DIVISION-BASED DR

Our division is allowed to make most of its own business decisions, including quality review of all products handled by its design, production, and sales departments. We have set up a separate DR department for this specific purpose.

DR BY PRODUCT CATEGORY

Recognizing that we deal with varying combinations of components and component sets, MEC has distinguished four new product categories, "A" through "D" (see Table 8-2) with separate DR methods for each (shown in Table 8-3).

DESIGN QUALIFICATION

Once a new product design is complete, the design department submits a qualification test request form (such as the example in Table 8-4) to the DR department. Test standards include the IEC 384-4 and JIS tests for aluminum electrolytic capacitors (Table 8-5 and Table 8-6, respectively), and the IEC 384-15 test for tantalum electrolytic capacitors. These help us determine test items, conditions, and minimum qualifying scores.

TABLE 8-2. New Product Categories

Category	Description
A	New products based on new design principles
B	Existing products with new materials, parts, structural design, or manufacturing methods 1. Products with improved performance or features 2. New applications
C	Existing products with new materials, parts, structural design, or manufacturing methods, where the revisions affect the entire product line
D	Existing products that are modified to suit specific applications where the revisions affect only certain models

TABLE 8-3. DR Methods for New Product Categories

Category	DR Method
A	Normal DR flow
B	DR and engineering departments jointly decide the review items and methods
C	DR and engineering departments jointly decide whether to conduct formal DR or to check quality just through first-run inspections and various tests
D	Quality is checked through first-run inspections and various tests without formal DR

Once they have compiled enough data and resolved any open technical issues, the design and DR departments may jointly elect to eliminate some of the tests. In addition, they can incorporate data from any tests the requesting department has already conducted, and if a standard series of components is involved, they need only to test representative samples of various rated values. For the example described in Table 8-7, we have selected samples according to IEC and JIS guidelines.

In this case we have selected four capacitors: one pair at minimum voltage (one each in minimum and maximum size) and one similar pair at maximum voltage. Notice that for the smallest 100V components there are several capacities available: 0.47, 1.0, 2.2, 3.3, and 4.7 microfarads. We would choose the maximum rating (the 4.7 μF component) because it is the most technically complex. These are the four selected:

Voltage	Capacity	Size
6.3V	100 μF	5 × 11(mm)
6.3V	15,000 μF	18 × 35.5(mm)
100V	4.7 μF	5 × 11(mm)
100V	470 μF	18 × 35.5(mm)

If all four pass the qualification tests, the entire series is qualified. If the voltage range of the series is 200V or more, we test two samples at intermediate voltages, which in this case would increase the total to six. Once qualification is complete, the DR department compiles the results into a report.

DESIGN QUALITY REVIEW

The DR department then appoints the design quality review (DQR) committee, selecting members with expertise in particular product functions. They adopt an impartial perspective in evaluating the design and recommending changes. Review items include the following:

- Electronic circuit technology
- Machine technology
- Physical and chemical functions
- Manufacturing technology
- Materials and purchasing
- Quality and reliability
- Standardization and patents
- Safety and environmental protection
- Sales and customer service

TABLE 8-4. Design Qualification Request Form

Design Qualification Request Form for
New Product
Revised Product

Requesting department: Section:

Date received: DD/ MM/ YY

Section chief	Supervisor	Person responsible

Date requested: DD/ MM/ YY

Section chief	Supervisor	Person responsible

Test subject		Category	A · B

(Purpose)

Characteristics (1. Quality 2. Cost 3. Manufacturability 4. Comparison to current products)

Technical improvements

Scope of application

Attachments
Product standards, product specs, manufacturing specs, part specs, material specs, development history, manufacturing history, qualification test result evaluation table, investigation results for new parts and materials

TABLE 8-4. (cont'd.)

Qualification test results and evaluations for technical items (item number/description, quantity, results, conditions)

Qualification test samples

Test items

Required = ○ Recommended = △ Not required = ×

Test item	Test status		Test item	Test status		Test item	Test status	
	Technical	Manufacturing		Technical	Manufacturing		Technical	Manufacturing
External structure and labels			Humidity load			Frequency characteristics		
Airtightness			Surge voltage			Salt spray test		
Excitation			Valve operation			High-frequency vibration		
Terminal strength			Voltage rise impact			Shock		
Soldering strength			Humidity resistance			Voltage rise time		
Electrostatic capacity			Solder heat resistance			(Reference tests)		
Capacitance loss			High/low temperature stability					
Force			Temperature and immersion cycle					
Current leakage			Aging effects					
Voltage resistance			Vibration resistance					
Insulation resistance			Attenuation					
High temperature without load			Overvoltage					
High temperature with load			Temperature characteristics					

Scheduled date for design qualification test: MM/DD [Signature]

TABLE 8-5. IEC 384-4 Qualification Test

Sampling Table and Allowable Defect Percentage for Qualification Test

Run No.		Test	Page number of this standard	Test samples (n) and allowable defect percentage (pd)						
				Capacitors (n) per voltage rating[3]	For capacitors with four or fewer ratings[3]			For capacitors with six ratings[3]		
					4n	pd	Total allowable defects Σ (pd)	6n	pd	Total allowable defects Σ (pd)
0		External inspection Dimensions Current leakage Electrostatic capacity Capacitance loss angle tangent Impedance[1]	4.2 4.2 4.3.1 4.3.2 4.3.3 4.3.4	30	120	1		180	2[2]	
		Spare samples		2	8			12	2	
1	1A	Terminal strength Solder heat resistance	4.4 4.5	3	12	1	4	18	1	6
	1B	Soldering strength Rapid temperature change Vibration Bump or impact resistance[1]	4.6 4.7 4.8 4.9 or 4.10	6	24	1		36	2[2]	
		Climate resistance	4.11	9	36	2[2]		54	2[2]	
2		Humidity resistance (normal conditions)	4.12	9	20	1		30	2[2]	
3		Durability	4.13	5	20	1		30	2[2]	
4 A		Surge voltage	4.14	5	8	1		12	1	
4 B		Reverse voltage[1] High-voltage safety[1]	4.15 4.16	2	8			12	1	
5 A		High-temperature storage[1]	4.17	2	8	1		12	1	
5 B		Low-temperature storage[1]	4.18	2	8			12	1	
6		Stability at high and low temperatures[1] Charging	4.19 4.20	3	12	1		18	2[2]	

1.Where the voltage rating is set by a specific standard.
2.No more than one defect allowed per voltage rating.
3.See section 3.4.1 regarding combinations of case sizes and voltages.

TABLE 8-6. JIS Qualification Test

(This quality qualification test can be used for special, ordinary, or abbreviated levels in testing aluminum electrolytic capacitors.)

Run	Test item	Applied section	Page number from JIS C 5102	Test samples[4]			No. passed[5]	
				Special	Ordinary	Abbre-viated		
I[1]	External inspection, structure, and dimensions[8]	6.1 6.2 6.5					Special level 0	
	Capacitance loss angle tangents	8.3	7.5				Ordinary level 1	
	Electrostatic capacity	8.2	7.4				Abbreviated level 2	
	Current leakage	8.1	7.3				0	
	Impedance[3]	8.4	7.7	90[2]	61[2]	38[2]		
II	Solder's heat resistance	9.4	8.3					2
	Impact resistance[3]	9.3	—					
	Vibration resistance	9.2	8.2					
	Salt spray test[3]	10.5	9.7					
	Temperature and immersion cycle[3]	10.2	9.3 9.4	18	12	6	1	
III	Soldering strength	9.5	8.4					
	Terminal strength	9.1	8.1	18	12	6	1	
	Surge voltage	8.5	7.10					
IV	Voltage resistance (sleeve)[3]	8.6.1	7.1					
	Insulation resistance (sleeve)[3]	8.6.2	7.2					
	Stability at high and low temperatures	10.1	9.11	18	12	6	1	
	Humidity resistance (for normal conditions)	10.3	9.5					
	Humidity resistance (for temperature and humidity cycle)[3]	10.4	9.6					
V	High-temperature loss (at maximum temperature used for rated voltage)	10.7	9.10	18	12	12	1	
VI	Attenuation[3]	10.6	9.8	18	12	6	1	
	Solvent resistance	6.6	6.2.1					

Notes:
1. Undamaged samples
2. Samples from run I are sorted this way because further tests will be done on subsequent runs (therefore, this number includes defects allowed for run I)
3. Where the voltage rating is set by a specific standard.
4. This number applies to one qualified run. According to the applicable standard, if that run includes multiple types or if the test is for a rated capacitor, the samples are sorted by type and rating. In such cases, the number may be higher or lower.
5. If one sample fails in two or more test items for the same run, it counts as only one defect.
8. Labels are tested only by external inspection and are judged defective if they are unclear, incomplete, or incorrect.

TABLE 8-7. Example of Product Series List

XX Series, Aluminum Electrolytic Capacitors

Dimension drawing

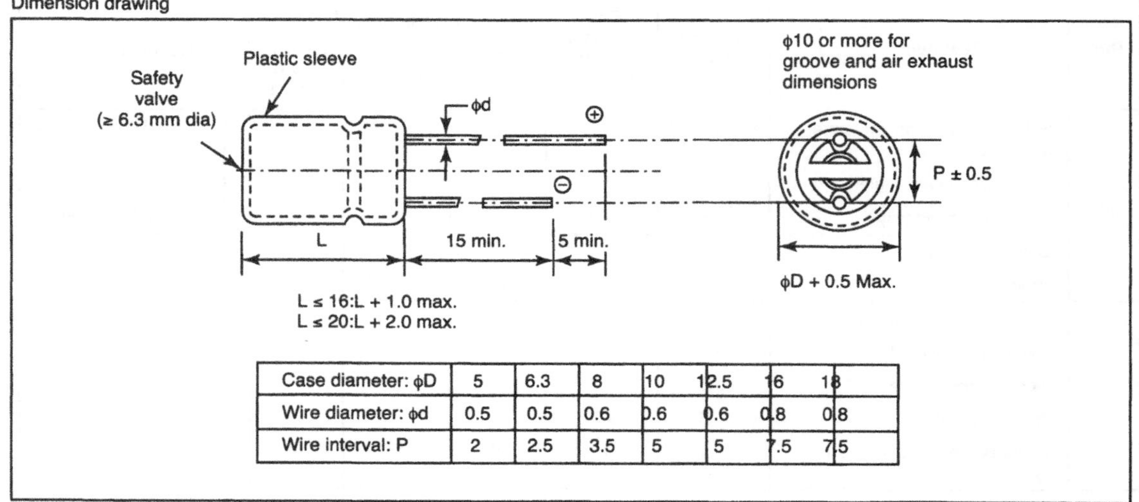

Case diameter: ϕD	5	6.3	8	10	12.5	16	18
Wire diameter: ϕd	0.5	0.5	0.6	0.6	0.6	0.8	0.8
Wire interval: P	2	2.5	3.5	5	5	7.5	7.5

Dimension table

ϕD × L (mm)

Electrostatic capacity \ Rated voltage	6.3 (OJ)	10 (1A)	16 (1C)	25 (1E)	35 (1V)	50 (1H)	63 (1J)	100 (2A)
0.1 (0R1)						5 × 11		
0.22 (R22)						5 × 11		
0.33 (R33)						5 × 11		
0.47 (R47)						5 × 11		5 × 11
1 (010)						5 × 11		5 × 11
2.2 (2R2)						5 × 11		5 × 11
3.3 (3R3)						5 × 11		5 × 11
4.7 (4R7)						5 × 11		5 × 11
10 (100)			5 × 11	5 × 11	5 × 11	5 × 11	5 × 11	6.3 × 11.2
22 (220)			5 × 11	5 × 11	5 × 11	5 × 11	6.3 × 11.2	8 × 11.5
33 (330)			5 × 11	5 × 11	5 × 11	6.3 × 11.2	6.3 × 11.2	10 × 12.5
47 (470)			5 × 11	5 × 11	6.3 × 11.2	6.3 × 11.2	8 × 11.5	10 × 16
100 (101)	5 × 11	5 × 11	6.3 × 11.2	6.3 × 11.2	8 × 11.5	8 × 12.5	10 × 12.5	12.5 × 20
220 (221)	6.3 × 11.2	6.3 × 11.2	8 × 11.5	8 × 12.5	10 × 12.5	10 × 16	10 × 20	16 × 25
330 (331)	6.3 × 11.2	8 × 11.5	8 × 12.5	10 × 12.5	10 × 16	10 × 20	12.5 × 20	16 × 25
470 (471)	8 × 11.5	8 × 12.5	10 × 12.5	10 × 16	10 × 20	12.5 × 25	12.5 × 25	16 × 31.5
1000 (102)	10 × 12.5	10 × 16	10 × 20	12.5 × 20	12.5 × 25	16 × 25	16 × 31.5	
2200 (222)	12.5 × 20	12.5 × 20	12.5 × 25	16 × 25	16 × 31.5	18 × 35.5		
3300 (332)	12.5 × 20	12.5 × 25	16 × 25	16 × 31.5	18 × 35.5			
4700 (472)	16 × 25	16 × 25	16 × 31.5	18 × 35.5				
6800 (682)	16 × 25	16 × 31.5	18 × 35.5					
10000 (103)	16 × 31.5	18 × 35.5						
15000 (153)	18 × 35.5							

DESIGN DEPARTMENT INPUTS

The requesting design department must prepare the following documents for the DQR committee:

- New Product Review Request Form (see Table 8-8)
- New Product Proposal Sheet (see Table 8-9)
- Development History (see Table 8-10)
- Self-Diagnostic Checklist (see Table 8-11)
- Previous test data
- Comparison data for existing and competitive products
- Proposed product standards and standards for materials, parts, manufacturing, and test methods
- Other documents deemed necessary by the DR department or by the requestor

PREPARATION

- As noted above, the DR department should select committee members for their functional expertise. Top priority goes to people familiar with the new product's key technologies.
- The requesting department should submit all relevant documents to the committee well before the DQR meeting, thus giving members enough time to study the review items.
- The DR department is also responsible for informing all committee members and the appropriate people in the requesting department of the DQR date and time (see Table 8-12).

EXECUTION

DQR generally starts with an overall review of every functional area, followed by ad hoc evaluation of key items by designated experts. The DQR committee covers these areas:

- Quality
- Performance
- Features
- Parts and materials

TABLE 8-8. New Product Review Request Form

To: QC Dept.

From:________________Division
________________Engineering Dept

[Signature]

New Product Review Request Form

The final design/project transfer for the following new product has been completed, and I therefore request a design quality/development management review based on the DR guidelines.

Signed:

1.New product name (new product category):

2.Projected product launch:

3.Proposed destination and application:

4.Documents to be presented to the QC department (due one week before review)

Documents	Available/Not available	Engineering Dept. comments
1. New product proposal		
2. Complete set of product standards and other applicable standards		
3. Development history and test data		
4. Product structural drawings		
5. Prototype sample (n = 1) and list of major components		
6. Documents (such as circuit diagrams) related to customer applications		
7. Performance comparison table for competitive products		
8. Self-diagnostic checklist		

TABLE 8-9. New Product Proposal Sheet (Example)

Date: MM/DD/YY

New Product Proposal Sheet						
Product name				Proposal No.		
Proposal summary						
Proposal objectives	Size			Quantity		
	Performance (electrical and mechanical)			Monthly volume		
				Sales period		
	Product life			Target price		
	Other					
Characteristics						
Applications/ Target market/ Benefits						
Depts. in charge	Design/Prototype			Manufacturing		
Design policy	(Design budget)					
Comments/ Related patents/ Competitive trends						
Master development schedule	Item	Development targets	Design/Prototype	Production process design	Pilot	Project transfer
	Completion date					

Notes: 1. The New Product Proposal is one of the most important documents in new product development. During DQR, the review committee uses it to check whether development targets have been met.

2. Since the information entered on this sheet is both strategic and proprietary, the requesting department must stamp it "confidential."

TABLE 8-10. Development History (Example)

Proposal No. (category)	New Product Technology Development History	Section chief	Supervisor	Person responsible
No.	Development project name: ______			

1. Process and progress management

Item / Step	Planning	Execution	Process and actions	Attached document nos.
Project start				
Design evaluation				
First test series				
Prototype build				
Production process design				
Second test series				
Pilot build				
Approval for production				
Transfer to production				
Approval for delivery				
Comments Proposal and schedule issues				

- Reliability
- Fitness for use
- Applications
- Safety
- Production process design
- Packaging design
- Data management

DQR follows this sequence:

1. The DQR committee asks the applicants (representatives from the requesting department) to provide prototype samples that illustrate product conformance in the above areas.
2. The applicants answer related questions from the committee.
3. The committee analyzes problems, recommends countermeasures, and makes an overall evaluation based on preliminary studies of the new product's functions.
4. Committee members combine historical information with their own specialized knowledge and experience to evaluate new product quality in depth.
5. Items not concluded by the review date are submitted to the appropriate department for qualification testing. The DQR committee can then incorporate the results of these tests into their findings and recommendations.

COMPILATION OF RESULTS

After the review is complete, each committee member submits a report to the DR department on his or her own field of expertise. This report addresses the new product's problem points, the relative importance of each, proposed countermeasures, and other relevant comments.

The DR department compiles all these individual reports into the New Product Review Report, which it then distributes to the review applicants and other parties concerned (see Tables 8-13 and 8-14).

TABLE 8-11. Design Department's Self-Diagnostic Checklist for New Product Evaluation

Evaluation items	Questions	Yes	No
1. Development planning	1. Are the development targets clearly stated in the new product proposal?		
	2. Are there any documents clearly stating company development policy?		
	3. Has a development budget been established?		
	4. Is the development project on schedule?		
2. Quality characteristics	1. Are there any documents clarifying how user quality requirements are reflected in the product dimensions, composition, and performance features?		
	2. Have applicable standards been established, such as for product planning, testing, and manufacturing?		
3. Parts and materials	1. Have parts and materials standards been established?		
	2. Have parts and materials suppliers been determined?		
	3. Can these suppliers meet the required quality, volume, and cost?		
	4. Have quality tests been carried out on the selected parts and materials and are the results available?		
4. Quality evaluation	1. Has the quality level of design prototypes been checked against the product standards?		
	2. Has the proposed product been compared (for advantages and disadvantages) with competitive products?		
	3. Does the product contain any technologies that merit applying for a patent?		
5. Reliability and environmental resistance tests	1. Have tests been carried out to verify that the product meets JIS electronic component standards for heat and humidity, impact, and vibration resistance?		
	2. Have 1,000-hour reliability tests been carried out for all of the product's major characteristics (for life cycle reliability tests if the product's guaranteed service life is less than 1,000 hours)?		
	3. Have reliability testing methods (duration, frequency, sample size) been determined?		
6. User application studies	1. Have studies been carried out on all electrical equipment and electronic circuitry used in the new product?		
	2. Have user cautions been clearly stated?		

TABLE 8-11. (cont'd.)

Evaluation items	Questions	Yes	No
7. Safety and regulatory compliance	1. Have studies been carried out on fire and electrical safety requirements?		
	2. Has safety been checked under various hazardous conditions?		
8. Production process design	1. Have purchasing arrangements been made for required production equipment and instrumentation?		
	2. Are current assembly process and operator capabilities in line with manufacturing quality standards?		
	3. Has all necessary information (on manufacturing engineering, manufacturing, quality control) been distributed among appropriate plant departments and have all task assignments been clarified to ensure a smooth transfer to full production?		
9. Packaging design	1. Is container design under way?		
	2. Has the container design been tested for packaging strength?		
10. Data management	1. Have dated files been kept to compile all relevant design data since the new product planning stage?		
	2. Have all problems for the current design stage been identified?		
11. In-house design quality check	1. Has the design department completed its in-house design quality check?		
	2. Have problems revealed during this check been addressed?		

Remaining problems	

Design department	Person responsible
Signature of division chief or plant manager	Signature

TABLE 8-12. DQR Notification Memo

TO:

FROM: QC Dept.,
Quality Engineering Section

DQR Notification

A design quality review meeting will be held on the date noted below as part of our new product review program. Please be sure to attend.

Signed:

Item	Description
1. Product name	
2. Date	MM/DD/YY, from ________:________ to ________:________ AM/PM
3. Place	
4. Prepared documents	
5. Schedule	
6. Participants (committee members with functional expertise)	

(Also distributed to the following individuals:)

Note: This DQR notification memo has been issued by the QC Department's DR Office. It should reach all committee members and applicants one week before the meeting.

TABLE 8-13. New Product Review Report (cover sheet)

Handling status:	Delivery No.:
CONFIDENTIAL	To:

No. ______________

New Product Review Report

(DQR)

Product name: XXXX capacitor

Category: A

Plant/Facility: Development lab

DD/MM/YY

Matsushita Electronic Components Company, Ltd.
New Product Review Committee
DROffice, QC Dept.

TABLE 8-14. New Product Review Report (blank form)

(Page _______ of _______)

Review date: MM/DD/YY

DR Results

Product name	
Severity*	**Findings**

* Severity codes:

Name of committee member:

X = Definitely requires improvements

△ =Needs further study

○ = Needs careful monitoring

□ =Suggestion/ comment only

DEPARTMENT RESPONSE

The requesting department plans and carries out any improvements identified by DR, informing the DR department upon completion. Their report should explain when and how the improvements were made, and why any may have been left out. The appropriate engineering department chief and/or manufacturing manager must then approve each of these.

Quality data compiled after the report is complete should be submitted as an attachment (see Table 8-15) or later as a separate document.

DEVELOPMENT MANAGEMENT REVIEW

The DR meeting after product launch looks at project results, with the primary intent of improving the development process. That is, it considers the question of whether the current approach to new product development achieves 100 percent of design quality goals at every stage from design to manufacturing. Sometimes the reviewers must go back upstream to modify the design or check on production capacities.

This development management review (DMR) covers everything from acceptance to shipment, including these topics:

- Documentation of policies, procedures, standards, and methods
- Management system for acceptance functions
- Management system for manufacturing processes
- Inspection system
- Management system for equipment and instrumentation
- Management system for quality evaluation and information

PREPARATION

Once the need for DMR is identified, committee members are selected. They meet to decide on a schedule and notify the original applicants from the DQR stage.

EXECUTION

Using previously submitted documents, the DMR committee then evaluates production management functions related to product launch, from parts acceptance to product shipment.

TABLE 8-15. Improvement Completion Report

TO: QC Dept.

No. ______________

Engineering Department Chief [Signature]

Plant Manager [Signature]

Improvement Result Report

Product name		Applicant			
DR Findings	**Cause(s)**	**Countermeasure(s)**	**Date Installed**	**QC Dept. approval date**	**QC Dept. comments**

Standards compatibility. Committee members check for discrepancies between the user acceptance drawings and applicable rated values and for compatibility with operating standards. They investigate how much leeway the rated values provide in terms of process capability.

Onsite investigations. The DMR committee goes onsite to evaluate the following management process chart items:

1. Supplier management
    - Raw materials acceptance inspection and quality check
    - Guidance for suppliers
    - Management of inspection equipment
    - Feedback data on processes
2. Manufacturing management
    - Management of key processes for quality
    - Management of key processes for safety
    - Process capability and control
    - Operation fail-safing
    - Enforcement of correct work methods
3. Inspection management
    - Inspection approach
    - Precision and relevance
    - Methods and interpretation of results
    - Data compilation and storage
    - Treatment of scrap and defects
4. Equipment management
    - PM and precision improvement efforts
    - Efficient utilization of machinery and tooling
5. Quality evaluation and information management
    - Management-directed testing
    - Analysis of process abnormalities and quality fluctuations
    - Management of daily, weekly, and monthly quality information
    - Management of user-oriented market feedback

The committee also uses this opportunity to confirm improvements from DQR. These onsite investigations are followed by Q&A sessions, after which individual members submit reports on their findings.

COMPILATION OF RESULTS

The DR department compiles all individual reports into the Product Project Review Report, which it distributes to the review applicants along with recommendations for further improvements. After carrying out these additional measures, the applicants submit an updated report to their division chief. Finally, the committee studies this report for any outstanding issues to be addressed.

DR AND JOINT DR FOR COMPONENT SETS

The reliability of electronic components, and also of electronic equipment as a whole, is influenced greatly by how the components are grouped together. A well-designed component set should be inexpensive and highly reliable. Accordingly, DR should also address set design and performance.

At MEC we go a step further by opening our DR meetings to other set manufacturers, so that we can jointly work out any problems in set configuration. These are the points we generally consider:

1. Electrical load
    - Are voltage, current, and power within specified tolerances?
    - Do any of the polarized components receive reverse voltage?
    - Is there a large ripple current?
    - Is the pulse voltage too high?
    - Is charging too frequent?
2. Thermal stress
    - Is the temperature within the rated value?
    - Are the components exposed to direct sunlight?
    - Are the components too close to a heat source?
    - Do temperatures run abnormally high or low during certain periods or seasons?
3. Installation methods
    - Is any excessive force required during installation?
    - Do any of the wires touch each other?

The reviewing committee issues a Set Analysis Report describing any problems and recommending specific countermeasures. The set manufacturers, whether in-house or external to the company, then work to carry out these improvements before their products reach the field.

EXAMPLE OF SET ANALYSIS

Analyzed set: ____________

Characteristics: Three power supply model, 25 percent smaller than conventional models

Manufacturing dept.: ________ Division, ________ Plant

Projected launch date: MM/YY

Analysis assignments: (see Table 8-16)

TABLE 8-16. Analysis Assignments

Analyzed component	Dept. where assigned	Assignee (section and name)
Transformers	Transformer Dept.	_____ section chief, ________
Coils	Transformer Dept.	_____ section chief, ________
Electrolytic capacitors	Capacitor Dept.	_____ section chief, ________
Fixed resistors	Fixed Resistor Dept.	_____ section chief, ________
Ceramic capacitors	Ceramic Dept.	_____ section chief, ________
Switches	Mechanical Components Dept.	_____ section chief, ________
Variable resistors	Mechanical Components Dept.	_____ section chief, ________
Integrated circuits	Integrated Circuit Dept.	_____ section chief, ________
(DR Office)	Quality Assurance Center	_____ section chief, ________

Analysis items: (see Table 8-17)

TABLE 8-17. Analysis Items

Analysis Item	Component	Problems	Severity	Proposed improvements
Electrical load	Aluminum electrolytic capacitor ECEAOJK 200 (6.3V 22 micro-F)	On at rated value of 6.3V, but then 8V added when off.	X	Replace 6.3V capacitor with 10V ECEAIAK 220 (10V, 22 micro-F) capacitor.
	Tantalum electrolytic capacitor ECSF 35 ER 47 (35V 0.46 micro-F)	Reverse voltage is applied.	X	Install the capacitor in the reverse direction.
	Fixed resistor ERQ 14 AJ 330 (1/4W 33 ohms)	Overcharges of 543% when main switch is on and 389% when off (effective value is 112%) damaging the line.	X	Replace 1/4W 33 ohm resistor with 1/2W 33 ohm model.
Thermal stress	Aluminum electrolytic capacitors (Qty: 3) ECEAIES 222 ECEAICS 100 ECET 50 R 222 SW	(Room temperature = 24°C) Measured temperature / Increase over room temperature 50°C 26°C 51°C 27°C 46°C 22°C	△	Measured temperature rises more than 20°C over the room temperature sometimes to over 60°C (compared to an estimated maximum of only 40°C). This causes no immediate problems, but will reduce the device's durability and reliability. Investigate alternative set configurations, various heat dissipation methods, or more heat resistant capacitors.
Installation methods	Semi-fixed resistor	Some semi-fixed resistors are either presently or potentially in contact with wire bundles. Contact: R17, R19 Contact risk: R11, R12	□	Arrange the wire bundles some other way to avoid contact with resistors.

Note: Severity codes X =Definitely requires improvements △ =Need careful monitoring and/or further study □ =Suggestion/ comment only

COMPONENT SET PROCESS IMPROVEMENTS

Recognizing the importance of process control, MEC long ago began a campaign to reduce the number of defective components. When one of these shows up in a set, the manufacturing department notifies the upstream parts department right away so that it can take corrective action. As part of our early warning system for new products, this closed loop helps us pinpoint the most critical design quality characteristics and test items.

MARKET FEEDBACK

MEC goes to these sources for quality information from the end user's perspective:

1. In-house component sets (manufactured)
   - Sales offices nationwide
   - Distribution centers
   - Matsushita Quality Headquarters
   - Leading quality consultants
2. External component sets (purchased)
   - Periodic surveys of major users
   - Quality focus groups

Thanks to these data-gathering efforts, each new product reflects at least one year's study of market quality requirements.

BENEFITS OF DR

Our biggest gain from DR is stabilization of quality. The practice of thorough design checks has brought us from frequent quality problems to virtually none. Most of what we still confront are manufacturing errors, generally more manageable than inherent design flaws. Product quality is determined foremost at the design stage, and the introduction of DR has allowed our design department to devote much more attention to product development. This has meant freeing our designers to address these market demands:

- High performance
- Downsizing (making the products smaller and lighter)
- Wide temperature range
- Long product life
- High reliability
- Low rate of defects and failure

PLANS FOR THE FUTURE

There is much more to be done. Each new generation of electronic components does more things faster and cheaper than the one before. There is no margin for waste. Meanwhile, applications for our products are broadening as life cycles shorten and the pace of new product development accelerates. The inevitable result is a proliferation of product types and a much heavier workload for our DR program.

We must therefore seek every way possible to carry out reviews more effectively and efficiently. This means continuous progress in these areas:

- Better management techniques and evaluation methods
- Automated measuring and data processing
- Stratification of new products for management purposes
- Application of emerging product and process technologies
- Application of new measuring, analyzing, and monitoring equipment
- Advanced physical analysis of failure modes

We look increasingly to statistical and reliability-oriented methods, and to FMEA and FTA in particular. Figure 8-1 and Table 8-18 show how MEC uses failure mode analysis data both to improve the design of its aluminum electrolytic capacitors and to identify desirable test methods.

Table 8-19 is a scoring table for three factors—frequency, detectability, and impact—that we multiply to measure failure severity.

We intervene with special measures as early as the design stage if any failure item has a total score of 27 or a score of 5 for any of the three factors. Although this evaluation method is somewhat subjective and therefore far from perfect, we have been using it extensively as we seek to refine it.

We need to develop more sophisticated testing methods and instrumentation, along with higher levels of technology. Furthermore, expanding the variety and length of our tests will yield more accurate estimates, giving us better quality evaluation capabilities.

Advances in product and process technologies are ushering in new materials, structures, and fabrication methods which require more specialized knowledge. We need people familiar with the physics and chemistry involved in failure analysis and with the operation of new instruments and monitoring equipment. In addition, automation of measuring and data processing tasks is a must for manipulating and analyzing failure data. Finally, we see product stratification as one tool that will enable us to undertake more and more development projects simultaneously.

In a nutshell, we hope to ensure quality with ever greater precision and efficiency. The foundation for this ongoing pursuit is matching the right people in terms of skill and experience with the right DR tasks.

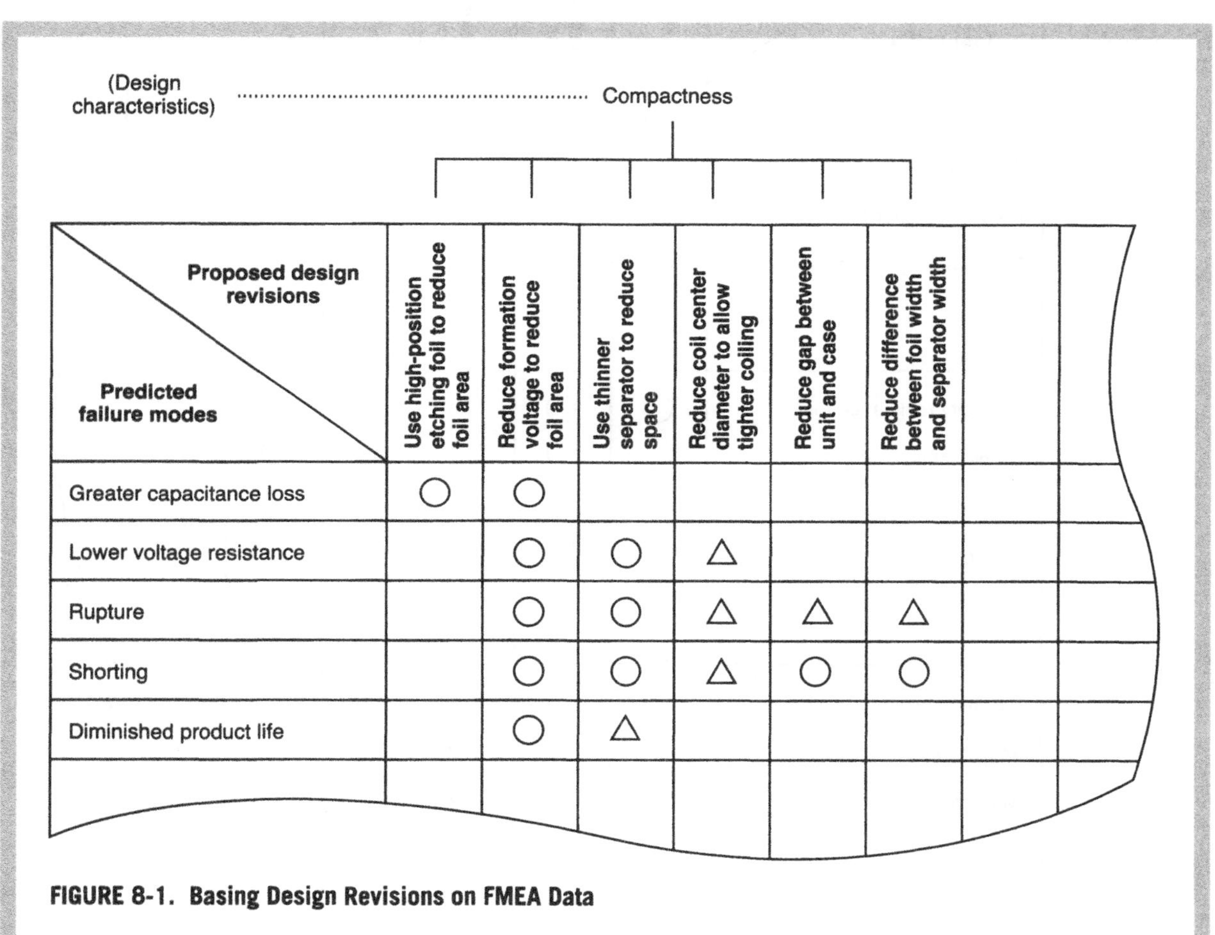

Proposed design revisions / Predicted failure modes	Use high-position etching foil to reduce foil area	Reduce formation voltage to reduce foil area	Use thinner separator to reduce space	Reduce coil center diameter to allow tighter coiling	Reduce gap between unit and case	Reduce difference between foil width and separator width		
Greater capacitance loss	○	○						
Lower voltage resistance		○	○	△				
Rupture		○	○	△	△	△		
Shorting		○	○	△	○	○		
Diminished product life		○	△					

FIGURE 8-1. Basing Design Revisions on FMEA Data

TABLE 8-18. Basing Test Methods on FMEA

Failure modes / Test methods	Greater capacitance loss	Lower voltage resistance	Rupture	Shorting	Diminished product life	
Start-up analysis	○	○			○	
Temperature analysis	○				△	
Frequency analysis	○					
Ripple heat generation	○	○				
⋮						
Humidity resistance test	○	○			○	
Surge voltage test	○	○	○	○	○	
High-temperature test	○	○			○	
Ripple load test	○	○	○	○	○	
⋮						
Vibration test			○	○		
Impact test			○	○		
Bump test			○	○		
⋮						

TABLE 8-19. Failure Severity Scoring Table

	Evaluation criteria	Points
Frequency	Failures occur rarely and only under special conditions	1
	Failures occur occasionally and only under special conditions	2
	Failures occur rarely under ordinary conditions	3
	Failures occur occasionally under ordinary conditions	4
Detectability	Failures are easily detected during ordinary process inspections	1
	Failures go undetected occasionally	2
	Failures can be detected during brief damage inspection	3
	Failures can be detected during extensive reliability tests	4
	Failures go undetected until a total breakdown occurs	5
Impact	External, visible abnormality with no impact on function	1
	Has a slight impact on functions, but can be easily repaired	2
	Interrupts at least one basic function, but can be easily repaired	3
	Interrupts at least one basic function and cannot be repaired	4
	Creates major safety problems (fire, electric shock, other hazards)	5

Note: Severity = frequency × detectability × impact

PART 3

DR ESSAYS

The essays in this part of the book address one or more of the following:

1. DR-related items and issues that have generated a lot of discussion and debate.
2. Traditional design tasks or other subjects which do not fall directly under DR but which are still of interest to DR participants.
3. Development management and other topics that are important for those managing DR.

I asked each of the authors to touch upon at least one of these areas. The idea was not to focus on DR itself, but rather on the relevance of these peripheral subjects for those directing and carrying out DR.

At the same time, all the essays include practical, specific guidance that should prove helpful in applying DR.

Tadashi Murata
University of the Ryukyus

9
AI and databases—DR tools for the future

WHAT IS ARTIFICIAL INTELLIGENCE?

To answer this question, let us first consider "real intelligence," which is how people think. Using a question as input and its answer as output, part (a) of Figure 9-1 shows what operations the human brain performs to convert input into output. The brain first analyzes the question, then goes through a series of reasoning processes that use the specialized and common knowledge it has accumulated. Some of this knowledge is instinctive, and some is gained through education. The final outcome of this reasoning is the answer.

Simply put, AI (artificial intelligence) is computer systems mimicking human thinking. In part (b) of Figure 9-1, the same question starts as computer input. The AI system uses a knowledge base into which information has been entered and stored to understand the meaning of the question and produce an answer (output) via an inference engine.

AI research began several decades ago amidst great expectations, but many soon grew pessimistic as cost constraints and underpowered computers slowed progress to a crawl. Consequently, AI projects faded quietly into the background.

Recently, however, AI-oriented programming languages such as LISP and PROLOG, coupled with ever improving computer performance, have breathed new life into AI research. The market for AI products is now growing steadily (see Figure 9-2). It was in the mid-1980s that applications really started mushrooming. Expert systems, natural-language software, CAI (computer aided instruction) software, and image recognition systems have been particularly successful. This trend is almost certain to continue as computer technology keeps advancing.

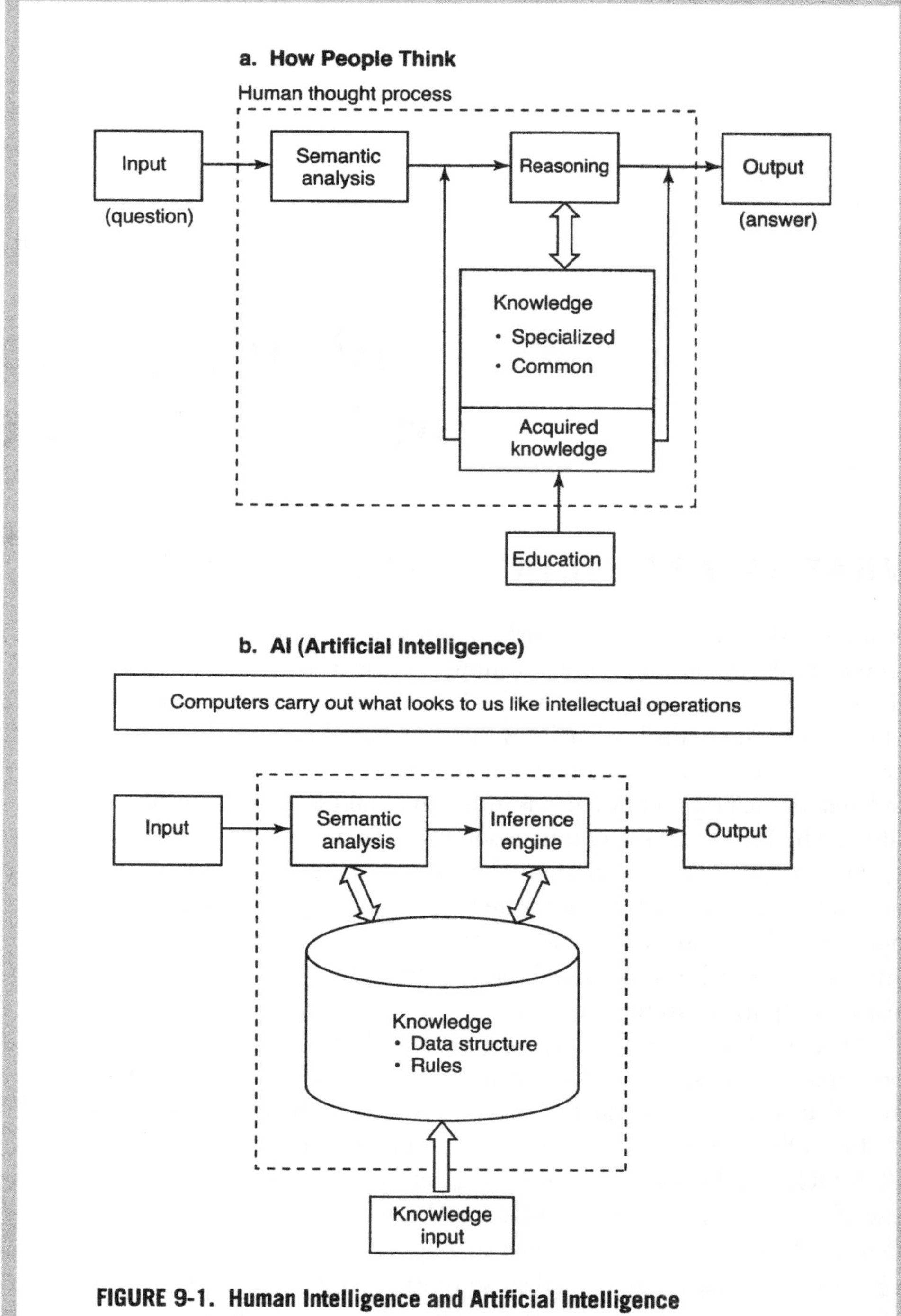

FIGURE 9-1. Human Intelligence and Artificial Intelligence

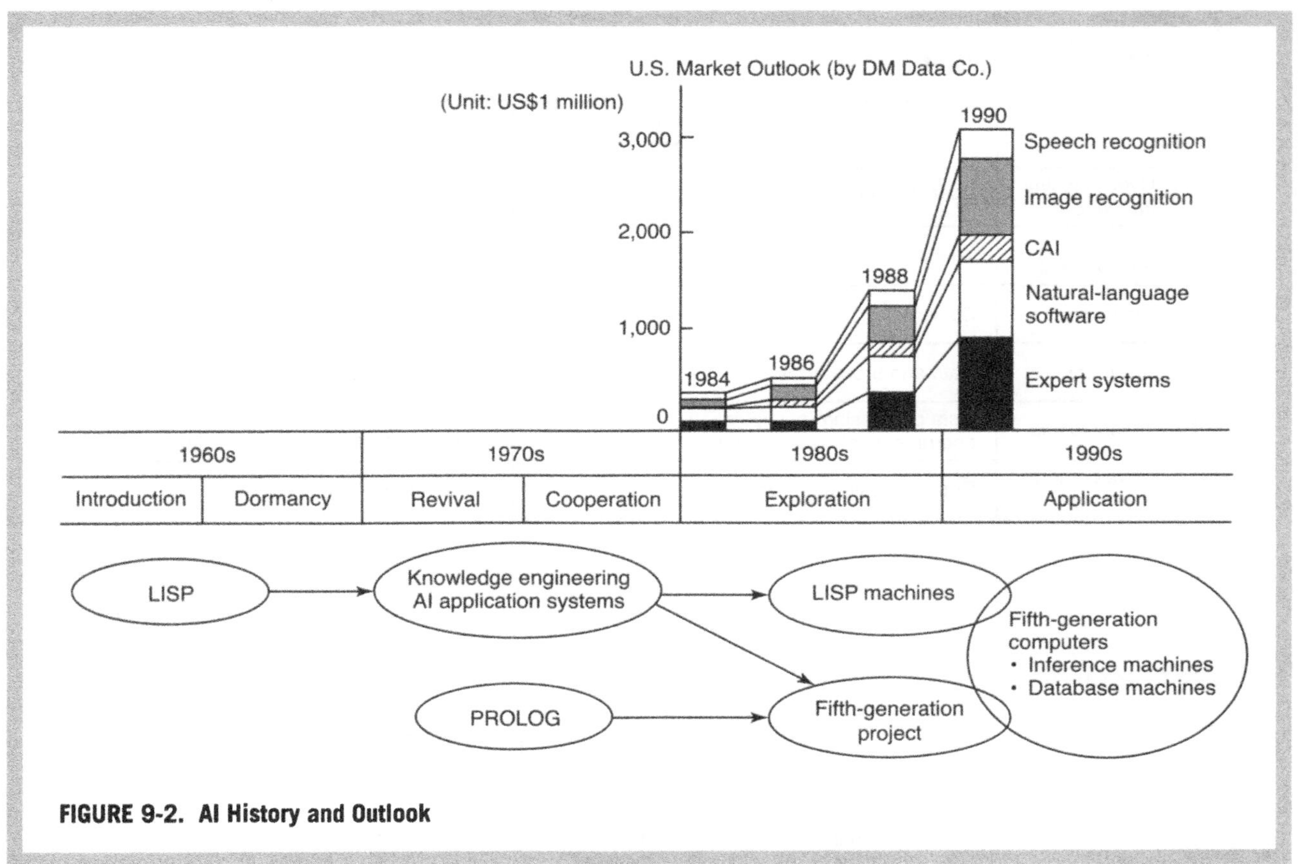

FIGURE 9-2. AI History and Outlook

Table 9-1 compares the features of AI and conventional information systems. In AI systems both hardware and software are designed to process knowledge data for human users.

EXPERT SYSTEMS

AI research can be broadly categorized into these major fields:

1. Natural languages
2. Machine translation
3. Expert systems

Because they make accumulated knowledge more accessible, expert systems have the greatest applicability to DR. Figure 9-3 shows how expert systems can be further categorized by areas of application.

TABLE 9-1. AI Features

	Conventional systems (high-speed data processing)	AI systems (knowledge data processing)
User-machine interface	Users work to suit the systems	Systems work to suit the users
Target environment	Well-structured	Ill-structured
Algorithms	Decisive	Indecisive
Programs	Data and procedures	Knowledge and inferences
Technologies	Data processing (manipulation and numerical calculations)	Symbolic processing (pattern matching and searching)
Development approach	Detailed system design	Trial-and-error method

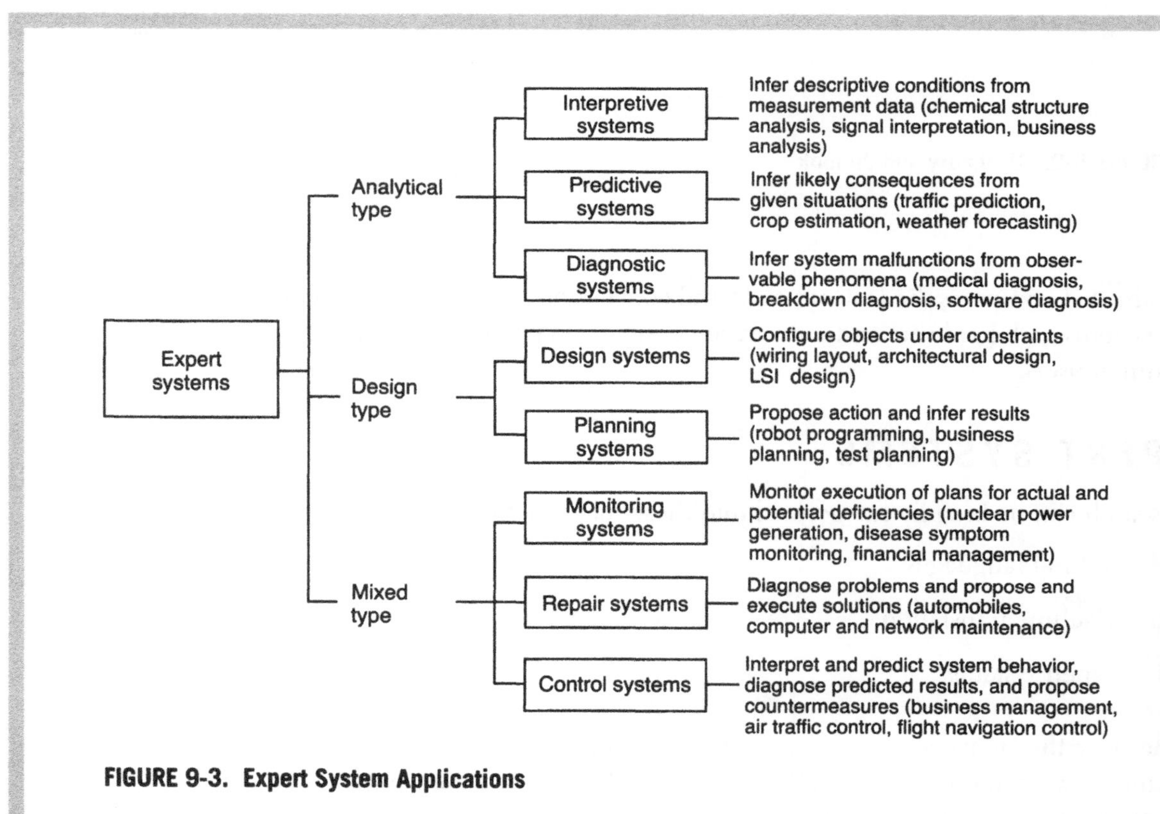

FIGURE 9-3. Expert System Applications

These are the main attributes of expert systems:

1. They use specialized knowledge from a particular field.
2. They use knowledge acquired from experts.
3. They handle very complicated and specialized problems.
4. They solve problems almost as well as the experts can.

Figure 9-4 illustrates expert systems in terms of a doctor-patient situation. Figure 9-5 outlines the structure of an expert system. Later we will discuss the databases and knowledge bases shown in these figures.

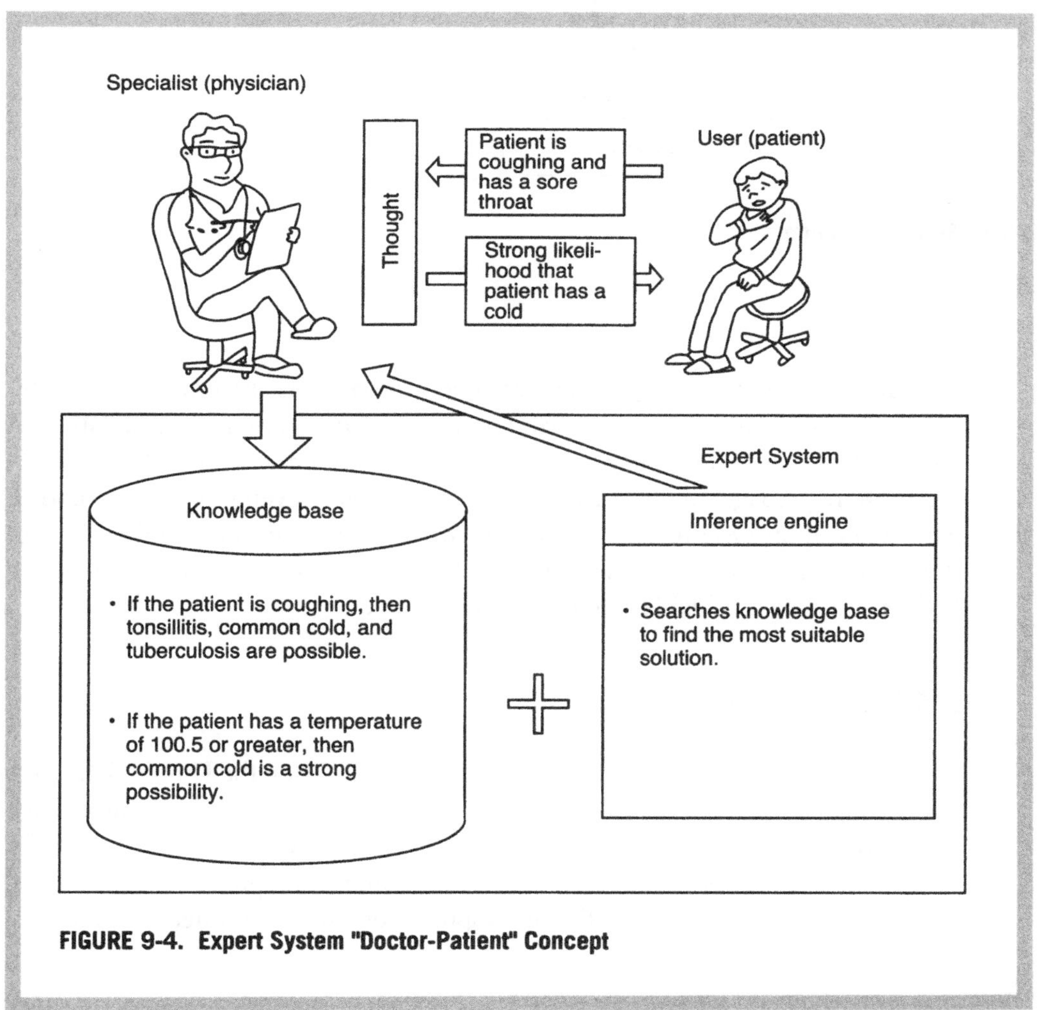

FIGURE 9-4. Expert System "Doctor-Patient" Concept

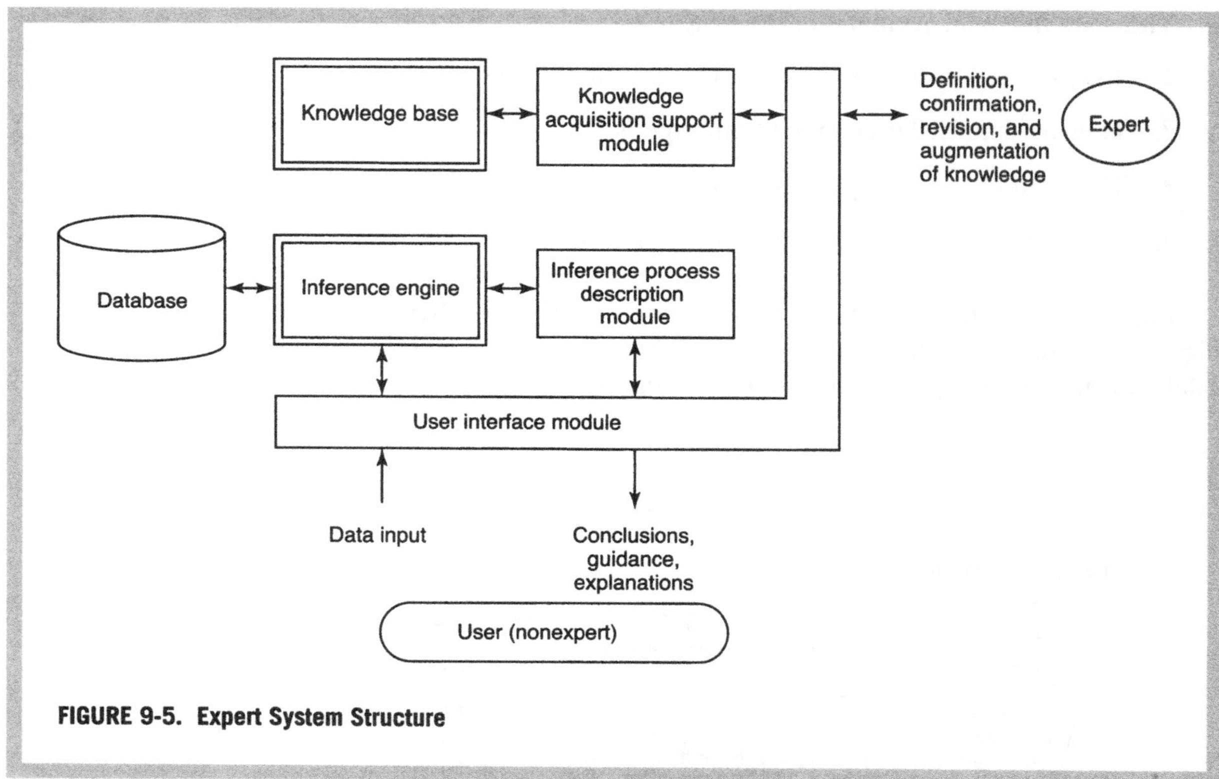

FIGURE 9-5. Expert System Structure

Many problems remain for expert system developers. Foremost is the difficulty of transferring extensive human knowledge and experience into a database. No matter how much memory and speed an expert system offers, GIGO "garbage in, garbage out" still applies. Researchers are developing various knowledge acquisition systems (see Table 9-2) to help eliminate this bottleneck, but these are still far from adequate. In this light, reliability-based techniques like FMEA can play a valuable role in the R&D process.

DATABASES

The term "database" originated during the late 1950s when the United States was trying to catch up with the Soviet Union in the space race. To boost its science and technology capabilities, the United States government stressed the need for greater volumes of commonly accessible information. The project they launched to achieve this objective led to the development of today's commercial databases.

More than just a mass of facts, a database must meet the following conditions:

1. Compile large volumes of data in a standardized, machine-readable format.
2. Search and retrieve data according to multiple criteria.
3. Allow quick access for either online or batch applications.

THE GROWTH OF DATABASES

As companies strive to keep pace with user demand and computer technology, databases play an increasingly pivotal role in our advanced information society. When skillfully applied, these powerful tools provide a wealth of information at a moment's notice. In Japan many independent companies specialize in database services for scientific organizations and businesses. Other new firms offer information retrieval services from a large number of databases. As the field of PC-based telecommunications moves forward in quantum leaps, we can only expect the demand for these services to keep growing.

DATABASE TYPES

Figure 9-6 lists common database types in terms of the information they provide.

DATABASE STRUCTURES

Databases are also classified by internal structure, as described in Figure 9-7 and depicted in Figure 9-8. The hierarchical model connects data units in a tree-like hierarchy that is limited strictly to vertical relationships. The network model is still primarily vertical, but it allows some cross-linkages.

The relational model, developed in the United States around 1970, is becoming increasingly dominant. Built on a two-dimensional table or matrix format, these databases can relate any two data units in the system. Since their mathematical foundation is excellent, relational databases are especially useful in research projects, including some that employ fuzzy logic.

According to a recent survey, commercial database usage in Japan breaks down as follows: 39 percent hierarchical, 17 percent relational, 17 percent network model, and 27 percent all others. More significantly, the percentage of databases in Japan that are imported is about 80 percent and climbing. This fact highlights a major challenge for Japan in the information age.

TABLE 9-2. Knowledge Acquisition Support Systems

System name	Main functions and characteristics	Comments
TEIRESIAS	**Characteristics** 1. Supports discovery and debugging of "rule bugs" 2. Supports rule input based on a rule model 3. Acquires new concepts **Weaknesses** 1. Knowledge level of support functions is not high 2. Difficult to use unless acquired knowledge is rule-based 3. Lacks ability to understand domains of problems	1. Used for MYCIN expert system 2. By studying the inference path that the TEIRESIAS system takes, experts can expand and refine the system's knowledge base.
SEEK	1. Refinement of rules in the SEEK system is based on two operations: common grouping and specialization. **Steps in knowledge refinement operations** 1. Input names of diagnosable diseases 2. Refine the names using the common-grouping and specialization rules 3. Select a refined version	1. SEEK semi-automatically reinforces the entire knowledge base. 2. Basically, by improving the rule base's overall diagnostic performance, SEEK acquires knowledge through rule refinements.
MORE	**Knowledge acquisition process steps** 1. Build an initial model through simple interviews 2. Refine the system's diagnostic knowledge by conducting interviews based on several questioning strategies 3. Generate diagnostic rules **Basic characteristics** 1. Includes a domain model 2. Generation of diagnostic rules from knowledge base 3. Advises experts based on strategic knowledge 4. Includes a diagnostic shell for testing its rule base 5. Can explain the roles played by various symptoms and background conditions	1. MORE differs from other systems in that its inference method uses cause-and-effect knowledge to make its diagnostic knowledge more accurate. Therefore, MORE promises to be a more powerful knowledge acquisition tool than other systems. 2. MORE functions only as a diagnostic system, a system that provides widely applicable strategic knowledge independent from the task's domain. 3. The model used in the MORE system allows for deeper knowledge that is possible with a rule-based system.
MOLE	**Process steps** 1. Static analysis • Avoids vagueness of the domain model • Streamlined determination of CF values • Refinement of domain model	1. MOLE is a revised version of MORE. One expanded feature is that MOLE enables input of vaguer information.

TABLE 9-2. (cont'd.)

System name	Main functions and characteristics	Comments
MOLE (cont'd.)	2. Dynamic analysis • Discovers inadequate knowledge • Supports correction of C_F values • Is more refined than the domain model	2. MOLE dynamically refines the knowledge base and makes knowledge acquisition more efficient.
ROGET	**System operation steps** 1. Determine task category 2. Determine general structure 3. Reconfigure general structure 4. Convert general structure to expressions used for tools **Types of tasks** 1. Determine problems (breakdowns) 2. Determine causes 3. Deduce countermeasures 4. Determine additional tests needed 5. Predict monitoring results 6. Evaluate symptoms and trends	1. Used for EMYCIN system 2. ROGET incorporates a variety of diagnostic concepts into a structured knowledge base that ties these concepts together to address specific tasks. 3. ROGET acquires knowledge to support its architecture by asking human experts about matters related to each diagnostic concept.
ETS	1. ETS is based on Personal Constructed Theory from the field of psychology. **Special interviewing techniques** 1. Taking three randomly selected subjects (such as three breakdown hypotheses), ETS groups two together and repeatedly asks which of their shared attributes are present or absent in the third subject. 2. ETS evaluates the subject for dependent relations among attributes. 3. ETS then displays these relations graphically for human expert confirmation. 4. If not satisfied with the results, the human expert can add other subjects and repeat the evaluation.	1. The ETS system has often been used at Boeing. 2. Personal Constructed Theory draws from human experience to develop theories about psychological responses to new environments. 3. ETS uses a psychology-based interview technique to build an analytical expert system.

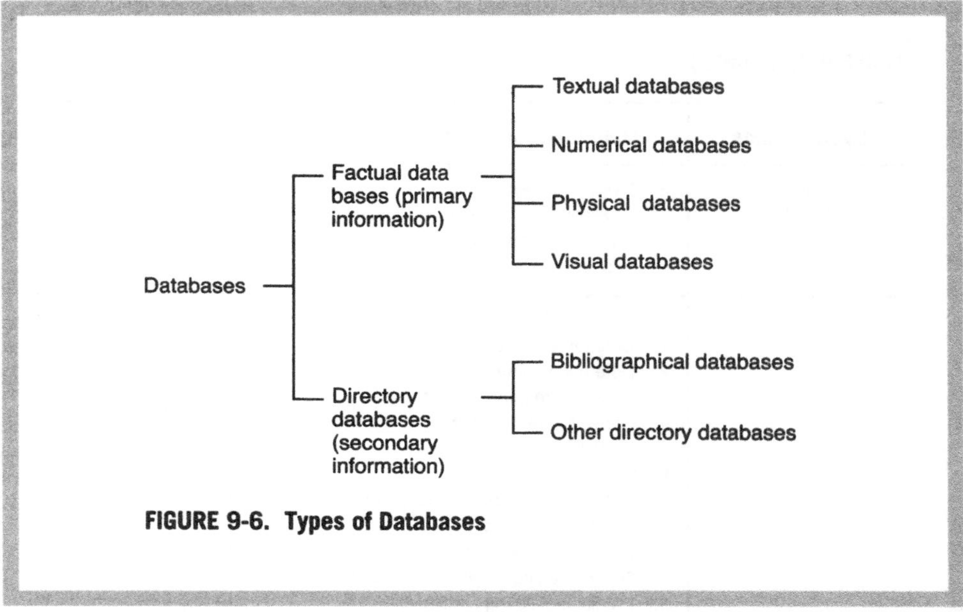

FIGURE 9-6. Types of Databases

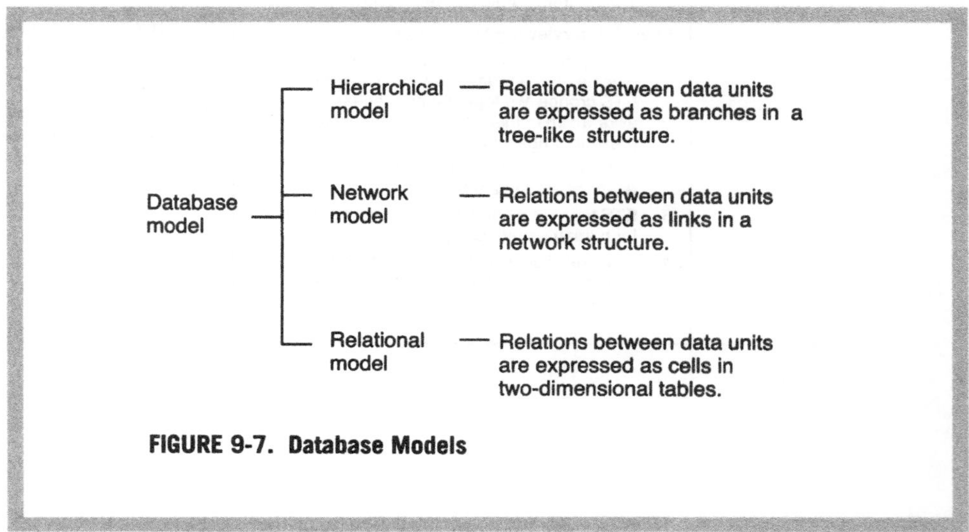

FIGURE 9-7. Database Models

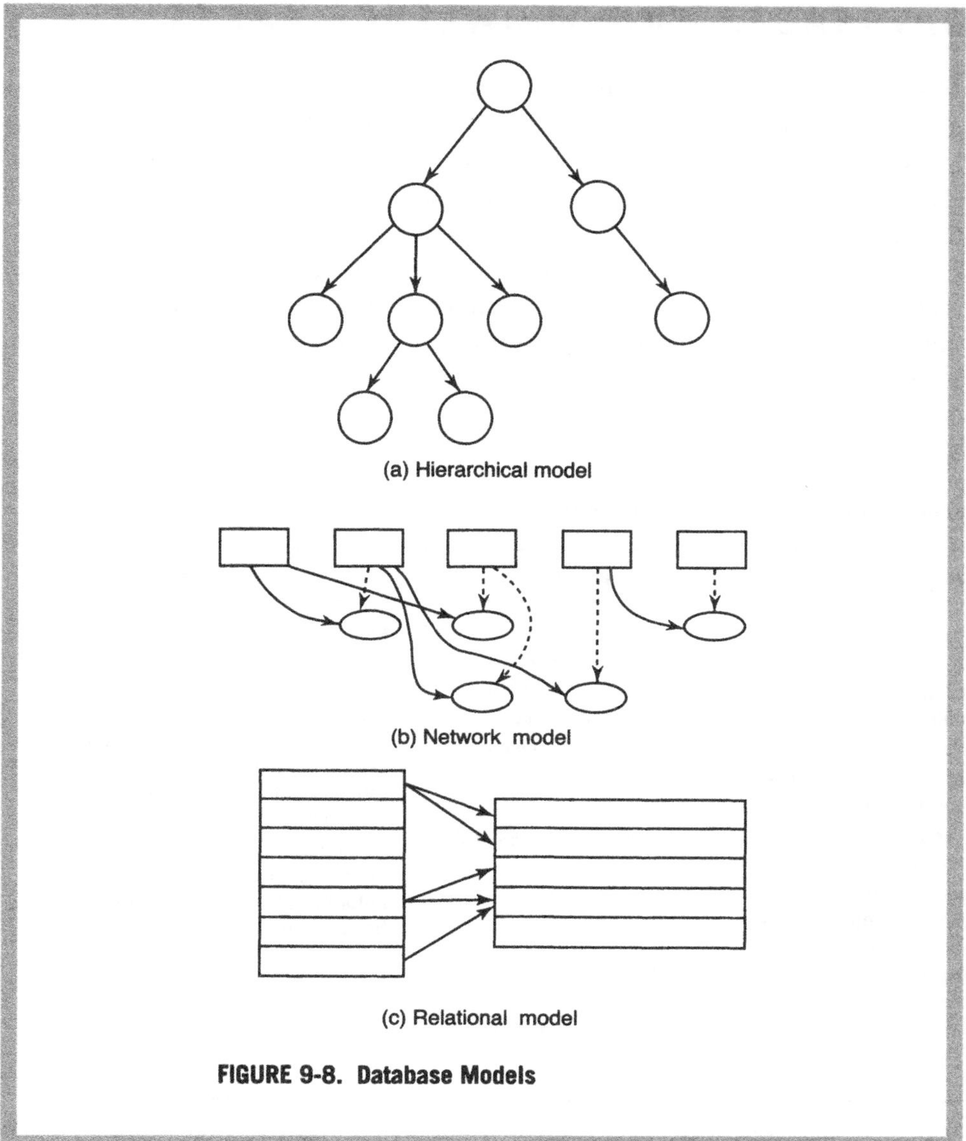

FIGURE 9-8. Database Models

DATABASES AND KNOWLEDGE BASES

The AI knowledge base is actually a database with an advanced reasoning element known as an "inference engine." Otherwise, databases and knowledge bases have much in common. While the two developed along separate lines, researchers in both fields have been working together to take advantage of mutual findings and improvements.

Table 9-3 compares databases and knowledge bases side by side. I have also included an illustration (Figure 9-9) of an expert system used for securities trading. The encircled numbers and arrows in the figure show the command sequence.

TABLE 9-3. Comparison of Databases and Knowledge Bases

Databases	Knowledge bases	Comments
1. Collections of data expressed as facts 2. Include detailed graphs and image-based information 3. Hold large volumes of data 4. Most data require frequent updates to reflect factual change 5. Database revisions and updates can be done rather easily 6. Primary data sources include textbooks, atlases, dictionaries, user manuals, and checklists 7. Driven by pregenerated data processing programs	1. Collections of rules, conditions, and knowledge derived mainly from human experience and expertise 2. Include highly abstract data 3. Hold less data than databases hold 4. Rules and restrictions do not change much over time 5. Revisions usually involve input by human experts 6. Primary data sources are documents (such as checklists and manuals) written by experts in specialized fields 7. Can be applied where algorithms are not sufficient for obtaining the desired information	1. Mutual research is aiding development of both databases and knowledge bases 2. Connections between databases and knowledge bases are enabling computers to handle routine data processing tasks previously done by people. 3. Researchers are now testing prototypes of a system that automatically builds knowledge bases from database contents

In this securities trading example, share prices for current holdings (in this case, Brand A) are recorded in the system's database every day. The knowledge base contains the rule "If current share price minus buying price is greater than profit margin, then output sales option." The system then plots the purchase price for the currently held shares on a graph with the specified profit margin. When the user presses the INQ (inquiry) key, the inference engine then draws information from both the database and knowledge base and generates the response "output sales option." Of course the actual decision of whether to sell or hold is still left up to the user.

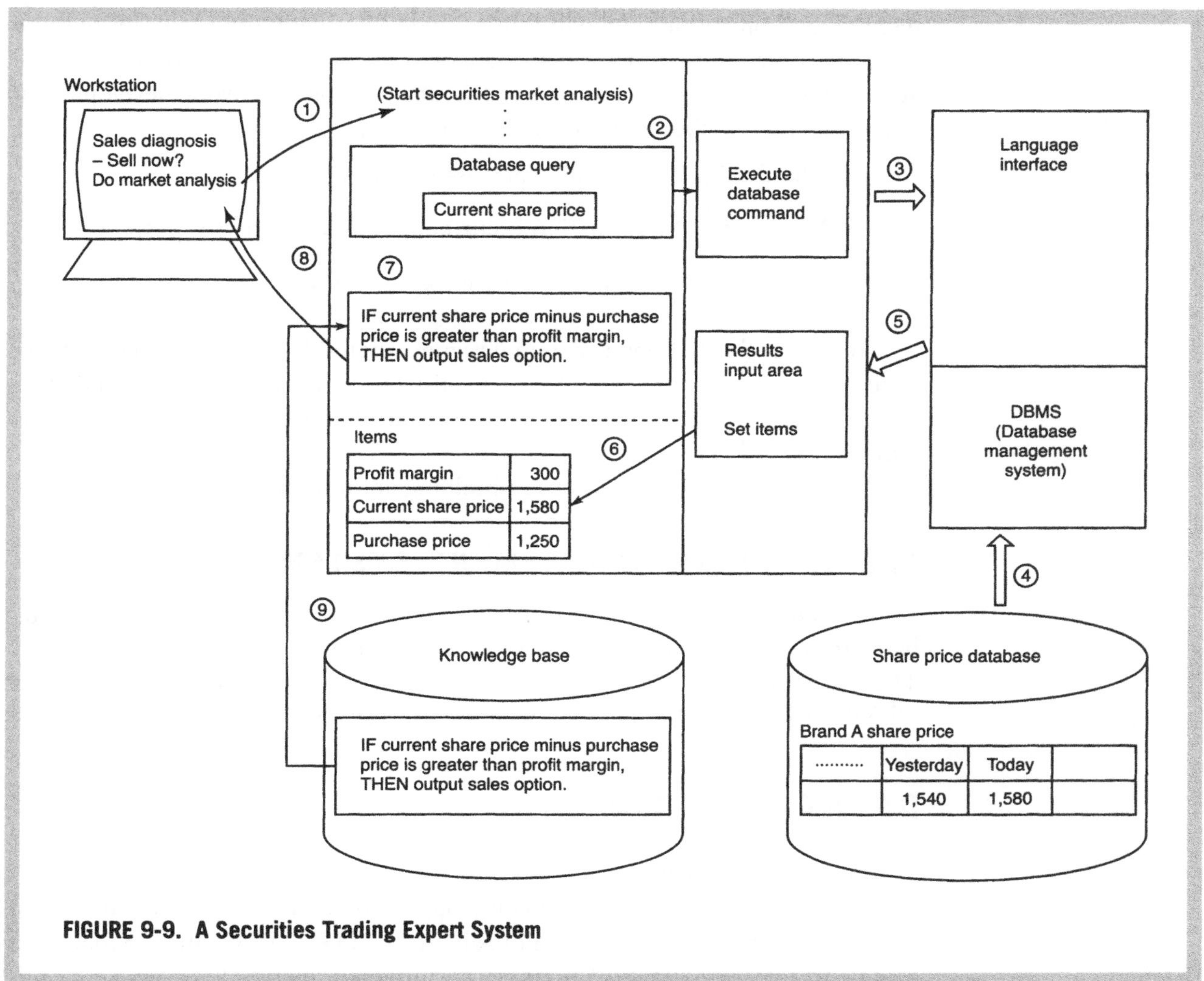

FIGURE 9-9. A Securities Trading Expert System

IN-HOUSE DATABASES

In recent years, private and public organizations and research centers have been setting up their own databases for the information they have acquired through surveys, research, or other means. This has enabled them to share useful knowledge with departments and individual employees, and in some cases with affiliates, suppliers, or other business partners.

DATABASE DESIGN GUIDELINES

We distinguish these in-house databases from commercial databases built to sell information. Most in-house databases are concerned with the company's research and operations and will thus exclude information not relevant to those concerns. One inherent risk is that changes in the business environment or management philosophy can render such a database obsolete. Anyone developing an in-house database should follow these guidelines:

- Clarify what purpose the database should serve.
- Make sure all information is current and relevant to this purpose.
- Make sure the database is easy to access and use.

In view of this last point, system designers should focus not on specific hardware or software features, but on user satisfaction. Their task will be aided by design input that clearly explains what users need and helps ensure that the system will serve those needs.

Figure 9-10 outlines the steps in building an in-house database.

THE DATABASE MANAGEMENT SYSTEM

The DBMS (database management system) connects users to an actual database. Its structure and operation should be a matter of common knowledge. There are several good references on the market which articulate how to make a DBMS easily accessible to as many target users as possible.

DR APPLICATIONS

When we view databases and knowledge bases in terms of DR and other quality assurance activities, the most obvious opportunities relate to generating and using checklists. But as we learn more about AI and expert systems, we may soon be able to automate design checking procedures completely. Even now, forward-thinking engineers and researchers are busy applying AI technology to develop more sophisticated CAD and design checking systems.

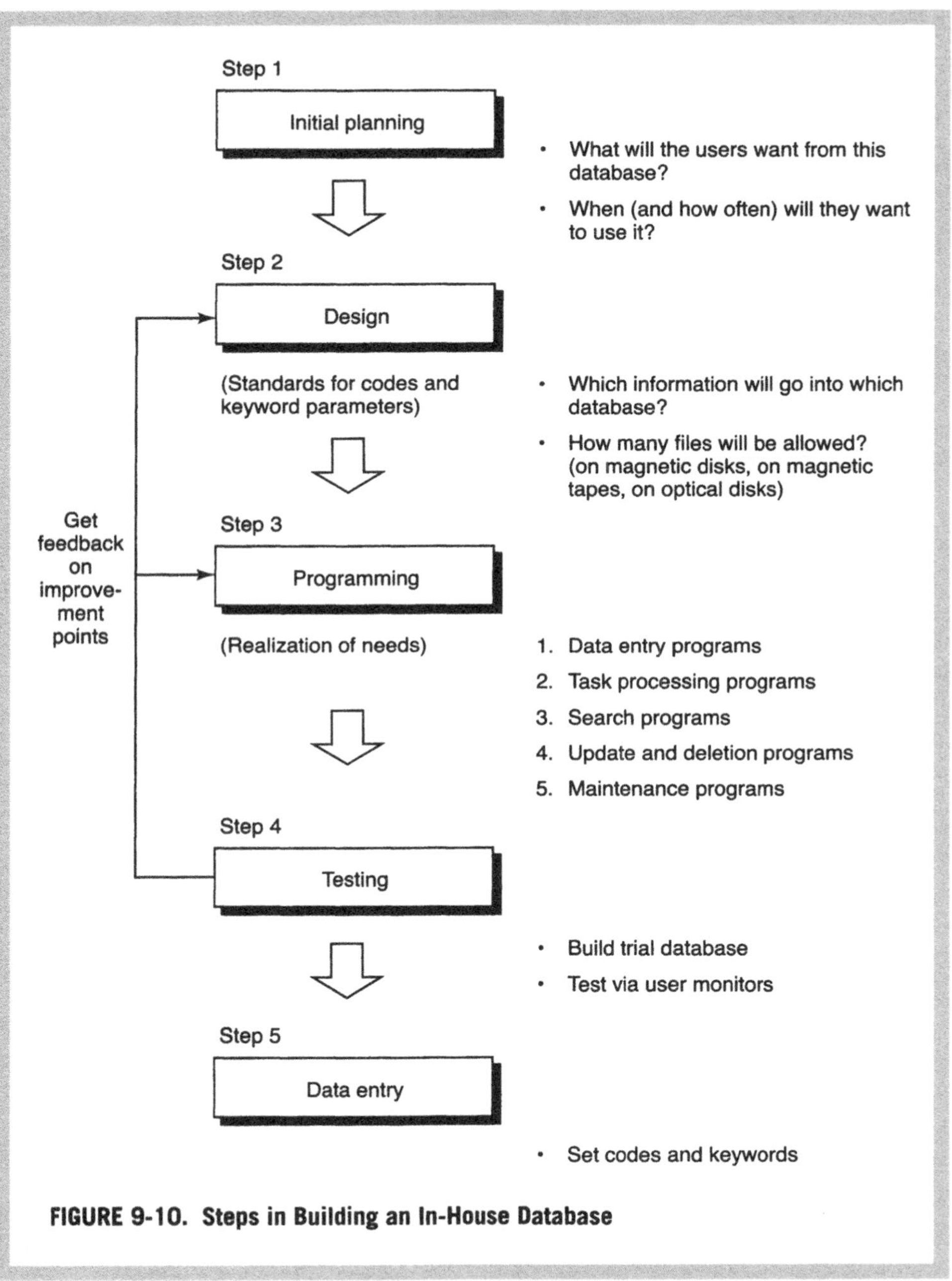
Step 1
Initial planning
What will the users want from this database?
When (and how often) will they want to use it?
Step 2
Design
(Standards for codes and keyword parameters)
Which information will go into which database?
How many files will be allowed? (on magnetic disks, on magnetic tapes, on optical disks)
Get feedback on improvement points
Step 3
Programming
(Realization of needs)
1. Data entry programs
2. Task processing programs
3. Search programs
4. Update and deletion programs
5. Maintenance programs
Step 4
Testing
Build trial database
Test via user monitors
Step 5
Data entry
Set codes and keywords

FIGURE 9-10. Steps in Building an In-House Database

Sadashige Morikawa
Tabai Espec

10
checklists and DR

WHAT ARE CHECKLISTS?

DR activities present many opportunities for using checklists. Responses to a September 1987 JUSE survey were divided as follows:

1. We always use checklists in our DR activities 41%
2. We sometimes use checklists in our DR activities 40%
3. We do not use checklists in our DR activities 18%

So the vast majority of these companies use checklists for at least some of their DR work (see question Q19 survey results from Part I, Chapter 2). This is not surprising, since checklists are one of the best organizing tools for complex or detailed tasks.

As the term "design review" implies, DR focuses mainly on the design stage of product development. Reviewers address performance features, functions, and reliability in their evaluation and recommended revisions. DR staff often facilitate this comprehensive process by listing review items on a standard list or table.

Checklists supposedly originated in England as a means of counting off voters on election day. You can define them as lists used to record or verify observations, comparisons, operations, tests, inspections, or compliance with standards, or more simply, as lists of planned or required activities. There is no single prescribed format, but their most important trait is comprehensiveness. Each checklist should list all target items in enough detail to ensure their precise completion. This naturally presents the risk of a list being too long to be practical. You can minimize that risk by limiting application and scope and by creating sublists for each item category.

IN-HOUSE TECHNOLOGIES, DR, AND CHECKLISTS

Use of in-house technologies is a key consideration when evaluating design quality. Suppose, for example, that environmental tests reveal a soldering defect in a printer circuit. When planning for the right countermeasure, do you stay with soldering, your in-house technology, or do you explore alternatives? Or is there a better approach to soldering? Improving reliability of a component or process sometimes calls for changes along these lines.

DR looks at in-house technologies as they affect performance and functions, manufacturability, serviceability, and cost effectiveness. Each of these characteristics is in turn covered by a list of review items. Where there are many technologies involved, checklists become invaluable. They can help you avoid both duplication and omission of items, making DR go that much more smoothly.

New checklists should accompany each DR meeting. Many companies conduct DR at only three stages (concept, general design, and detailed design), but the ideal is to apply it throughout product development. If you prepare and use checklists for the unique array of in-house technologies and characteristics at each stage, it can only aid your efforts to improve reliability.

CHECKLIST DEVELOPMENT

The potential applications for checklists are virtually endless, since you can use them for anything that requires checking, but this discussion will examine only the types used in DR..

Even without knowing all target items in advance, you can usually get enough information to draw up the checklist. This involves arranging potential subjects in some kind of order and then selecting which belong on the list. Each target item should be as comprehensive and detailed as possible, but should also fall within the scope of the project. It may be helpful to think of the checklist as a large fishnet, big enough to cover a wide area but fine enough to catch even small fish.

GATHERING DATA

The composition of the checklist depends partly on what DR activities it is supporting. For example, if you are building checklists for environmental tests, you can consult the target product's operating profile. This will give you some idea of the stress imposed on various components by the full range of operating conditions. Such data are well worth including in a DR checklist.

Results of breakdown analyses such as FMEA carried out at the design stage can also be a very useful reference. Critical parts and sensitive mechanisms are especially important check items, since they constitute "weak links" in the product.

Sometimes the best source of information is simply your own experience. For instance, the checklists should include failure modes and abnormalities that have shown up with any kind of frequency.

ORGANIZING DATA

The key to organizing data is finding a format that works for you. I have found the following approach to be both reliable and effective:

1. Clearly restate the purpose of the checklist.
2. Establish the product's operating conditions and physical limitations.
3. Identify target parts or a range of target characteristics.
4. Use all the above as boundaries in composing the checklist.

You will still need to define your own specific format. If several people will be using the checklist (which is often the case), write it clearly enough to prevent misunderstanding and confusion among these multiple users. Tailor the level of technical terminology to your audience: high enough to be accurate and low enough to be understandable.

PRE-CHECKLISTS

Sometimes the best way to organize one checklist is to create another. Here is one example of a "pre-checklist":

Heading information:

[ ] checklist title

[ ] Originator(s)

[ ] Originating manager

[ ] Approval and revision dates

Users:

[ ] Senior manager

[ ] Originating manager

[ ] R&D manager

[ ] Engineering staff

[ ] Line operator (from Manufacturing or Plant Services)

[ ] Testing and Inspection staff

[ ] Materials or Purchasing staff

[ ] Sales and Service staff

[ ] Transportation and Installation staff

[ ] Other (please specify)

Target product development stages (including support activities):

[ ] All stages

[ ] Market planning

[ ] R&D

[ ] Product design

[ ] Production process design

[ ] Testing and inspection

[ ] Transportation and installation

[ ] Sales

[ ] Maintenance and repair

[ ] Service

[ ] Disposal

[ ] Education and training

[ ] International operations

[ ] Other (please specify)

Target area:

[ ] Common

[ ] Division

[ ] Individual

[ ] Special

Target items:

[ ] Materials

[ ] Parts

[ ] Stand alone components

[ ] Small systems

[ ] Large systems

[ ] Software design

[ ] Programming

[ ] System design

[ ] Other (please specify)

Input mode:

[ ] Descriptive entry

[ ] Check mark entry

[ ] Point-based evaluation

[ ] Other (please specify)

Type of operations:

[ ] One-time

[ ] Repetitive

[ ] Other (please specify)

Type of checking:

[ ] Evaluation meetings

[ ] Inspection or confirmation

[ ] Self-checking

Major concerns (rank in order of importance):

[ ] Reliability

[ ] Safety

[ ] Security

[ ] Delivery

[ ] Cost

[ ] Trade-offs

[ ] Other (please specify)

Since the above does not go into much detail, the pre-checklist you use to build checklists in your own company will probably need to be more comprehensive.

VISUAL AIDS

Some check items require clarification through supporting figures and tables. Line drawings, matrices, pie charts, 3-D diagrams, flowcharts, FMEA and FTA charts, cause-and-effect diagrams, and quality tables (see next chapter) are all useful tools that make checking easier. You may also want to incorporate technical illustrations, photographs, or even samples to show external characteristics such as shape, color, appearance, or texture.

DESCRIPTIVE TERMINOLOGY

Finally, be as clear and precise as possible when describing items that must be checked physically. It helps to use everyday terminology. For example, you can express operating limits as "too bright to look at without blinking," "too dark to distinguish one object from another," "too loud to bear listening to," or "too quiet to be heard." While these may seem too subjective at first, remember that the *final* evaluation—the user's—typically relies on similar standards.

ORGANIZING CHECK ITEMS

Once you have gathered all the check items, organize them according to intended use. This may mean sorting them by relative importance or checking requirements while working to keep the total number of check items manageable. Feedback from designated users will help ensure that the checklist meets their needs. This is especially true when the checklist serves manufacturing or other standard operations. Few things are more irrelevant than a checklist designed by someone unfamiliar with its application.

IDENTIFYING ESSENTIAL ITEMS

To recap, a checklist should be broad enough in scope and deep enough in detail without being too long. The most important aspect of this balancing act is identifying essential items. If any of these are missing, the list is practically worthless. Conversely, as long as you cover all of the items in adequate detail, you are more than halfway there. Typically the two best sources for essential items are FMEA results and personal experience.

HELPFUL TIPS

Here a few more important points to consider when developing checklists:

- Target items can be tangible or intangible.
- Express items in question format.
- Use yes/no (Y/N) questions where possible, so as to minimize subjective, open-ended responses.
- Try to offer multiple-choice responses, such as "excellent/good/fair/poor," "complete/incomplete," or "high/medium/low," when requiring the user to check the status or amount of something.
- Some DR checklists need to be tailored to a particular design stage (concept, general, detailed), others to a level of management or supervision (group, department, section).

CHECKLIST MAINTENANCE

An effective checklist is never really complete. Like any other standard, it requires constant updating, or else it will grow obsolete. You can either designate someone to carry out routine checklist maintenance or simply revise and replace the list as the need arises. Any of the following will likely generate a need for revisions:

1. Regulatory changes: especially relating to safety or environmental protection
2. Changes in market trends: major technological advances, shifts in user requirements
3. Demographic changes: especially age distribution among the user population
4. Company policy changes: diversification, joint ventures, overseas production

5. New materials, parts, or manufacturing processes: including ceramics, optical fibers, new semiconductor devices

When any new parts or processes are introduced, related checklists must be either abandoned or substantially revised. It is best to accomplish these revisions before the new products reach the production stage.

None of the above changes directly affect product design, but all are critical from a market planning standpoint. Many companies have expanded their perspective to include international trends as well.

Since DR considers all these factors, and since checklists help facilitate the DR process, you need to identify and complete any list updates before DR begins. For example, if you omit a new industrial safety regulation from a DR checklist, you run the risk of having to redo the entire product design later or at least to make some very expensive changes. Checklist revisions should be an integral part of product development at your company, for even minor changes can have a major impact on other development items.

CHECKLISTS AND AI

Checklists have been used extensively in AI since its early days, specifically in building expert systems, databases, and knowledge bases.

Researchers in this field of reliability engineering have developed numerous effective methods for diagnosing, predicting, and preventing equipment and system breakdowns. Alongside other valuable technologies such as FMEA and FTA, checklists provide the experience and insight of experts in various disciplines. However, most conventional checklist formats are incompatible with computer databases and knowledge bases, so the check items need to be reorganized into a hierarchical, network, or relational data model.

These checklists of the future will comprise a powerful element of expert systems used for reliability engineering.

CHECKLIST EXAMPLE

The Operating Conditions/Environmental Test Checklist below is typical of the checklists used in DR:

OPERATING CONDITIONS

1. Has a profile been written for all the product's potential operating conditions?

2. Does the profile specify regions where the product will be used (global environment)?
3. Does it specify individual locations where the product will be used (local environment)?
4. Does it specify installation conditions?
    a. Unrestricted (can operate under all outdoor conditions)
    b. Sheltered (can operate outdoors if protected from rainfall and direct sunlight)
    c. Indoors
    d. Outer space
5. Can the product be moved, or have handling methods been investigated?
6. Will the product be moved on land, underground, on water, underwater, in the air, or in space?
7. Have the following environmental parameters been evaluated for degree of impact?
    a. Temperature (high, low, normal)
    b. Temperature changes (gradual, rapid)
    c. Temperature cycle (day and night)
    d. Humidity (normal humidity and temperature/humidity cycle)
    e. Atmospheric pressure (low, high)
    f. Changes in atmospheric pressure (gradual, rapid)
    g. Changes in ambient medium (such as air or water), including movement relative to product such as wind force
    h. Rain, snow, hail, water drops, water spray, dew, water jet, waves, floodwater, moisture content
    i. Radiation (solar and other), ionized radiation
    j. Seawater, salt spray, sulfur dioxide, hydrogen sulfide, nitrogen dioxide, ozone, organic hydrocarbons, ammonia
    k. Sand, dust, dirt
    l. Cyclical vibrations (sine waves, bumps)
    m. Random vibrations
    n. Impact

- o. Free falling, falling over
- p. Rolling, pitching, yawing
- q. Sonic vibrations
- r. Acceleration (concentric or linear)
- s. Electrical and magnetic interference (electric field, magnetic field)
- t. Microorganisms, mold, animals, plants
- u. Any combination of the above

PRODUCT EFFECTS

1. High temperature:
   - **a.** Thermal aging (oxidation, cracking, chemical reactions)
   - **b.** Softening, melting
   - **c.** Sublimation, vaporization
   - **d.** Viscosity loss, elongation
2. Low temperature:
   - **a.** Brittleness, freezing
   - **b.** Increased or jelled viscosity
   - **c.** Loss of mechanical strength
   - **d.** Physical contraction
3. High humidity:
   - **a.** Water absorption or adherence
   - **b.** Swelling
   - **c.** Loss of mechanical strength
   - **d.** Chemical reactions, corrosion,
   - **e.** Electrolysis, insulation loss
4. Low humidity:
   - **a.** Moisture loss (brittleness)
   - **b.** Loss of mechanical strength
   - **c.** Physical contraction
   - **d.** Increased friction in moving parts
5. High pressure:
   - **a.** Compression, distortion
6. Low pressure:
   - **a.** Elongation
   - **b.** Reduction in static electricity

   c. Corona and ozone increases
   d. Reduction in cooling effects

7. Sunlight:
   a. Surface deterioration
   b. Brittleness
   c. Color fading
   d. Increased ozone
   e. Increased differential heat (such as between the exposed and hidden sides of a space satellite)
   f. Differential mechanical stress

8. Sand, debris, and dust:
   a. Friction loss
   b. Clogging
   c. Adhesion
   d. Thermal insulation
   e. Charged particles

9. Chemical atmosphere:
   a. Corrosion
   b. Electrolysis
   c. Surface deterioration
   d. Increased conductivity
   e. Increased resistance between materials at contact points

10. Wind:
   a. Fatigue
   b. Clogging
   c. Friction loss
   d. Induced vibration

11. Rain:
   a. Water absorption
   b. Thermal shock
   c. Erosion
   d. Corrosion

12. Hail:
   a. Friction loss
   b. Thermal shock
   c. Mechanical distortion

13. Snow/ice:
    a. Mechanical load
    b. Moisture absorption
    c. Thermal shock
14. Abrupt temperature changes:
    a. Thermal shock
    b. Impact of differential heat increases
15. Ozone:
    a. Rapid oxidation
    b. Brittleness (particularly in rubber)
    c. Reduction in static electricity
16. Constant acceleration, vibration, impact, or bumps:
    a. Mechanical stress
    b. Fatigue
    c. Resonance

ENVIRONMENTAL TESTS

1. Are test containers large enough to hold the specimens?
2. Has temperature/humidity distribution been measured inside the empty containers to make sure the variation is within the specified range?
3. Has the container dehumidifier water been tested for purity, and has the filter been changed as specified in the standards?
4. Have the container temperature and humidity gauges been calibrated as specified in the standards? Is the margin of error within the specified range?
5. Does the water used in the humidity test containers meet applicable standards?
6. Can container temperature changes be controlled as required?
7. Do the containers have reliability warranties?
8. Do the containers have a fail-safe structure?
9. Does the pH value of the water used in the test containers meet applicable standards?

10. Have partitions or racks in the containers been contaminated with volatile matter from previous specimens?
11. Have fully adequate safety measures been established in the event of a container explosion?
12. Are the containers under a maintenance contract?
13. Have fully adequate safety measures been established in the event of toxic gas leakage from a corrosive atmosphere test container?
14. Do the jigs used to fasten down the test specimens possess ample structural strength and temperature and humidity resistance? Are they suitable from the standpoint of heat conductivity?
15. Are test specimens fastened down so as not to block air flow in between?
16. If an electric charge is to be applied in a container, do the wires possess ample temperature, humidity, and corrosion resistance?
17. If an electric charge is to be applied in a container, has an acoustic shield been installed to prevent induction of external noise?
18. If active devices are being installed, are they positioned to prevent resonance from one another or from wiring interference?
19. If two containers are being stacked to save space, have ample anti-vibration measures been taken?
20. Has the vibration test device been calibrated as specified for measuring waveform, frequency, and amplitude?
21. Are the jigs used to fasten down test specimens in the vibration test device built to ensure reliable transmission of vibrations from the source?
22. Can the vibration test device accommodate the largest and heaviest specimens?
23. Is the vibration test device's overall frequency response within the specified range?
24. Has the vibration test device been installed so as to filter out external vibration and noise?
25. If an electric charge is to be applied during a vibration test, has an acoustic shield been installed to prevent induction of external noise?

26. In sine wave resonance tests, have ample precautions been taken to make sure resonance point sensors are monitored within the specified frequency range?
27. If conducting random vibration tests, has the vibration frequency corresponding to the specified response been checked by dummy loading?
28. If conducting random vibration tests, has specimen fault detection been checked for various parameters (electrical, mechanical, others)?
29. Has the impact test device been confirmed to be capable of the required impact and waveform?
30. Are the speed changes for all waveforms produced by the impact test device within the specified tolerance?
31. Were the most appropriate pulse waveforms and magnitude selected for the test specimens?
32. Have the measured pulse values at the observation point been confirmed as being within the specified tolerance?
33. Is a jig being used to ensure that the impact test device's moving platform collides with the test specimen correctly?
34. Has the impact test device been installed so as to filter out external vibration and noise?
35. If an electric charge is applied during an impact test, has an acoustic shield been installed to prevent induction of external noise?
36. Have ample safety measures been established for impact tests?
37. Are fastening devices for vibration and impact tests free from resonance within the specified frequency range? Has the sound flux transmission path been confirmed as being within a quarter wavelength?
38. In vibration and impact tests, are specimen fastening methods as close as possible to actual conditions?

TEST PERSONNEL

1. Have test personnel been thoroughly instructed in duplicating stress effects from environmental tests?
2. Have test personnel recognized that some environmental tests call for prolonged duration?
3. Environmental testing requires strict procedures and should lead to product technical improvements. Have the test personnel been trained to work well under these demands?
4. Are test personnel continuously checking into the worst possible operating conditions and misuses the product may experience?
5. Are test personnel kept trained in maintenance procedures for environmental test equipment, and are they prepared for quick and proper response in the event of a breakdown?
6. Have test personnel been taught how to draft an efficient testing schedule?
7. Are test personnel kept informed of changes to environmental test standards (JIS, IEC, ISO, MIL, DIN, BS), and do they understand and practice the proper filing procedures for these standards?

Masaru Watanabe, Daihen Corporation
Yōji Akao, Tamagawa University

11 quality function deployment and DR

INTRODUCTION

An effective DR program generally follows this pattern:

- Set up the DR organization.
- Clearly define the review items at each product development stage.
- Thoroughly prepare committee members and other participants for their various tasks.
- Carry out DR systematically.

With respect to preparation, the data packages handed out before DR meetings are critical. We want to ensure that the information in these packages will help build in quality at the design stage. This chapter describes quality function deployment (QFD), perhaps the most powerful source of such information for DR.

QUALITY FUNCTION DEPLOYMENT

QFD is an objective method for ensuring quality from the earliest stages of product development. The aim is to create a product that will fully satisfy users by relating their requirements to design characteristics all the way downstream to production.

Quality deployment consists of these elements:

- Conversion of user quality requirements into design characteristics
- Determination of those characteristics most critical to product quality
- Conversion of product quality characteristics into supporting characteristics in and among subassemblies and parts

Figure 11-1 includes such elements as technology, reliability, and costs under QFD.

USE OF QUALITY TABLES

The QFD table (section 1-I in the figure, top left) organizes and categorizes customer requirements for quality planning and then converts these requirements into design quality characteristics. This quality table matrix format starts with a systematic listing of words expressing the true qualities required by users. These are then related to design characteristics. This table therefore provides input for design quality.

In section 3-I of Figure 11-1 we convert product quality characteristics into characteristics for subassemblies and parts, setting up QA tables for the parts determined most critical. Each QA table shows the part's design specifications (standard values) and the impact on the product when the part does not meet those specifications. These tables play a very important role in product development, since items marked here as critical characteristics are added to QC process tables for both parts making and assembly. So QFD is a systematic approach that ensures quality at every stage up to full production.

CASE STUDY A: AIR PLASMA CUTTER

This case study describes a recent application of QFD at Daihen for development of a new air plasma cutter. This equipment, which cuts metals electrically with plasma arc technology, is easier to use and much more effective than conventional gas or mechanical cutters.

DEFINING MARKET NEEDS

For a current assessment of the metal cutting market, we distributed information feedback cards to our staff in every sales district as part of a market survey. We organized the feedback data into a matrix built around four elements:

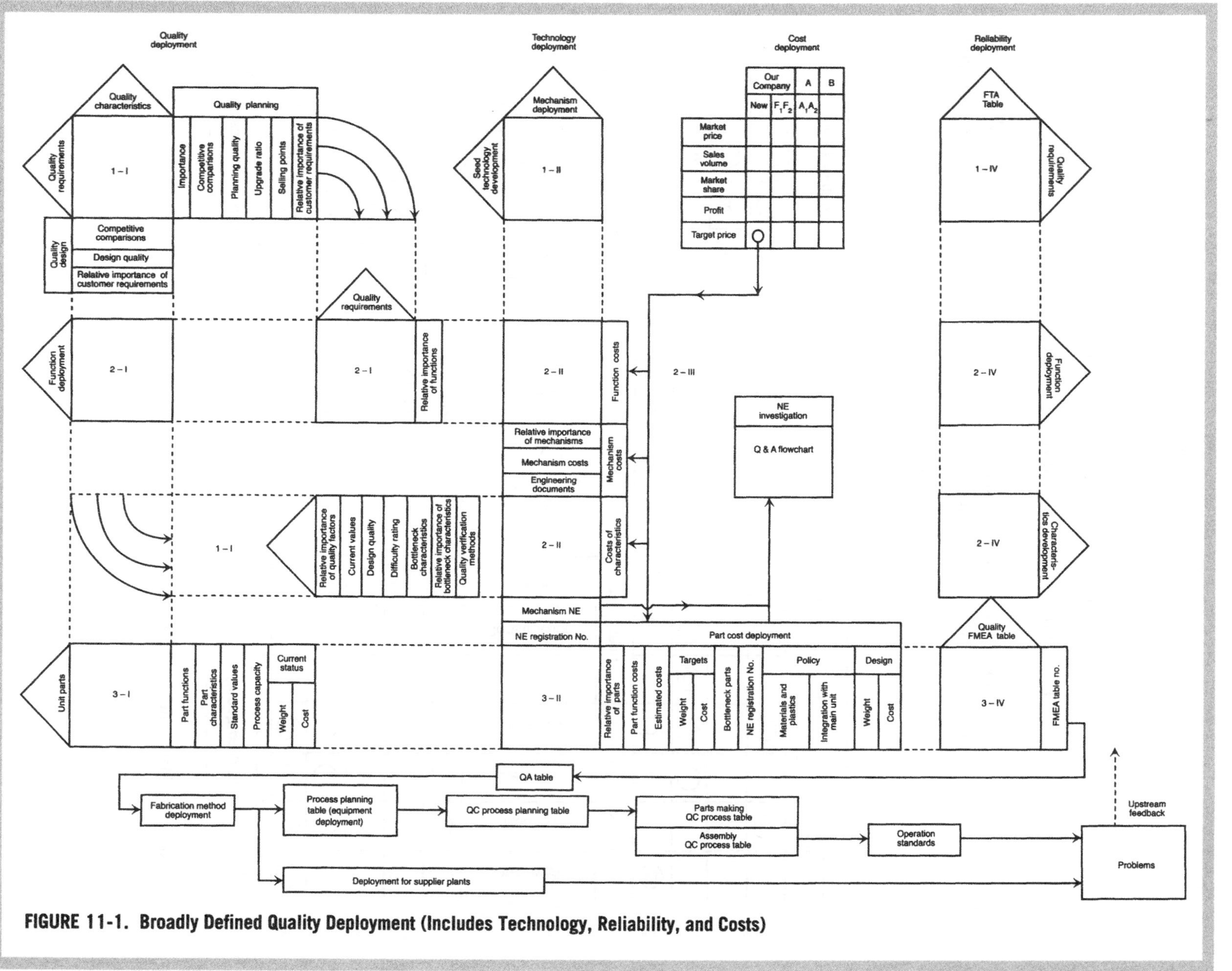

FIGURE 11-1. Broadly Defined Quality Deployment (Includes Technology, Reliability, and Costs)

1. Customer's field of business
2. Types of metals to be cut
3. Customer's needs for metal cutting
4. Cutting methods used by customers

In this market analysis matrix (see Figure 11-2), organizing the data by metal thickness helped us define what needs an expanded product line would serve.

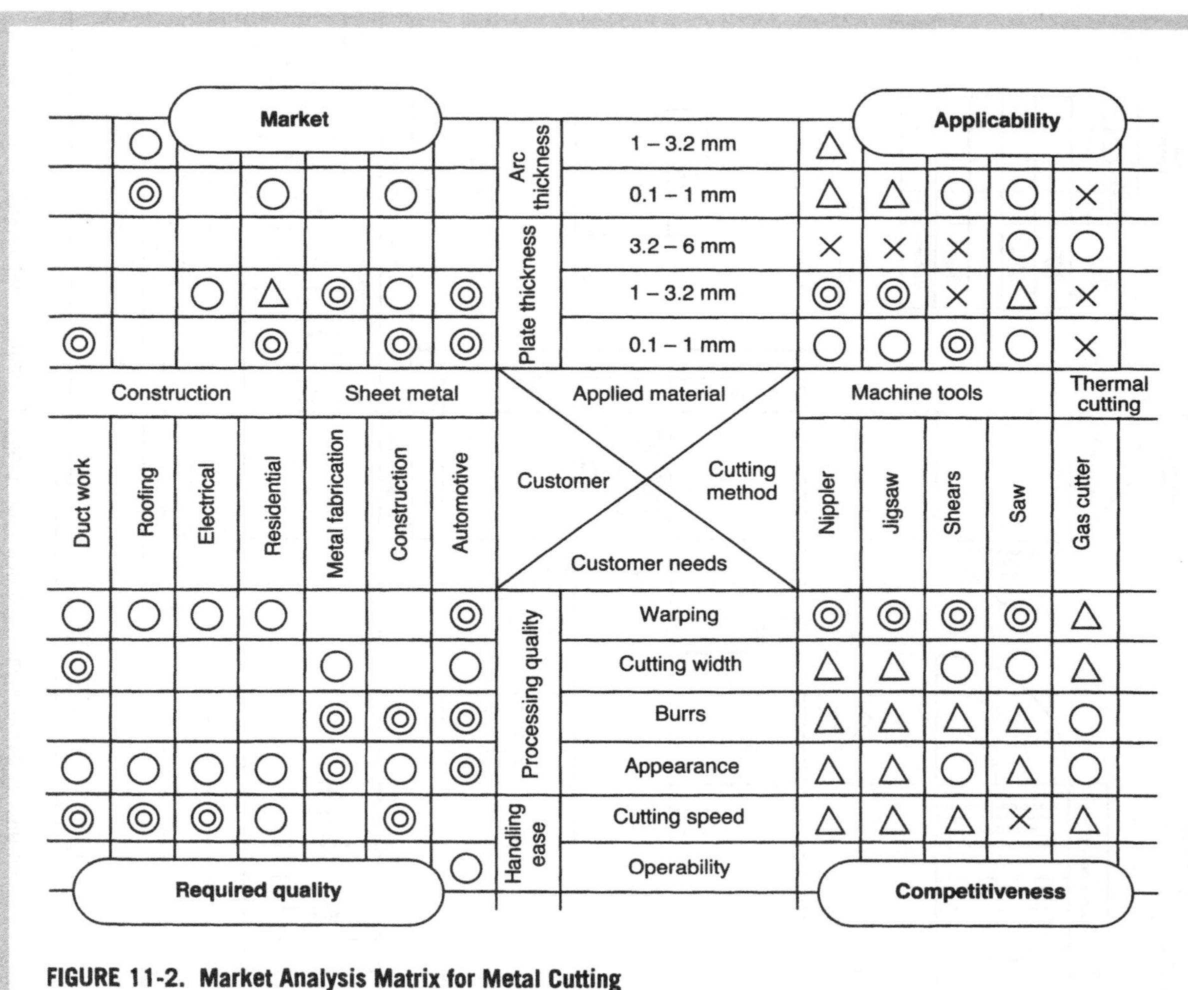

FIGURE 11-2. Market Analysis Matrix for Metal Cutting

COLLECTING USER NEEDS DATA

Once these market needs were defined, we sent sales staff and product development engineers directly to the customers for a firsthand look at their facilities. Our people were able to observe product applications and to talk with operators and technicians on the shop floor. This onsite approach has proven very effective for collecting live data and uncovering previously unknown customer needs. It has resulted in some new ideas that have been very well received. Figure 11-3 shows several of the forms we use when making these kinds of surveys.

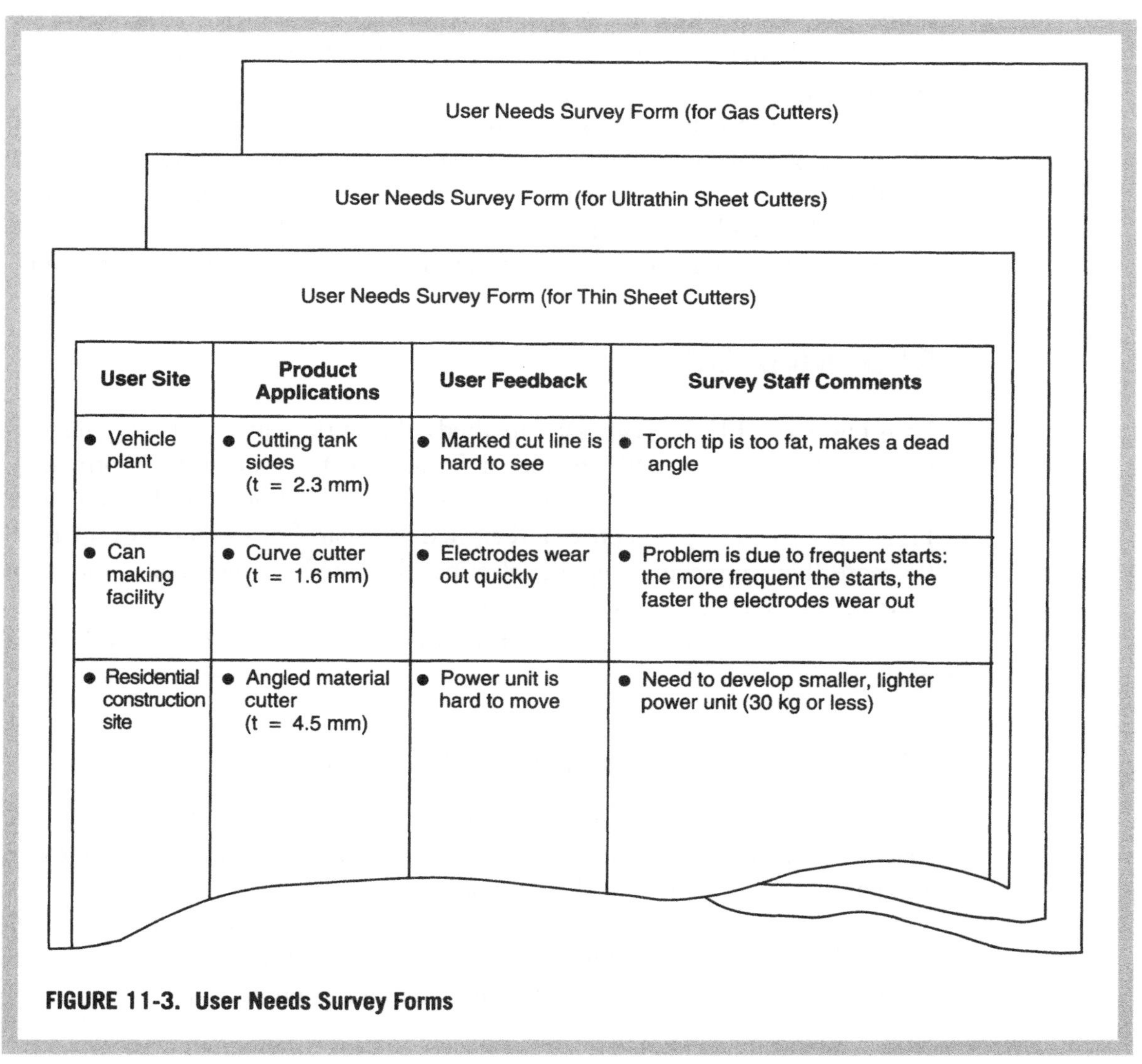

User Needs Survey Form (for Gas Cutters)

User Needs Survey Form (for Ultrathin Sheet Cutters)

User Needs Survey Form (for Thin Sheet Cutters)

User Site	Product Applications	User Feedback	Survey Staff Comments
• Vehicle plant	• Cutting tank sides (t = 2.3 mm)	• Marked cut line is hard to see	• Torch tip is too fat, makes a dead angle
• Can making facility	• Curve cutter (t = 1.6 mm)	• Electrodes wear out quickly	• Problem is due to frequent starts: the more frequent the starts, the faster the electrodes wear out
• Residential construction site	• Angled material cutter (t = 4.5 mm)	• Power unit is hard to move	• Need to develop smaller, lighter power unit (30 kg or less)

FIGURE 11-3. User Needs Survey Forms

APPLYING QFD

We next restated the user needs data as quality requirements, defined the product design characteristics needed to satisfy those requirements, and organized all this information into a quality table (see Figure 11-4).

The upper part of Figure 11-4 depicts a quality table for an air plasma cutter used on thin metal sheets. Aside from tying quality requirements to design quality characteristics, this table also helped us set target values for the more critical characteristics.

Setting quality target values meant identifying which functions and features would give our products a competitive advantage and which selling points we should emphasize. The people we assigned to this task found the quality table very helpful.

Part of QFD is identifying the obstacles to achieving these quality targets. Identification of technical bottlenecks (shaded sections in Figure 11-4) helps narrow this search by relating quality characteristics to specific mechanisms or subsystems. Meanwhile, reliability deployment uses design FMEA to assess product reliability. These activities are explained in further detail in the next case study.

QFD AND DR

Both DR and QFD are systematic methods of ensuring quality at every stage of product development. DR provides a framework for evaluating information, while QFD helps pull together all the information that needs to be evaluated. From the designers' perspective, DR carried out apart from QFD ends up as little more than nitpicking, superficial criticisms based on personal opinions or preferences. Needless to say, that is not effective DR.

Table 11-1 shows where QFD fits into DR at each stage as part of the data package.

FOCUS ON CRITICAL CHARACTERISTICS

QFD involves the concept of critical characteristics. We not only make sure that designers hand over data free of errors and omissions, but also make clear to DR participants which items they should evaluate most closely.

The data packages that DR participants receive in advance contain the various quality tables. These tables help them understand the design from a quality perspective and thus come up with better ideas for improvement.

Quality characteristics

Quality requirements: Primary	Secondary	Tertiary	Power unit		Power unit: Outer dimensions	Power unit: Weight	Air unit		Torch: Electrode life	Torch: Viewing angle	Torch
Easier to use than previous products	Good cutting quality	Can cut large thicknesses									
		Cuts neatly									
	Low oper. costs	Consumable parts have long life							◎		
	Easy to handle	Marked cutting line is easy to see								◎	
	Easy to move	Small width			◎						
		Can be carried in one hand				◎					
Charac-teristic values		Previous product			330	72			300	35	
		Competition's product			280	26			300	37	
		Target value			Width: 189 mm	16.5 kg			1,500 starts	50	

Seed technology

Mechanism deployment: Primary	Secondary	Tertiary	Electrical/electronic: Electronic	Current control	Noise abatement		Mechanical: Assembly and processing	Plasma charge	Thermal resistance		Power unit		Outer dimensions	Weight	Air unit		Electrode life	Viewing angle	
Cutter power unit	Power circuit																		
		Inverter unit	◎										◎	◎					
	Control circuit																		
		DC reactor		◎									◎	◎					
		Inverter control circuit		◎													◎		
Torch	Arc generator																		
		Electrode					○	◎	◎								◎		
		Tip					○	◎	◎									◎	
		Shield cap					○	○	○									◎	
Technical bottlenecks		In-house technology									○----	---○			○----	---○		○	
		Bottleneck technology											◎	◎			◎		

(Legend:)
◎ Highly revelant
○ Relevant

Note: This table highlights previously overlooked ease-of-handling issues, such as "small width" and "can be carried in one hand." To address this user requirement, we established a design quality standard of 189 mm width and 16.5 kg weight, which compare to 280 mm and 26 kg, respectively, for our competitor's product. This standard was both a response to on-site survey feedback and an initiative to set our company apart from the competition. This and other selling points drew much interest from customers and contributed to expanded sales.

FIGURE 11-4. Quality Table for Product A

TABLE 11-1. QFD Application for DR

Step	DR Flowchart	QFD Elements	Review items based on QFD
Product planning	Quality assurance policy → Collection and analysis of market data → New product planning → Product planning review (DR-1)	○ Quality requirements deployment	○ Understand customer needs ○ Review competitive advantages ○ Identify selling points ○ Establish planning quality
Product design	Design concept → Design concept review (DR-2)	○ Quality characteristics deployment ○ Identification of technical bottlenecks ○ Cost deployment	○ Establish design quality characteristics ○ Set quality target values ○ Analyze technical bottlenecks ○ Identify solutions
	Prototype design → Initial design prototype review (DR-3)	○ Reliability deployment ○ Quality characteristics evaluation table from quality characteristics deployment ○ Cost deployment	○ Review reliability check items and corresponding target values ○ Approve/reject reliability test items ○ Approve/reject quality characteristics evaluation methods ○ Review cost estimates
	Prototype testing → Final design prototype review (DR-4)	○ Quality characteristics evaluation table ○ CR/QA deployment (correlation between cost reduction items and quality based on prototype test results)	○ Evaluate design quality based on quality characteristics evaluation table ○ Review cost/quality tradeoffs
	Final product design → Final product design review (DR-5)	○ QA table (from quality characteristics deployment) ○ Cost deployment	○ Evaluate suitability of quality characteristic control points for production ○ Review cost estimates
Production setup	Production process design → Production process design review (DR-6) → DR VI	○ Process-planning table and QC process table, both based on QA table	○ Tie together QA table, process-planning table, and QC process table.

Note: DR includes other review items, but this example shows only those related to QFD.

MORE COMPREHENSIVE DATA PACKAGES

No one can deny that data package preparation is a key aspect of DR, particularly where the package contents concern design quality. With QFD we can establish clear links between design quality and technology, reliability, and cost (refer back to Figure 11-1). The table in Figure 11-5 illustrates the link between quality and reliability. It tracks quality characteristics from prototype to launch, making it very useful for DR quality evaluation.

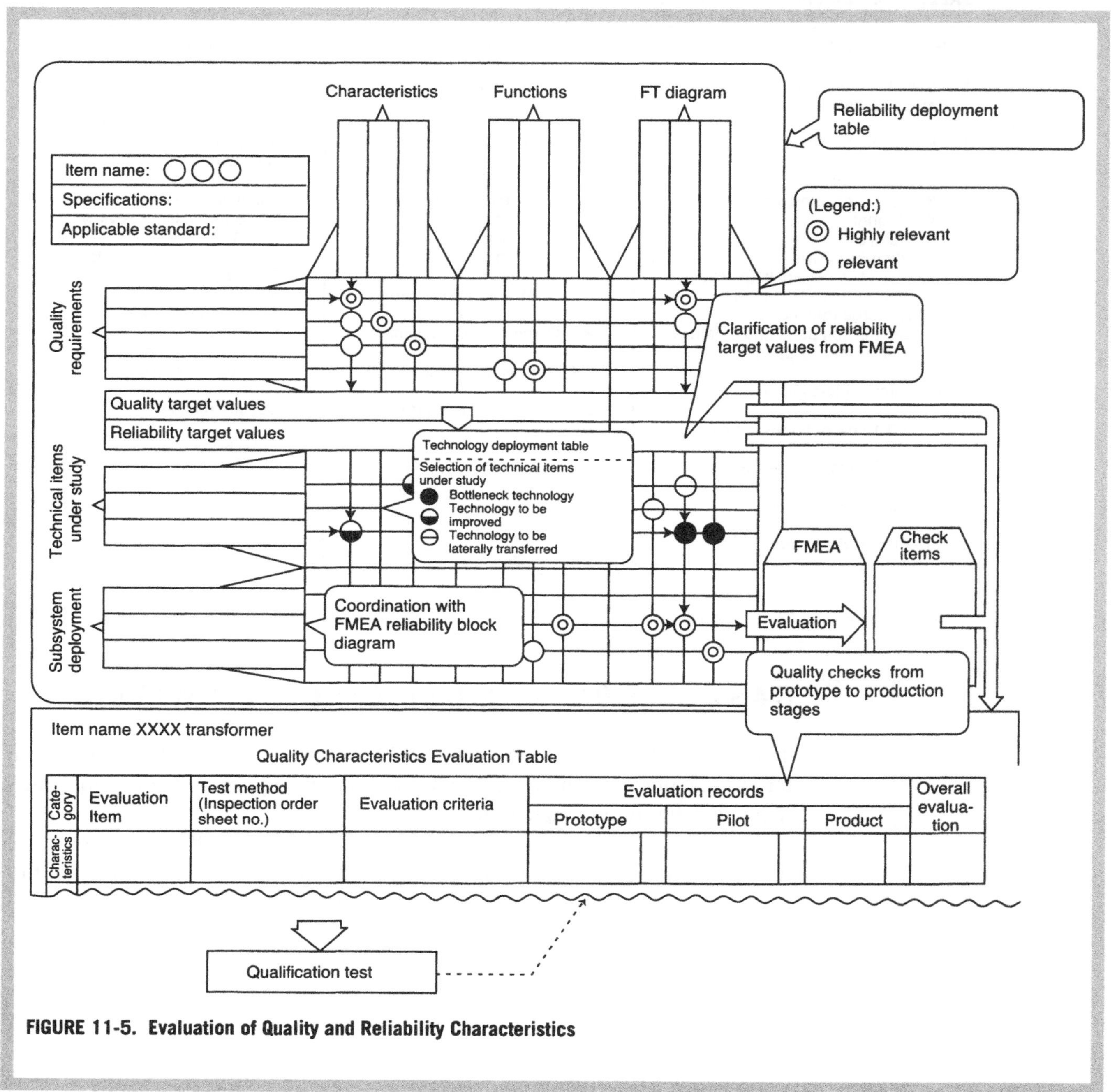

FIGURE 11-5. Evaluation of Quality and Reliability Characteristics

REVIEW OF DR CHECKLISTS

Effective DR checklists require frequent updating. Much of this occurs naturally in the course of DR deliberations, but we also can and should use QFD data to review these checklists and make sure nothing has been left out. Tables 11-2 and 11-3 show examples of checklists:

TABLE 11-2. DR Checklists (Table of Contents)

1. Electrical check items 1.1 Selection and evaluation of parts and materials 1.2 Parts and materials 1. Resistors 2. Capacitors 3. Semiconductors and diodes 4. Magnets 5. Relays and switches 6. Vacuum valves 7. Insulation materials (plastic insulators, rods, barriers, recharge materials) 8. Connection parts and materials 9. Miscellaneous parts 1.3 Circuit-related items 1.3.1 Low-voltage circuits 1.3.2 High-voltage circuits 1.4 Reliability analysis 1.5 Electrical interference	2. Mechanical check items 2.1 Selection and evaluation of parts and materials 2.2 Parts and materials 1. Nails and rivets 2. O-rings 3. Bearings (roller and slide) 4. Paints 5. Plating 6. Welding 7. Packing 8. Miscellaneous parts 2.3 Common design items 2.4 Reliability analysis 2.5 Mechanical interference	3. Safety factors 4. Operability 5. Ergonomics (in handling, packaging, transportation, storage) 6. Value engineering 6.1 Specifications review 6.2 General VE 6.3 Manufacturing costs 6.4 Machine design 6.5 Structural design 6.6 Standardization 6.7 Testing 6.8 Items purchased from outside suppliers 7. Documentation 8. Patents

CASE STUDY B: MULTICIRCUIT SWITCH

This section describes how we used QFD to develop a new multicircuit switch for our line of electric power products. As its name implies, this device integrates many switches into a single unit.

Many of Japan's electric power companies have recently been very active installing underground power lines. The multicircuit switches described in this case study are used to divide and branch these lines.

TABLE 11-3. DR Checklist Example

Target item	Multicircuit switch

Check items	Further study required		Standards and specifications	Design contents	Documentation	DR results				Corrective action
	Yes	No								
1. Electrical check items										
1.1 Selection and evaluation of parts and materials										
(1) Have appropriate standards been consulted?										
(2) Can nonstandard parts and materials be excluded or replaced with standard items through redesign?										
(3) Have vibration and impact testing been addressed?										
3. Safety factors										
(1) Has a safe deenergizing method been established for emergencies?										
(2) Are the hazardous external parts safely grounded?										
(11) Does the product have adequate structural strength to keep it from obstructing vehicular traffic?										

Quality Table

Quality requirements: Primary	Secondary	Tertiary	Quality characteristics (Primary: Transportation/installation; Secondary)			Enclosure lid strength	Enclosure lid weight				
No public hazards											
	Vehicles can pass	Does not hit lid				◎					
		Does not fall if lid slips				○	◎				

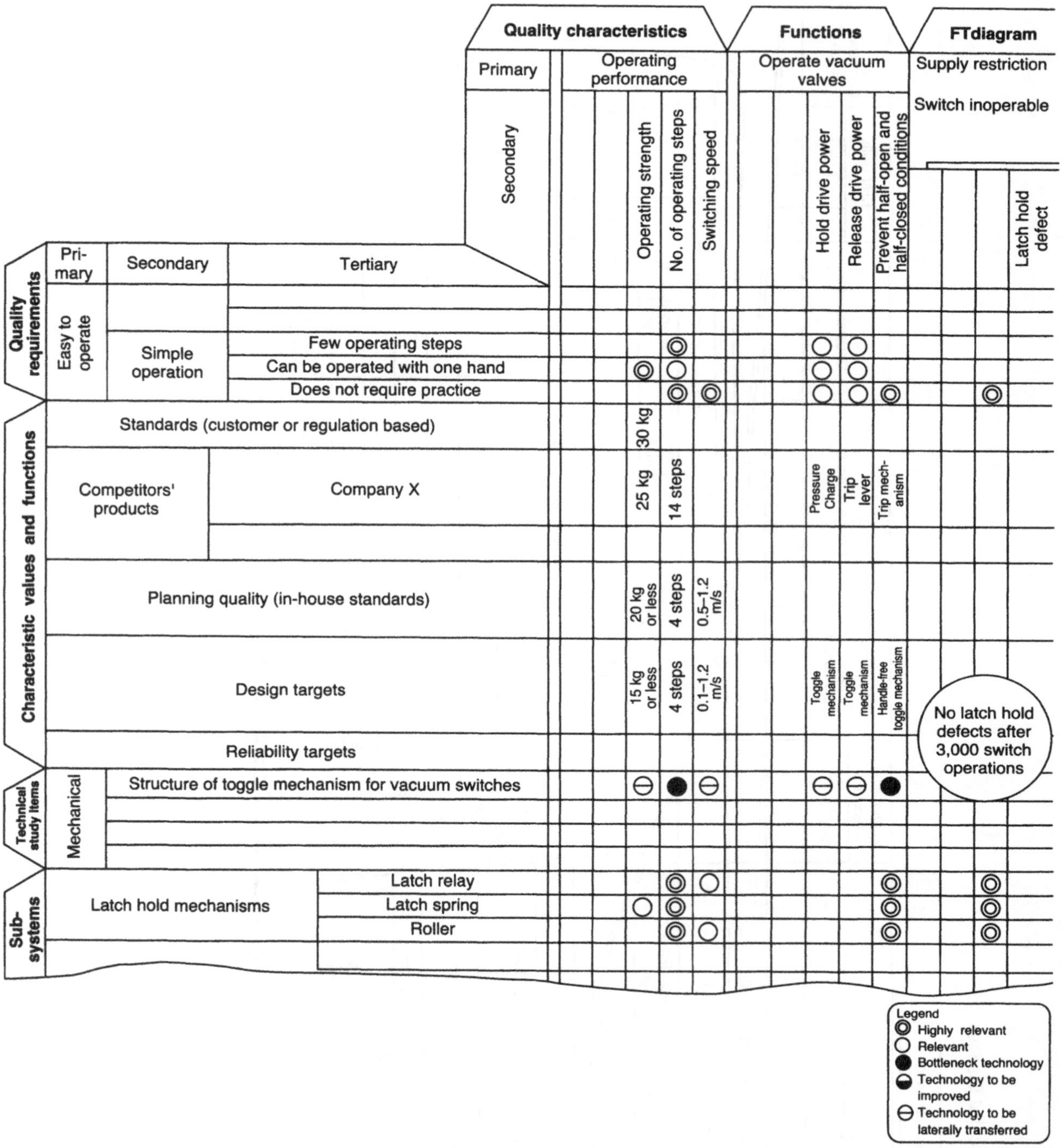

Quality requirements / Characteristic values and functions (Primary / Secondary / Tertiary)	Quality characteristics: Operating performance — Operating strength	Operating performance — No. of operating steps	Operating performance — Switching speed	Functions: Operate vacuum valves — Hold drive power	Operate vacuum valves — Release drive power	Operate vacuum valves — Prevent half-open and half-closed conditions	FTdiagram: Supply restriction — Switch inoperable	Switch inoperable — Latch hold defect
Quality requirements — Easy to operate — Simple operation — Few operating steps		◎		○	○			
Quality requirements — Easy to operate — Simple operation — Can be operated with one hand	◎	○		○	○			
Quality requirements — Easy to operate — Simple operation — Does not require practice		◎	◎	○	○	◎	◎	
Characteristic values and functions — Standards (customer or regulation based)	30 kg							
Characteristic values and functions — Competitors' products — Company X	25 kg	14 steps		Pressure Charge	Trip lever	Trip mechanism		
Characteristic values and functions — Planning quality (in-house standards)	20 kg or less	4 steps	0.5–1.2 m/s					
Characteristic values and functions — Design targets	15 kg or less	4 steps	0.1–1.2 m/s	Toggle mechanism	Toggle mechanism	Handle-free toggle mechanism		
Characteristic values and functions — Reliability targets							No latch hold defects after 3,000 switch operations	
Technical study items — Mechanical — Structure of toggle mechanism for vacuum switches	⊖	●	⊖	⊖	⊖	●		
Sub-systems — Latch hold mechanisms — Latch relay		◎	○			◎	◎	
Sub-systems — Latch hold mechanisms — Latch spring	○	◎				◎	◎	
Sub-systems — Latch hold mechanisms — Roller		◎	○			◎	◎	

Legend
◎ Highly relevant
○ Relevant
● Bottleneck technology
◓ Technology to be improved
⊖ Technology to be laterally transferred

Note: To convert actual quality requirements such as "Does not require practice" (under "Simple operation") to equivalent characteristics, we can use something measurable like "number of operating steps." This in turn presupposes the functions "Operate vacuum valves" and "Prevent half-open and half-closed conditions." The technology needed to tie all these together is embodied in "Handle-free toggle mechanism." Since the company lacks the in-house resources to provide this mechanism, it is marked as a technical bottleneck for further study.

FIGURE 11-6. Quality Table for Product B

RELIABILITY-BASED PRODUCT DEVELOPMENT

The electric power supply business has a large public-sector component (electric power companies) with a social obligation to prevent power outages. Not surprisingly, reliability—specifically, zero breakdowns—is our top priority for switches and other power supply products.

Reliability is best measured over periods of extended use, making it difficult to assess through preshipment inspections. Instead we must do our best to predict what kind of wear, deterioration, or other age-related stresses will occur, and then build the product to handle them. What this means for us in new product development is pinpointing failure modes and conducting experiments to confirm reliability.

IDENTIFYING TECHNICAL BOTTLENECKS

Figure 11-6 shows part of the quality table we used when developing a new multicircuit switch. As you can see, the format is different from the one shown in the earlier case study. The reason is that mechanical functions were much more important for the air plasma cutter than for the switch, so that table included function and technology deployment sections.

In both case studies, our developers asked themselves what mechanisms were needed to achieve the desired product functions. Then they asked whether or not those mechanisms could be made using in-house technologies. Any mechanism that could not was listed as a "technical bottleneck."

Figure 11-7 shows a Q&A Flowchart, a brainstorming aid which helped us work out a satisfactory toggle mechanism and thus resolve a technical bottleneck. We were constrained by the mechanism design proposals and by target values for quality characteristics. This Q&A Flowchart plays a useful role in DR, as we shall see later.

Identification of technical bottlenecks is also a part of FMEA (failure mode and effects analysis), which is the next step in QFD.

RELIABILITY DEPLOYMENT

The deployment we have described so far has been aimed at creating products that will sell. This perspective alone does not adequately address the causes of failures and other problems during development. Consequently, we carry out a separate deployment to ensure product reliability.

Adopting the FT (fault tree) diagram from the QFD table, we selected reliability items to be checked at each stage of product development. This involved looking for correlations between FT failure mode data and design quality characteristics. For example, in Figure 11-6, the failure mode corresponding to "Does not require practice" is "Latch hold defect." This also shows us the relations between quality characteristics and functions and enables us to set more realistic reliability targets.

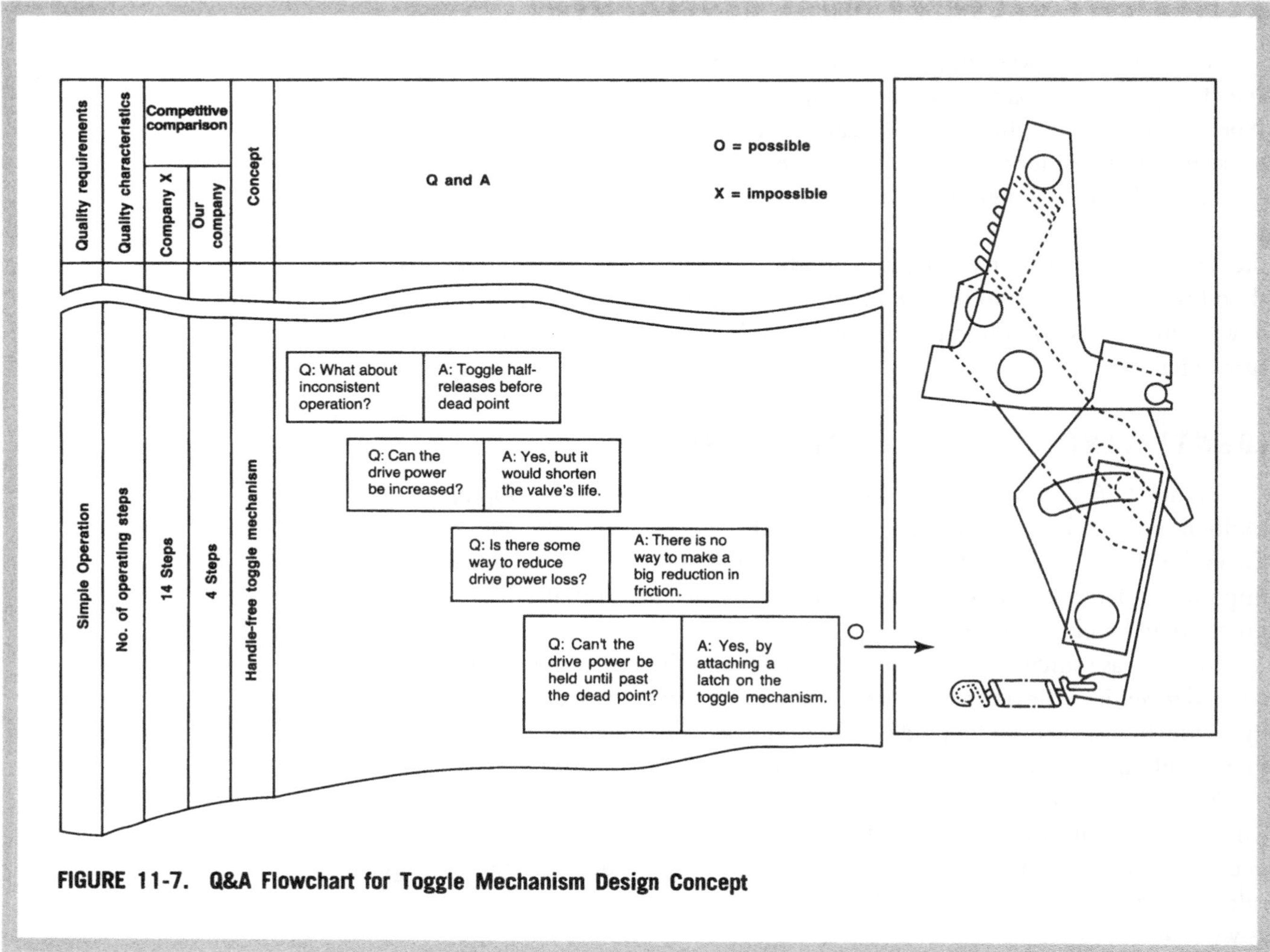

FIGURE 11-7. Q&A Flowchart for Toggle Mechanism Design Concept

The issue of technical bottlenecks is certainly relevant to achieving the desired quality characteristics, but it is also worth reexamining failure modes to identify technical obstacles to reliability targets.

We next draw up a matrix to relate failure modes, such as the latch hold defect mentioned above, to function deployment items, such as the latch hold mechanism mentioned in Figure 11-6. At the detailed design stage this will allow us to link these relations with FMEA studies, evaluating the reliability of each item's design elements, such as materials, shape, dimensions, and finish. Then we are ready to make a comprehensive reliability deployment list. Figure 11-8 shows the FMEA table for the latch mechanism, while the response table in Figure 11-9 lists policies and action plans for preventing latch hold defects.

System: Power line
Subsystem: Multicircuit switch

FMEA Table

	Component	Failure mode	Suspected cause of failure	Probability of occurrence	Impact on subsystems	Defect detection method	Detect-ability	Impact on system	Severity of impact	Criti-cality code	Failure ranking
1.0	1.1										
3.0	3.1 Toggle mechanism	1. .... : 6.									
	3.3 Latch mechanism	1. Latch hold defect	1. Lever/ roller dimension defect	1	Unstable breaking speed	Dimension measurement	2	Accidental short-circuit		8	III
			2. Lever/ roller finishing defect	1		Appearance inspection	1			4	IV
			3. Latch spring load defect	2		Weight measurement	3			24	II
			4. Latch position adjustment defect	1		Dimension measurement	2			8	III

FIGURE 11-8. FMEA Table for Latch Mechanism

Table of Critical Items

	Failure Mode	Impact on subsystem	Impact on system	Suspected cause of failure	FMEA page	Failure ranking	Prevention policy	Action
3.2	1. Latch hold defect	Unstable breaking speed	Accidental short-circuit	(1) Lever/roller dimension defect	5	III	1.	1. .... 2. ....
				(3) Latch spring load defect	5	II	1. Measure spring characteristics	1. Set minimum operating load at 5 kgf 2. Copy to QA table (1)
							2. Check operating characteristics	1. Register on quality characteristics evaluation table
				(4) Latch position adjustment defect	5	III	1.	1. .... 2. ....

Figure 11-9. Response Table for Latch Hold Defect

DR SEQUENCE

DR-1 (product planning review) for Product A centered on the quality tables shown in Figures 11-2 and 11-4. We looked at the proposed product in terms of customer needs, competitive advantage, specific selling points, and other quality planning considerations.

During DR-2 (design concept review), the DR staff evaluated the same Product A with reference to the quality table shown in Figure 11-4, and Product B according to the items listed in Figure 11-6. They also found the Q&A Flowchart (Figure 11-7) expedient for resolving technical bottlenecks. Up to this point, DR had dealt mainly with the results of previous studies, but this flowchart enabled the DR staff to see the reasoning process behind the design concept. This gave their DR work a much more solid base.

The cost deployment and quality characteristics evaluation tables in DR-3 (initial design prototype review) listed all quality characteristics that require checking. Included were reliability items identified by QFD and by the reliability deployment table based on the failure modes in Figure 11-6. The DR focus on reliability was particularly well supported by correlations between quality requirements and failure modes, as well as by other data that clarified the design department's reliability goals. The FMEA table (Figure 11-8) and response table (Figure 11-9) also helped make DR-3 successful.

The agenda for DR-4 (final design prototype review) started with an evaluation of the results from the quality characteristics evaluation table. When current prototype cost estimates exceeded targets, the DR staff employed value engineering to work out a VE-based cost reduction policy. They backed up this policy with a CR/QA deployment table to check for quality consistency. DR-5 (final product design review) revolved around the QA table, consisting mainly of data from the previous quality table. The QA table was used again for DR-6 (production process design review), along with studying the QC process table, which clarifies production and/or inspection management methods.

What we see, therefore, is that quality function deployment plays an important role at each stage of DR.

BENEFITS

We have experienced two primary benefits from QFD:

1. It was our first systematic attempt at finding out customer needs. The information we gleaned helped us improve both the development process and the new product itself.

2. The emphasis on each product's distinctive and critical characteristics has served to reduce errors and omissions in establishing product design quality and has also made for more useful pre-DR data packages.

CONCLUSION

Both on its own merits and in relation to DR, the goal of quality function deployment is to ensure design quality throughout product development. The more fully QFD is carried out, the more effective DR becomes.

Shogo Yamamoto
Hamanako Electric Company, Ltd.

12 new DOE methods for reliability

INTRODUCTION

One vital question in DR is how to confirm the reliability of each design parameter value. We need to know if these values represent the optimal mix of quality, cost, and delivery (QCD).

Since probably over 80 percent of product reliability is determined before production, designers apply much of their expertise to setting parameter values. They use methods such as FMEA and FTA, followed by confirmation experiments for suspected problem areas. To make these experiments more accurate and efficient, we have added DOE (design of experiments) methods to our DR program.

CONVENTIONAL DOE APPLICATIONS

We have traditionally used DOE for problem solving. First we identify causal factors for characteristics requiring improvement. Then we set benchmarks for these factors and enter the values in matrices. We next design and conduct experiments based on these values, applying deductive statistical methods such as variance analysis to the results. While this has helped us improve existing products and processes, conventional DOE methods are not geared toward designing new products for reliability.

Because these conventional methods are rooted in deductive statistics, data distribution is always an issue. But for new designs, we do not have any physical test data on hand. Moreover, the established methods address reliability of manufacturing processes, not technical reliability at the front end.

We have therefore had to rely on durability tests and other physical evaluation methods, which are both time consuming and costly. Solutions have mostly involved switching to more expensive materials and parts or applying stricter process controls.

PARAMETER DESIGN

Dr. Gen'ichi Taguchi has recently developed an alternative approach, based on both Fisher and Schwarz (management chart methodology) but no longer tied to statistics. More and more engineers worldwide are using his parameter design to investigate reliability during the design phase.

DEPARTURE FROM DISTRIBUTION

The most distinctive aspect of parameter design is how data is handled. We are accustomed to squaring event observation data before doing conventional variance analysis. Take the common example of electric energy, in which measurements such as current and voltage are compared in terms of their square values. In parameter design, though, we are not doing simple statistical analysis. Data distribution becomes irrelevant.

This means we are not restricted to the results of physical tests. Parameter design can use theoretical or calculated data. Specifically, it can use combinations from an allocation matrix that contains benchmark values for control and noise (non-control) factors. If, for example, the reliability equation contains many parameters, we can use large matrices such as L_{36} or L_{54} and then let a computer do the calculations.

The characteristic used to evaluate reliability is the S/N (signal-to-noise) ratio, which enables us to evaluate both average values and variation apart from statistical distributions.

With parameter design you can set aside variance analysis, verification, inference, and contribution factors. While you need a certain level of understanding to calculate S/N ratios from the given data, after that they themselves become the target characteristic data. We can examine average values by drawing graphs for each level of factors. As a result, engineers with little or no background in statistics can master this approach.

HIGH RELIABILITY AT LOW COST

JIS-Z 8815 defines reliability as the quality of an item in terms of its ability to perform all required functions under specified operating conditions throughout its design life. Figure 12-1 illustrates this definition.

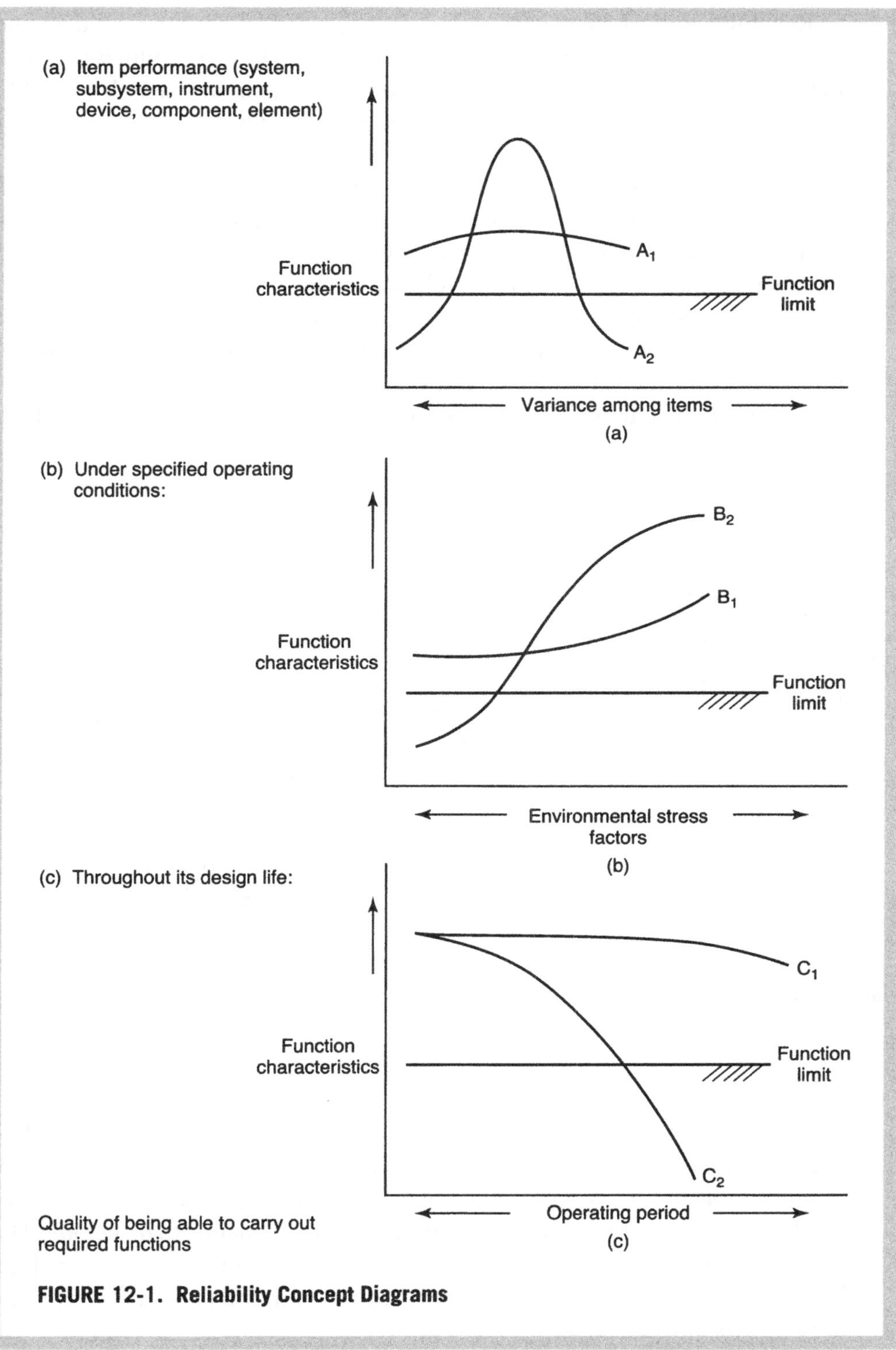

FIGURE 12-1. Reliability Concept Diagrams

Reliability is most often associated with long service life (represented by line C_1), but environmental resistance is just as important. Today's products toil in all kinds of environments around the world, sometimes even in space. If we fail to consider the full range of conditions, our design will not be adequately robust. As shown by line B_2, the product will not hold its tolerance.

Of course, the basis for parts B and C is part A, the item or product itself. Even if we use inexpensive components subject to wide variation, a design that ensures function characteristics such as those shown by line A_1 will be easy to manufacture and will also result in a reliable product.

Parameter design using new DOE methods is the best way to achieve high reliability at low cost. This involves studying the relation between parameters A and B (characteristic values for several elements in the system, such as parts or materials) and the required final characteristic value "y," as shown in Figure 12-2.

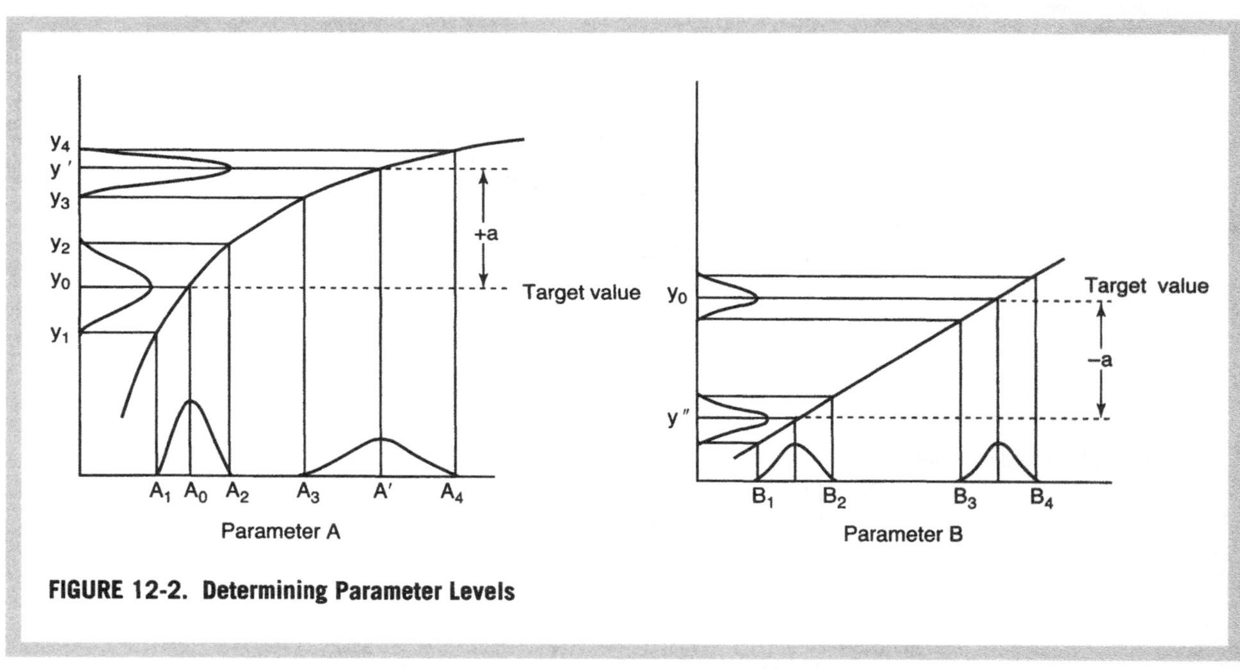

FIGURE 12-2. Determining Parameter Levels

We first set parameter A equal to A_0, corresponding to target value y_0. The range of variation from A_1 to A_2 produces the range from y_1 to y_2. Notice that while the range for A′ (A_3 to A_4) is about twice that for A_0, the range (y_3 to y_4) for y′—the system's final characteristic value—is much smaller than before. The central value in this range is larger than the target value only by $+\alpha$. Meanwhile, the graph for parameter B shows a linear reduction in the target value with the range of variation unchanged.

The more complicated a system becomes, the greater the variety of parts and/or materials it will require. This in turn means more factors to be optimized, which brings us back to the advantages of using the S/N ratio to quantify reliability.

CASE STUDY A: DESIGNING FOR ENVIRONMENTAL RESISTANCE

As mentioned earlier, reliability in the face of changing operating conditions is a key ingredient in design specifications. What we do in parameter design is carry out product definition experiments for each control factor and noise factor and then adjust the control factor benchmark values for the smallest possible variation between the characteristic value and noise factors.

FACTOR ALLOCATION

In one case we carried out various predictive experiments and finally identified control factors A (2 levels), B (4 levels), and C (2 levels). P, Q, R, and S were the noise factors we used to evaluate product reliability. We also established a standard value, upper limit, and lower limit for each control factor.

To determine the optimum values for A, B, and C, we allocated them into a three-dimensional array and allocated noise factors P, Q, R, and S into an L_9 (3^4) matrix. Our product-definition experiments based on the formula "three-way layout times L_9" yielded the data shown in Table 12-1. The desirable characteristic is the one with the smallest negative S/N ratio.

VARIANCE ANALYSIS

Table 12-2 shows the results of conventional variance analysis on this raw data.

Look at the interaction of the control factor and noise factor (see Figure 12-3). Control factor α_1 is optimal around noise factor ϕ_2, while α_2 is preferable over the entire range from ϕ_1 to ϕ_3.

Such detailed analysis of the interaction between control and noise factors is important, but it also requires extensive, time consuming calculations. We also need to draw graphs such as those in Figures 12-3 and 12-4 to clarify this interaction.

Further studies from an in-house technology perspective can help us confirm optimum control factor levels.

TABLE 12-1. Allocation and Data

S	4		1	2	3	3	1	2	2	3	1		
R	3		1	2	3	2	3	1	3	1	2		
Q	2		1	2	3	1	2	3	1	2	3		
P	1		1	1	1	2	2	2	3	3	3		
Factor	Column No.		1	2	3	4	5	6	7	8	9		
												Total	S / N ratio (dB)
A_1	B_1	C_1	28	46	45	40	7	6	14	7	5	198	–28.83
		C_2	54	38	29	22	5	9	8	7	5	177	–28.18
	B_2	C_1	22	20	18	23	4	3	20	4	3	117	–23.86
		C_2	22	24	22	49	4	24	15	12	6	178	–27.40
	B_3	C_1	27	25	20	12	2	3	3	3	3	98	–23.33
		C_2	29	28	28	8	4	8	6	7	1	119	–24.67
	B_4	C_1	7	10	13	16	2	3	4	4	2	61	–18.40
		C_2	9	11	13	15	4	13	8	11	2	86	–20.33
A_2	B_1	C_1	30	44	40	33	6	3	6	3	4	169	–27.96
		C_2	43	28	36	11	5	13	4	8	3	151	–26.82
	B_2	C_1	19	14	10	11	6	2	8	3	3	76	–20.00
		C_2	15	14	15	15	3	11	4	9	3	89	–20.90
	B_3	C_1	22	24	25	12	2	2	3	2	2	94	–23.14
		C_2	30	24	23	8	5	9	6	9	1	115	–24.06
	B_4	C_1	8	9	11	10	1	2	3	3	2	49	–16.40
		C_2	10	12	12	13	5	14	6	15	1	88	–20.63
Total			375	371	360	298	65	125	118	107	46	1865	

TABLE 12-2. Variance Analysis Table

Parameter	f	S	V	S'	ρ (%)
A	1	286.17	286.17	274.49	1.41
B	3	2422.24	807.41	2387.20	12.24
C	1	138.06	138.06	126.38	0.65
A × B	3	271.86	90.62	236.82	1.21
A × C	1	6.68	6.68	—	—
B × C	3	219.08	73.03	184.4	0.94
e_1	3	63.01	21.00	—	—
P	2	7821.10	3910.55	7797.74	39.98
Q	2	897.56	448.78	874.20	4.48
R	2	314.89	157.44	291.53	1.49
S	2	812.68	406.34	789.32	4.05
A × P	2	12.93	6.46	—	—
A × Q	2	125.39	62.70	102.03	0.52
A × R	2	66.89	33.44	43.53	0.22
A × S	2	49.68	24.84	—	—
B × P	6	3240.90	540.15	3170.82	16.26
B × Q	6	283.11	47.18	213.03	1.09
B × R	6	153.28	25.55	—	—
B × S	6	115.16	19.19	—	—
C × P	2	12.54	6.27	—	—
C × Q	2	19.50	9.75	—	—
C × R	2	520.17	260.08	496.81	2.55
C × S	2	10.79	5.40	—	—
A × B × P	6	30.63	5.10	—	—
A × B × Q	6	111.16	18.53	—	—
A × B × R	6	33.16	5.53	—	—
A × B × S	6	88.37	14.73	—	—
A × C × P	2	14.26	7.13	—	—
A × C × Q	2	10.88	5.44	—	—
A × C × R	2	26.72	13.36	—	—
A × C × S	2	0.52	0.26	—	—
B × C × P	6	178.57	29.76	108.49	0.56
B × C × Q	6	44.28	7.38	—	—
B × C × R	6	381.11	63.52	311.03	1.59
B × C × S	6	497.15	82.86	427.07	2.19
e_2	24	224.18	9.34	—	—
T	143	19504.66			100.00
(e'	88	1027.73	11.68	1670.24	8.56)

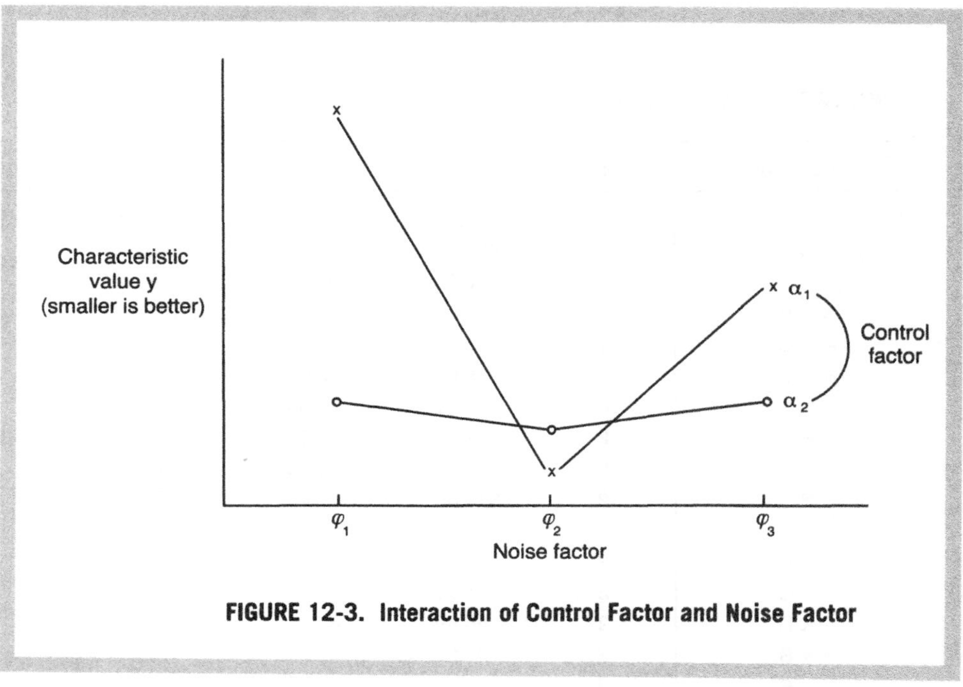

FIGURE 12-3. Interaction of Control Factor and Noise Factor

S/N RATIO ANALYSIS

Analysis using the S/N ratio is more comprehensive and objective than conventional variance analysis, and more manageable as well.

In this kind of product definition experiment, each combination of control factors (A, B, and C) has its own combinations of noise factors (P, Q, R, and S). This gives us nine different conditions to evaluate. We need a characteristic value that can be judged in terms not only of the averages resulting from the nine noise factors, but also of the amount of variance. The S/N ratio developed by Dr. Taguchi meets this requirement.

A small negative value represents the best S/N ratio in experiments like this one. The optimum average value is the one closest to zero, which also happens to mean the smallest possible variation. We can therefore evaluate the S/N ratio as follows:

$$\eta = -10 \log V_T$$

Where

$$V_T = \frac{y_1^2 + y_2^2 + \cdots\cdots + y_n^2}{n}$$

In this experiment, a three-dimensional array of control factors A, B, and C results in 16 combinations. Using the nine sets of data from the nine combinations of noise factors P, Q, R, and S as allocated on an L_9 matrix, we can calculate the S/N ratios as expressed in the above equation.

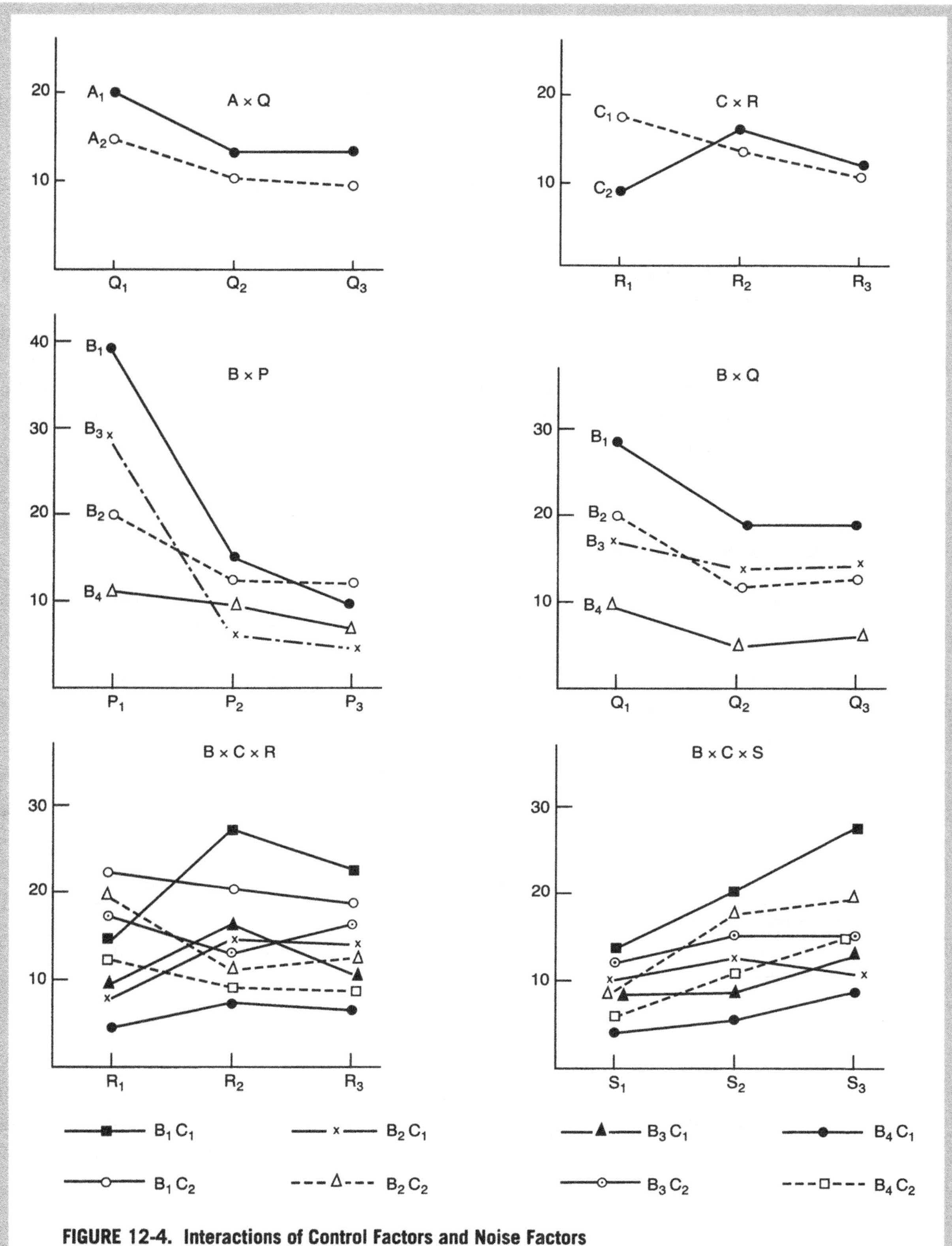

FIGURE 12-4. Interactions of Control Factors and Noise Factors

For example, to find the S/N ratio for the "A_1 B_1 C_1" combination:

$$V_{T(A_1B_1C_1)} = \frac{28^2+46^2+45^2+\cdots\cdots+7^2+5^2}{9} = 764.4$$

$$\begin{aligned}\eta_{(A_1B_1C_1)} &= -\ 10 \log V_T = -\ 10 \log 764.4\\ &= -\ 28.83 \text{ (dB)}\end{aligned}$$

The far right column in Table 12-3 lists the results of similar calculations for 16 S/N ratios.

We next use these S/N ratios as the characteristic values to find the optimum solution: the levels for A, B, and C that result in the largest possible S/N ratio.

Table 12-3 lists the results of this S/N ratio analysis. From this point on, the calculations are extremely simple and take only a fraction of the time required by the conventional method.

TABLE 12-3. Variance Analysis of S/N Ratios

Parameter	*f*	S	V	S'	ρ (%)
A	1	14.23	14.23	13.44	6.34
B	3	163.43	54.48	161.06	75.95
C	1	7.66	7.66	6.87	3.24
A × B	3	14.73	4.91	12.36	5.83
A × C	1	0.10 ○	0.10	—	—
B × C	3	8.83	2.94	6.46	3.05
e	3	3.07 ○	1.02	—	—
T	15	212.05			100.00
(e'	4	3.17	0.79	11.85	5.59)

Circle indicates pooled data

Another advantage of this new method is that graphs showing the effect of the S/N ratio on the parameters (see Figure 12-5) are easy to understand. In this case, the "A_2 B_4 C_1" combination clearly yields the optimum (largest) S/N ratio.

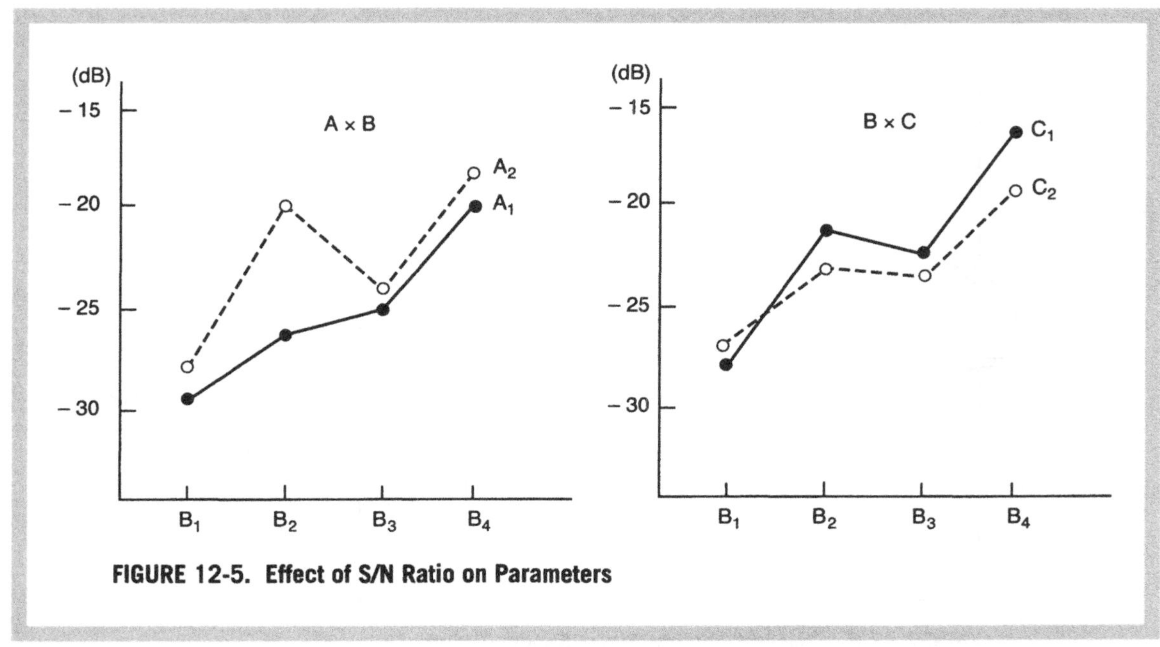

FIGURE 12-5. Effect of S/N Ratio on Parameters

CASE STUDY B: RELIABILITY DESIGN FOR ELECTRONIC POWER SUPPLY UNITS

We shall now look at how parameter design can handle more complex experiments. Our solution is a compound factor that reduces the external noise factor to three conditions: standard, worst-case positive, and worst-case negative.

OBJECTIVE

Figure 12-6 is a diagram of the power supply circuit in question. One of its requirements is to provide a stable supply of constant voltage.

The purpose of this experiment is to meet that requirement in the face of destabilizing conditions. These include external changes in battery voltage, load, and ambient air temperature, deterioration of various circuit elements, and variation in their internal constants. The parameter design establishes the target value for each parameter in as few test runs as possible.

EXPERIMENT DESIGN

Using an L_8 matrix with circuit elements as control factors, we draw the line/point graph shown in Figure 12-7 and allocate the conditions as shown in Table 12-4.

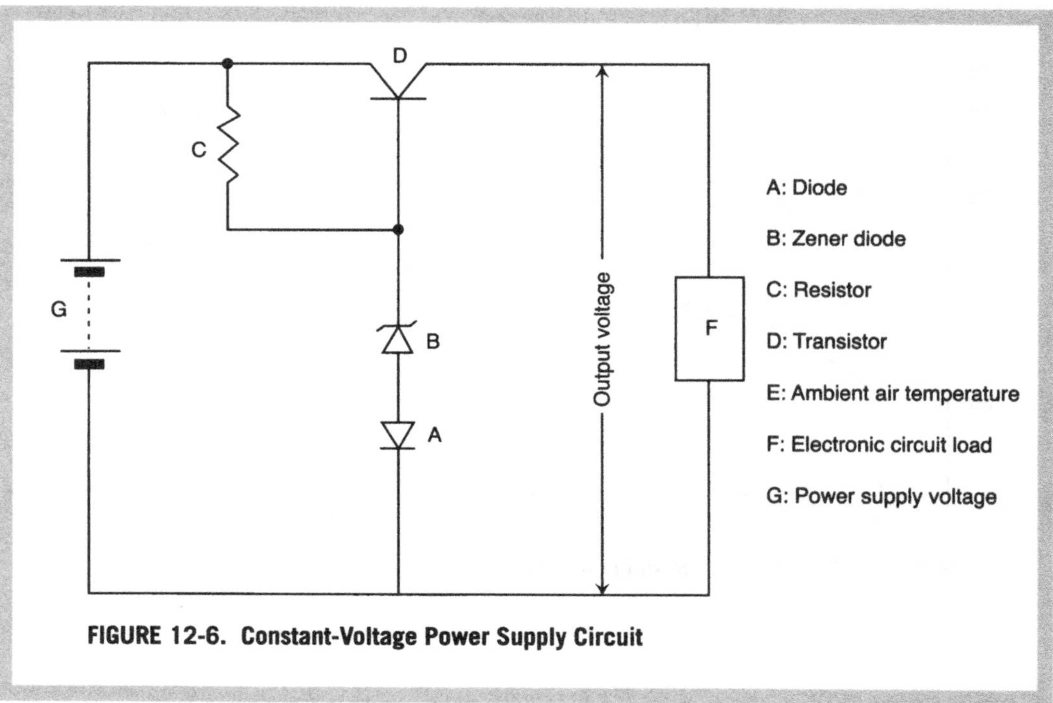

FIGURE 12-6. Constant-Voltage Power Supply Circuit

Control factor		Noise factor		
Matrix	$L_8(2^7)$	Compound factor		
Allocation method (line/point graph)	(Factor simulation method) 1 3 2 B′ (A_1) A ○——○ B″ (A_2) C e (A × C) e D ○ ○ ○ ○ 4 5 6 7	N_1	N_2	N_3
		E_1 F_1 G_1	E_2 F_2 G_2	E_3 F_3 G_3
		Minimum voltage condition	Standard condition	Maximum voltage condition

FIGURE 12-7. Internal Matrix Allocation and External Compound Factors

TABLE 12-4. Experiment Conditions for Each Factor

<table>
<tr><th colspan="5">Control Factor</th><th colspan="5">Noise Factor</th></tr>
<tr><th colspan="3"></th><th colspan="2">Level</th><th colspan="2"></th><th colspan="3">Level</th></tr>
<tr><th colspan="2">Symbol</th><th>Factor</th><th>1</th><th>2</th><th>Symbol</th><th>Factor</th><th>1</th><th>2</th><th>3</th></tr>
<tr><td colspan="2">A</td><td>Diode</td><td>Do not use</td><td>Use</td><td>E</td><td>Ambient air temperature</td><td>Low</td><td>Medium</td><td>High</td></tr>
<tr><td rowspan="2">B</td><td>B′</td><td>Zener diode Z_1 with A_1</td><td>Small</td><td>Large</td><td>F</td><td>Electronic circuit load</td><td>Small</td><td>Medium</td><td>High</td></tr>
<tr><td>B″</td><td>Zener diode Z_2 with A_2</td><td>Small</td><td>Large</td><td>G</td><td>Power supply voltage</td><td>Low</td><td>Medium</td><td>High</td></tr>
<tr><td colspan="2">C</td><td>Resistor</td><td>Small</td><td>Large</td><td rowspan="2"></td><td rowspan="2"></td><td rowspan="2" colspan="3"></td></tr>
<tr><td colspan="2">D</td><td>Transistor h_{FE}</td><td>70</td><td>140</td></tr>
</table>

We next establish conditions for combining air temperature, circuit load, and supply voltage standard values. These will comprise compound factor N_2.

From there we find the worst possible negative and positive (low and high) levels of our target characteristic value (output voltage), which we call N_1 and N_3, respectively. For example, the condition for N_1 is that a drop in ambient air temperature causes a drop in voltage. We can turn that around and use N_1 to set the power supply unit's minimum operating temperature.

Table 12-5 lists the results of our product-definition experiment using the L_8 matrix allocation of control factors and the three-level compound factor N.

ANALYSIS

We conduct our analysis via the following process. The characteristic values from Table 12-5 are expressed as output voltage (V), and the rated value is 6.6 ± 0.8 V. For each run number in the L_8 matrix, we use the equations below to calculate values for three S/N ratios (S_m, S_T, and η) and sensitivity (S). Here, η is the evaluation criterion for design reliability and S for the characteristic value itself.

$$S_m = \left(\sum_{i=1}^{3} y_i\right)^2/3$$

TABLE 12-5. Allocation Table and Experiment Result Data

	Control factor							Noise factor		
Column no.	1	2	3	4	5	6	7	Compound factor		
Experiment run no. \ Parameter	A	B		C	e	e	D	N_1	N_2	N_3
1	1	1	B′	1	1	1	1	6.13	6.55	6.90
2	1	1		2	2	2	2	5.89	6.25	6.60
3	1	2		1	1	2	2	6.52	6.98	7.39
4	1	2		2	2	1	1	5.89	6.61	6.91
5	2	1	B″	1	2	1	2	5.94	6.46	6.95
6	2	1		2	1	2	1	5.88	6.23	6.62
7	2	2		1	2	2	1	6.25	6.78	7.28
8	2	2		2	1	1	2	6.21	6.56	6.98

$$S_T = \sum_{i=1}^{3} y_i^2 - S_m$$

$$\eta = 10 \log \frac{S_m}{S_T/2}$$

$$S = 10 \log S_m$$

For example, we obtain the following results for Run 1:

$$S_m = (6.13+6.55+6.90)^2/3 = 127.792$$

$$S_T = (6.13^2+6.55^2+6.90^2) - S_m = 0.297$$

$$\eta = 10 \log \frac{127.89}{0.297/2} = 29.35 \quad \text{(dB)}$$

$$S = 10 \log 127.792 = 21.06 \quad \text{(dB)}$$

Similar results for Runs 2 through 8 are shown in Table 12-6.

Next, we carry out S/N ratio analysis with the various characteristic values for η and S from Table 12-6. The results are shown in Tables 12-7 and 12-8. Meanwhile, Tables 12-9 and 12-10 show factor estimates representing the highest contribution ratio for η and S.

TABLE 12-6. Data Analysis Results

Experiment run no.	S_m	S_T	η (dB)	S (dB)
1	127.792	0.297	29.35	21.06
2	117.062	0.253	29.66	20.68
3	145.464	0.379	28.85	21.63
4	125.583	0.549	26.60	20.99
5	124.808	0.510	26.90	20.96
6	116.938	0.274	29.31	20.68
7	137.499	0.530	27.15	21.38
8	130.021	0.297	29.42	21.14

TABLE 12-7. Variance Analysis Table for η

Parameter	f	S	V	S'	ρ (%)
A	1	0.3528	0.353	—	—
B′	1	3.1684	3.168	2.6099	22.5
B″	1	0.0324 ○	0.032	—	—
C	1	0.9384	0.938	0.3799	3.3
D	1	0.7320 ○	0.732	—	—
e (A × C)	1	5.4780	5.478	4.9195	42.4
e	1	0.9112 ○	0.911	—	—
T	7	11.6132			100.0

Circle indicates pooled data

(e′)	3	1.6756	0.5585	3.7038	(31.8)

TABLE 12-8. Variance Analysis Table for *S*

Parameter	*f*	S	V	S'	ρ (%)
A	1	0.005 ○	0.005	—	—
B'	1	0.194	0.194	0.181	24.6
B"	1	0.194	0.194	0.181	24.6
C	1	0.296	0.296	0.283	38.4
D	1	0.011 ○	0.011	—	—
e	2	0.037 ○	0.018	—	—
T	7	0.737			100.0
Circle indicates pooled data					
(e')	4	0.053	0.013	0.092	12.4

Combining the estimated η value and the most economical level results gives us A_1 $B_{1'}$ C_1. There is no need to specify a value for D, which is the transistor (an hFE value). Using the data in Table 12-9, we estimate S/N ratio η for the optimum level of A_1 $B_{1'}$ C_1 via the following equation:

TABLE 12-9. Estimated η Values for Factors with High Contribution Ratios

Parameter			Average level (dB)
A	A_1	C_1	29.10
		C_2	28.13
	A_2	C_1	27.02
		C_2	29.36
B"		B_1'	29.50
		B_2'	27.72

TABLE 12-10. Estimated *S* Values for Factors with High Contribution Ratios

Parameter		Average level (dB)
B′	B_1'	20.87
	B_2'	21.31
B″	B_1''	20.82
	B_2''	21.26
C	C_1	21.03
	C_2	20.87

$$\hat{\eta} = \widehat{A_1C_1} + \overline{B_{1'}} - \overline{T}$$

$$= 29.10+29.50-28.615$$

$$= 29.985 \quad \text{(dB)}$$

Therefore, if we set the standard condition for an optimal (A_1 $B_{1'}$ C_1) power supply unit at 6.6 V, we can expect a worst-case range of 6.24 to 6.96 V. In contrast, the range of variation for the least reliable combination (A_1 $B_{2'}$ C_2) is 1.4 times greater.

CONCLUSION

Compound factors can keep parameter design manageable, even with many control factors and large matrixes. Also, S/N ratios are simple to calculate, and if we use mixed matrixes like L_{18} or L_{36}, we do not have to consider factor interactions. Since that lets us confine our analysis to primary input-output effects, we believe that the entire process can be mastered by people with no statistical background.

This brief overview has highlighted DOE methods that can be very useful in defining technical reliability at the front end of product development. These serve to complement other methods targeted more at manufacturing processes. If space permitted, we could discuss these new methods in even more detail.

Katsuyuki Shimodaira
NASDA

13
configuration control—managing product development

INTRODUCTION

DR as a program falls under the broader heading of configuration control. This term covers all management tasks concerned with product development. By reviewing configuration control and its various elements, this chapter should help tie together what you have learned so far about DR and new product quality assurance.

INITIATING DEVELOPMENT PROJECTS

Any attempt at DR must first address two questions:

- What is its objective?
- At what stage should it be applied?

To answer either of these questions, we must first define the development project. Product development starts with identification of target users and their needs and then applies staff employee-hours to translate those needs into product functions. Once we know these things, we can formulate appropriate design goals. We then make concrete development plans based on achieving these goals.

This is where we decide if the product is worth developing and if the company has the technical and financial resources to do so. Middle managers must ask these questions as information is gathered:

- Does this product meet customer requirements?
- Is it commercially viable?
- Is it technically feasible?
- Will it be profitable for the company?
- Are there any built-in deficiencies?
- Can it be made user-friendly?
- Have we overlooked anything?

They should answer these questions in a feasibility report as early as possible. After appropriate studies and analyses, top management will either adopt or drop the plan. Even when the decision is to go forward, managers must monitor progress and identify needed plan revisions, and at the end of each stage, development can only continue with top management approval.

MANAGING DEVELOPMENT PROJECTS

Configuration control is also known as "development management." As it tracks the product from design concept to full production and beyond, its main objective is more efficient development projects.

Design management is at the heart of configuration control, since it is designers who drive the new product project. DR and design management are closely intertwined. Other people from throughout the company play supporting roles along the way from initial concept to full production. Each stage is then supported by documentation such as manuals, graphs, memos, and orders, culminating in the production manual.

PRODUCT DEVELOPMENT FLOW

Product development starts with planning:

- Decide what you are going to make.
- Figure out how to make it.
- Estimate how long it will take and how much it will cost.

Next comes the design work itself, followed by prototype build and testing, product documentation, and finally full production. Figure 13-1 outlines this overall development flow.

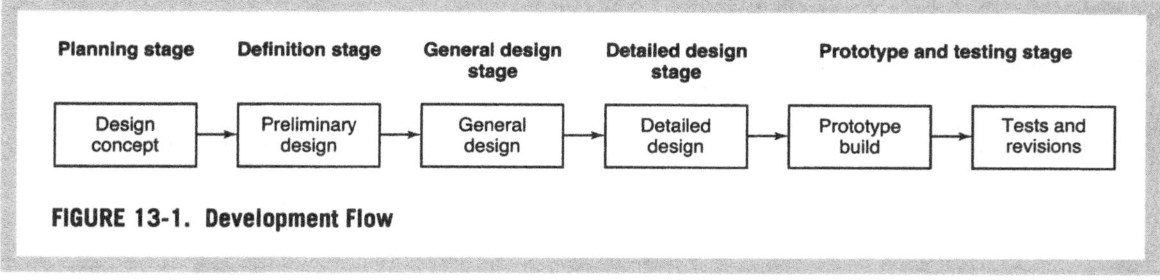

FIGURE 13-1. Development Flow

Activities associated with each stage are as follows:

Concept stage: Formulate the design concept from published data, experience, and analysis.

Definition stage: Identify quality requirements, write the baseline report, and start framing the preliminary design.

General design stage: Work through the product's general (overall) design, using the project baseline as a guide. Take care not to miss any important elements.

Detailed design stage: Draft the documentation for each component to move from general to detailed design. After that, double-check the design against quality requirements.

Prototype and testing stage: Build a prototype from the detailed design, test it, verify the results, and turn the project over to production. Although we apply the term "product development" to the entire product life cycle, the actual development process ends here.

THE PROJECT BASELINE

The baseline report (see Figure 13-2) is a planning document that lays out the development goals by stage. It is updated at each stage as additional details are filled in.

- *Results* based on strict adherence to the baseline
- *Proposed revisions* to correct problems found in the baseline
- *Proposed improvements* to make baseline goals more effective and appropriate

We then take any immediate action needed and make our baseline revisions.

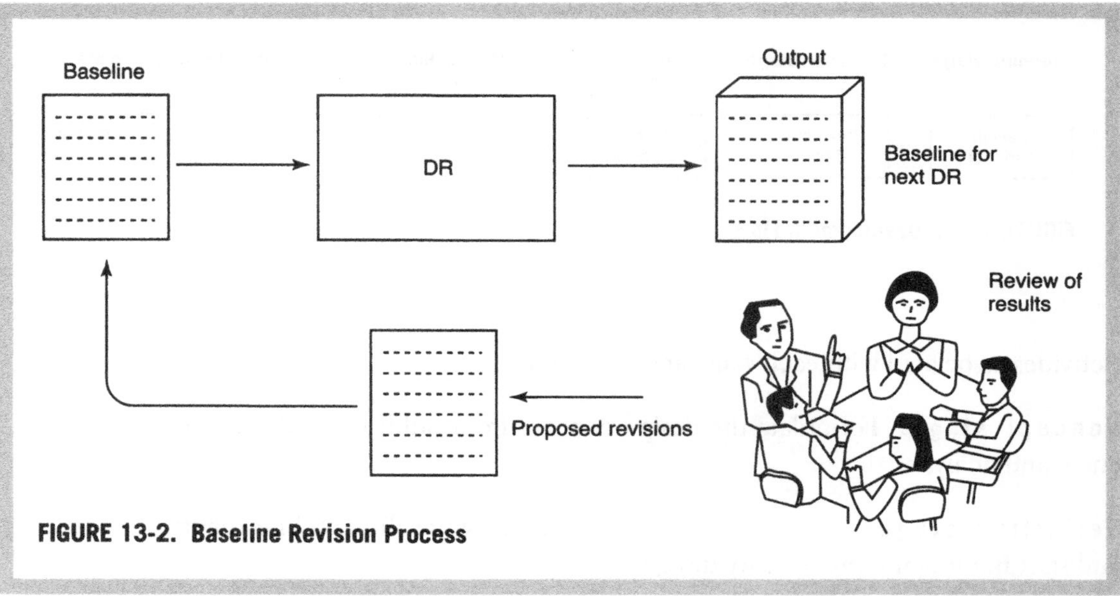

FIGURE 13-2. Baseline Revision Process

DESIGN REVISIONS

Once these revisions have been reviewed, we submit the results via a formal ECP (engineering change proposal). Once approved, this ECP is distributed to all affected parts of the organization so that they can incorporate these changes into their activities. The final results become part of the baseline report for the next stage.

The volume of revisions and ECPs is greatest during the early stages of development, tapering off later. If the reverse occurs, you can be sure that something is wrong. For one, the development process was probably not very well organized, or perhaps the increased changes reflect persistent errors due to a lack of skills or information. Also, some of the ECPs may simply supersede earlier ones. In other words, there may have been errors in the revisions themselves.

In any case, when ECPs keep popping up after prototype build and testing are underway, revisions become much more expensive. You are now undoing much that has already been done. Figure 13-3 shows how the cost per design revision escalates steeply as ECPs are put in later and later. At the beginning of the project these changes involve no more than some extra documentation, but before long, high capital costs start to kick in.

DEVELOPMENT GOALS

This high cost of delays reinforces why DR is especially important towards the front end of product development. It also underscores these points:

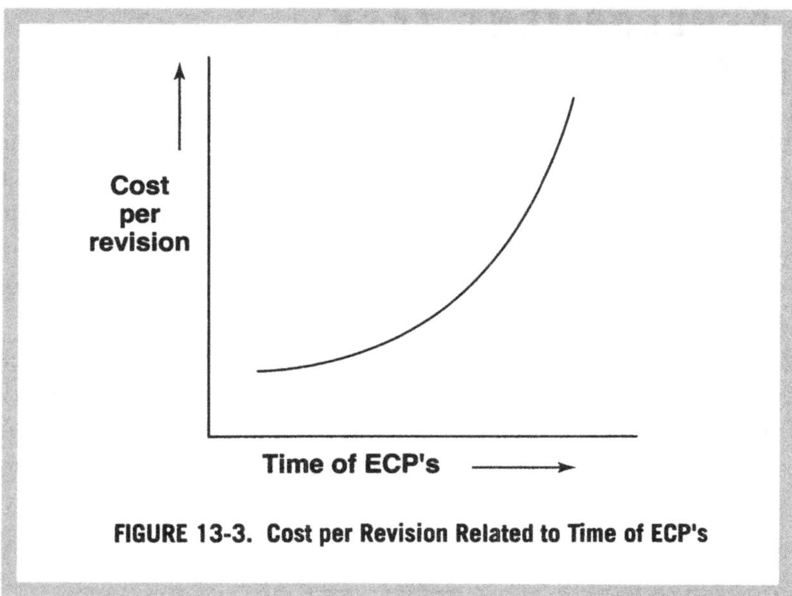

FIGURE 13-3. Cost per Revision Related to Time of ECP's

1. Initial development goals should be not only new and original, but also feasible.
2. Dividing development into well-defined stages makes it easier to do a thorough job with DR.

All companies derive a certain amount of their strength from their investment in R&D, where they learn, develop, and apply new technology. But when it comes to goals, the down side of innovation is complexity. New or unproven design elements should be factored into the initial feasibility analysis. They usually claim added time and resources for technology development, capital expenditures, organizational support, and training. Today's strongest companies are those that have built this sort of planning into product development.

DEVELOPMENT STAGES

I recommend the stages shown in Figure 13-1. If you subdivide them further, review work starts taking up too much of the total project effort. If a project is especially complicated or breaks a lot of new ground, you can always hold additional DR meetings. For instance, you may need to involve a wider circle of people in making corrective responses. It is also advisable to set up a system for formally reporting abnormalities both before and during the prototype and testing stage.

THE DEVELOPMENT TASK BREAKDOWN STRUCTURE

We must identify all tasks directly or indirectly related to developing the target product and then organize them into a plan and schedule. Figure 13-4 shows how one product, System 1000, was broken down into four subsystems numbered 1100, 1200, 1300, and 1400. Similarly, subsystem 1200 was broken down into components 1210, 1220, and 1230. This can continue down to individual parts and materials if necessary.

This kind of configuration chart, known generically as a "work breakdown structure," is usually created at the planning or definition stage. In this context we call it a DTBS (development task breakdown structure). Number designations are subject to revision as product requirements or design elements change.

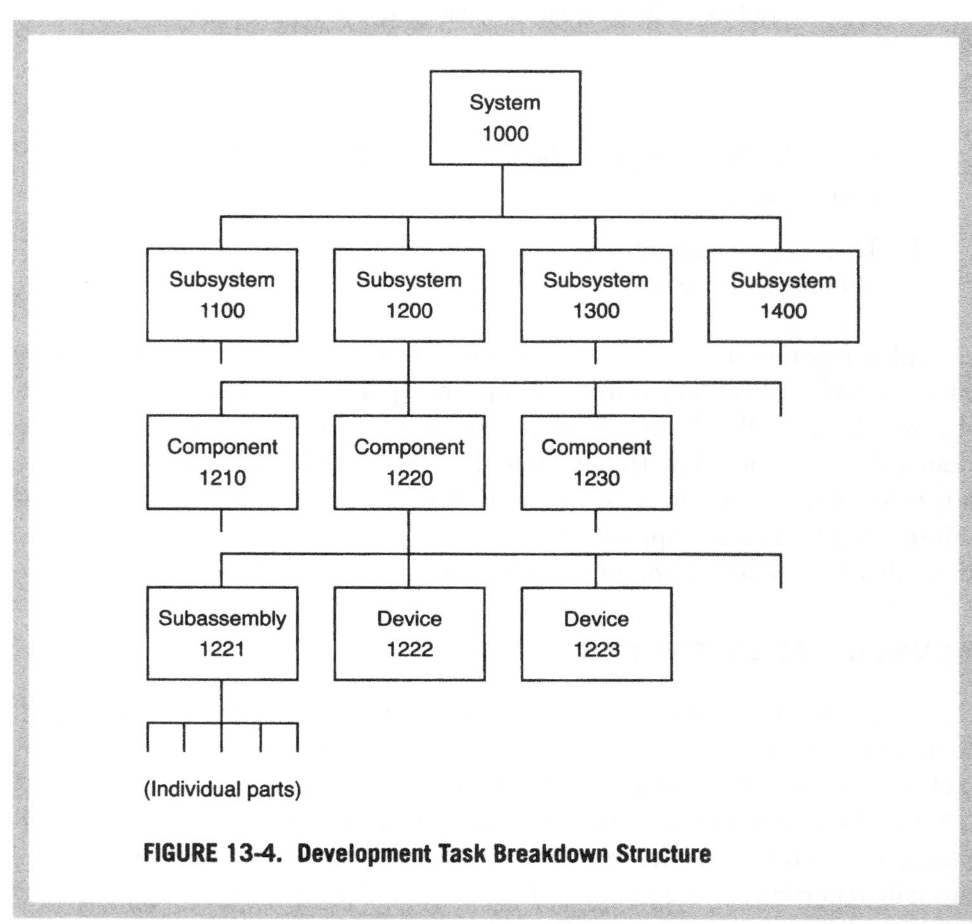

FIGURE 13-4. Development Task Breakdown Structure

The DTBS helps ensure a comprehensive approach by laying out the entire range of required development tasks. Similar charts show tasks for related research, software development, facilities and logistics support, staff training, and other administrative work. The main purpose of the DTBS is to prevent delays due to overlooked tasks that surface later in the project.

We assign numbers to components so that corresponding tasks can be identified by a matching control number on vouchers, instruction forms, and product documentation. Computer databases also use these control numbers to track employee-hours, losses, investments, and other information.

It is best to use multiples of 10 or 100, so that additional components or tasks can be inserted downstream as required. To avoid confusion, we never reassign a number from a canceled component to a new one. Also, if you start with relatively low numbers on the initial DTBS, that will allow a greater spread as the development schedule fills in. This progression also makes the numbers easier to look up.

INGREDIENTS OF A SUCCESSFUL DEVELOPMENT PROJECT

Product development is about keeping a company competitive by introducing successful new products. The end result should be enough profit to justify funding the next development project. New products that lose money place the future of the company at risk.

If a project looks otherwise unprofitable but offers some clear benefit to society as a whole, it may lead to a public/private joint venture. In any event, development should serve clear goals and objectives. Where waste is tolerated, any project will fall short of expectations regardless of its merits. You also need good project estimates to know what those expectations should be.

SYSTEM-ORIENTED DEVELOPMENT

Some development projects are organized ad hoc, pooling people into a task force structure. Top management sets the goals and then divides up design work along systems lines. This “system-oriented development” normally follows the outline of Figure 13-1. The baseline is centered on system requirements, against which the product design will be compared. Project managers then weed out any tasks that do not serve these system-oriented goals.

INFORMATION SUPPORT

All development projects require information support, starting with meaningful estimates. These estimates in turn depend on techniques to organize, store, and retrieve source data. We also need information from outside sources, in-house research, and just plain experience. The bulk of this support network is already in place when a new product project begins.

Figure 13-5 shows how to obtain and prepare information for project estimates.

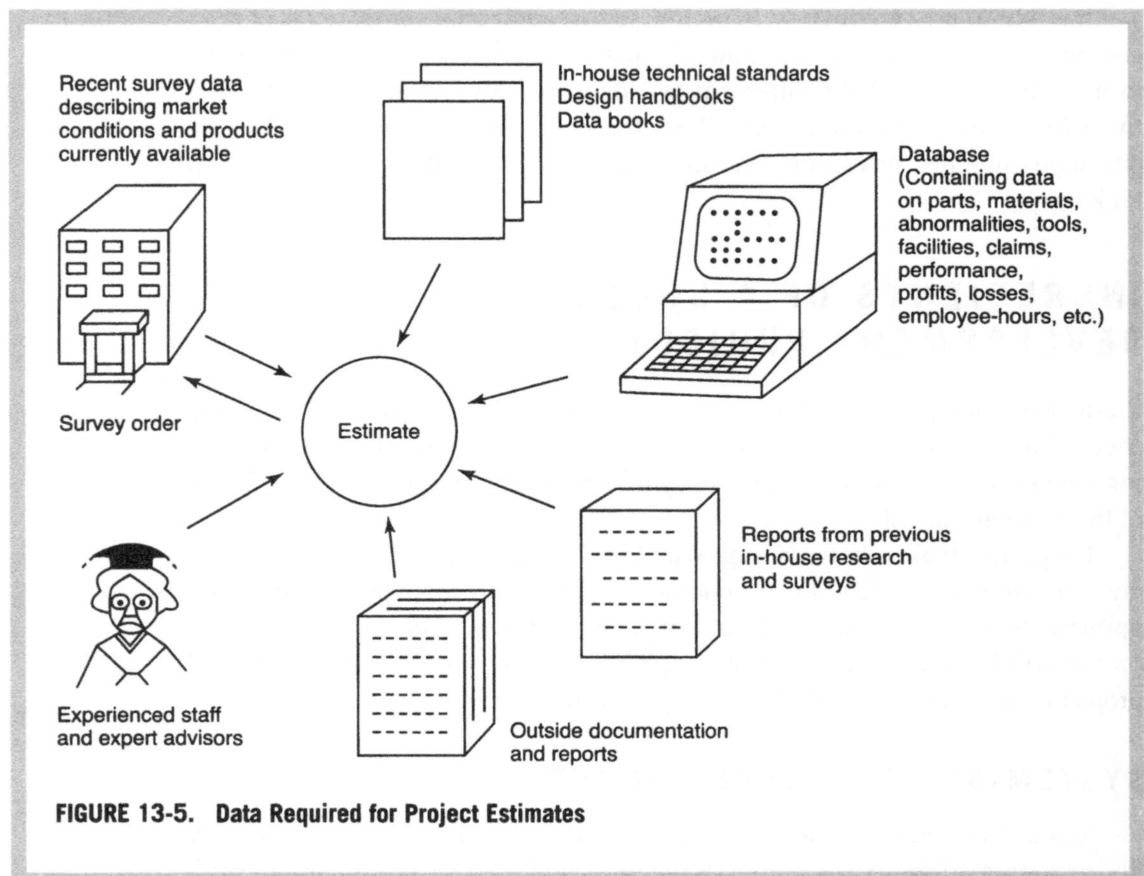

FIGURE 13-5. Data Required for Project Estimates

In-house technical standards, design handbooks, data references, lists, and other records are important assets for any company. How well a company maintains and uses these assets is to some extent indicative of how well it is run overall. A good technical library can be a key resource in overcoming design limitations.

COMPUTERIZED DATABASE MANAGEMENT

Working with large volumes of detailed statistics is especially time consuming, so we store that kind of information in a computer database to minimize access and processing time. Data on parts, abnormalities, costs, and other current project concerns should be continuously transferred to this database for reference on future projects. Keyword search capability can make it easy for engineers and others to retrieve what they need.

USE OF TECHNOLOGY

State-of-the-art technology is a key ingredient. Its presence does not guarantee success, but its absence all but ensures failure. If related data have been organized into a standard documentation system, the company can find out immediately what new technology, if any, might apply to a given project or, conversely, what is lacking. They can then factor this technology into the project estimate and adjust the schedule, cost, and performance targets accordingly.

R&D EMPHASIS

Companies must also maintain new offline research and survey studies to stay ahead of the game. When company managers see everything in pure profit-and-loss terms, they tend to lose sight of creativity, originality, and uniqueness. Investment in R&D is investment in people, ensuring that the next generation of researchers will be well trained and experienced. Such forward-looking investment should correspond to at least 20 percent of a company's profits, or from 2 to 4 percent of its gross sales.

Companies should set aside funds for purchasing reference materials and for sending representatives to seminars and conferences. Even in the absence of immediate direct benefits, companies can make good use of all the information gained.

TRAINING AND ORGANIZATIONAL DEVELOPMENT

As valuable as information can be, a company's employees are an even greater asset. The success of development projects depends above all on the participants, and the need to develop people is fundamental. Managers must offer more than job security (which is rapidly disappearing anyway). They should rotate newer employees among different positions to gain experience, sponsor research projects and R&D conferences and meetings, and establish some sort of accreditation system for employee skills improvement.

EXAMPLE OF PROJECT ESTIMATING

A good project estimate uses both current and historical sources. Many companies have done little to organize and store project historical data, only to invest large sums on market surveys, product trends and predictions, and other needed information when a new project begins. Confining development work within the strict boundaries of initial requirements is also risky, since customer specifications are subject to change.

WORKING WITH THE CUSTOMER

Consider a situation where product development is driven by single orders from major customers. Whoever receives such an order should view it as one more piece of market feedback. Armed with this perspective, he or she can then work with the customer toward a more reliable estimate of the development project. Since these discussions normally take place under tight lead time constraints, companies have all the more reason to maintain up-to-date, easily accessible marketing databases.

USING PERT

A company thus prepared can make fast, reliable estimates of product development projects, including responses to customer orders. Table 13-1 lists project planning estimates, and Figure 13-6 shows a corresponding PERT (program evaluation and review technique) diagram.

TABLE 13-1. Development Project Estimate Data

Subsystem	Complexity rating	Technical level	Estimated development lead time	Advanced R&D	Total development lead time	Action plan
A	40	In-house technology	30 months	None	30 months	*
B	50	High level	56 months or more	Feasibility study (12 months)	68 months or more	**
C	120	In-house technology	35 months	None	35 months	**
D	40	"	30 months	None	30 months	*
E	50	High level	56 months or more	Parts development (12 months)	68 months or more	***
	300					

* = Delay start of development ** = Start feasibility study and development *** = Start parts development and advance R&D

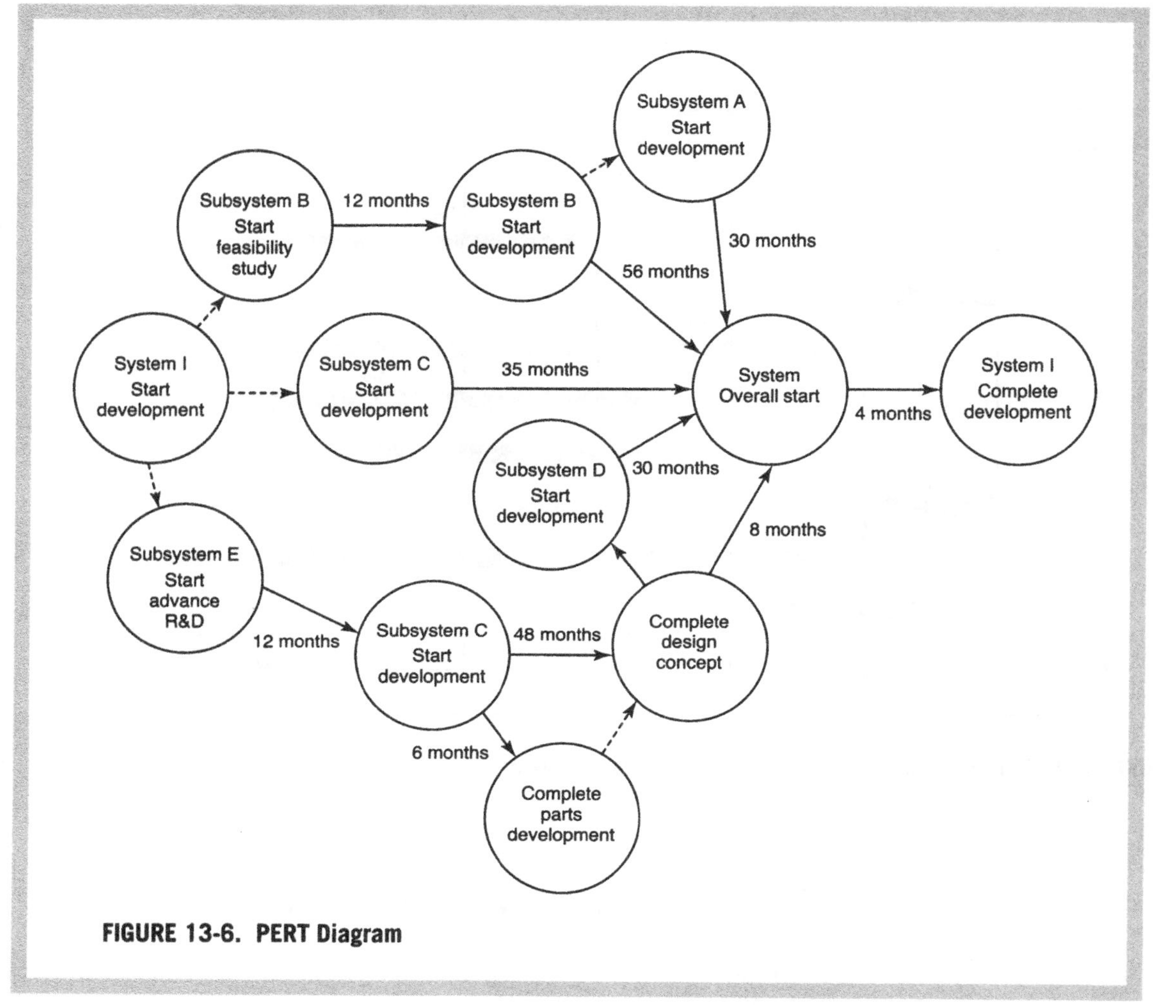

FIGURE 13-6. PERT Diagram

System I consists of five subsystems (A, B, C, D, and E). In-house technology appears adequate for subsystems A, C, and D, so development can start anytime.

Subsystem E requires an R&D project to develop one or more new parts. As for subsystem B, a feasibility study will explore how to obtain or develop some new hardware that is not readily available. The end result is a development lead time of 68 months for System I. This PERT diagram is really just a reconfiguration of Table 13-1, as is the bar graph in Figure 13-7.

KEEPING INFORMATION ACCESSIBLE

I encourage managers to post relevant tables and charts in project offices or on bulletin boards, frequently updating them to reflect development progress and DR-related changes. I also recommend storing them in the company's database for ready access by engineers and other managers.

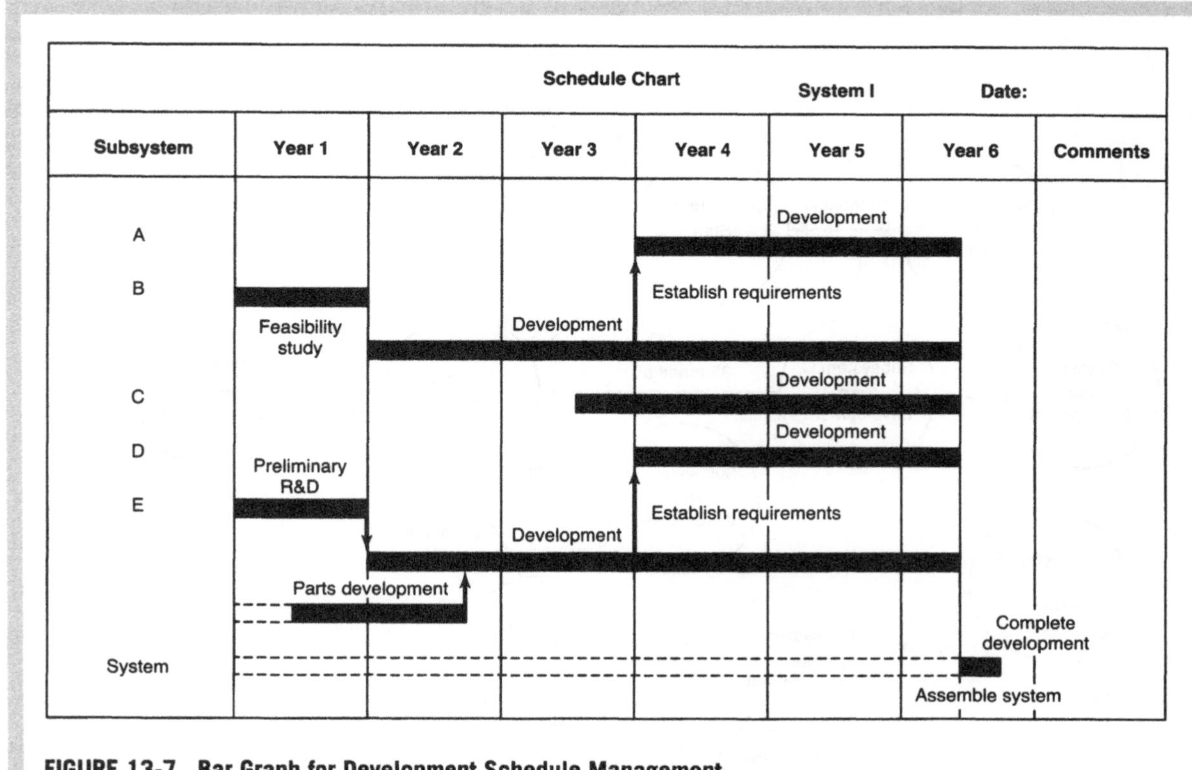

FIGURE 13-7. Bar Graph for Development Schedule Management

DEVELOPMENT ACTIVITIES BY STAGE

Let us now examine the main activities at each stage in the overall context of product and system development (see Figure 13-8).

CONCEPT STAGE

Primary activities revolve around survey studies, estimates, and tradeoffs among QCD factors. We are seeking to identify optimal conditions for the new product. This stage culminates in the development plan (Figure 13-9).

In our organization, small-scale development plans in response to customer orders must be completed within three to five days. That compares with one month for medium-scale plans and from six months to a year for large-scale plans, such as those for buildings, signaling systems, and space satellites. "Scale" is measured by the precision required in the target system and by the number of trade-offs involved.

Table 13-2 spells out key check items for making a development plan.

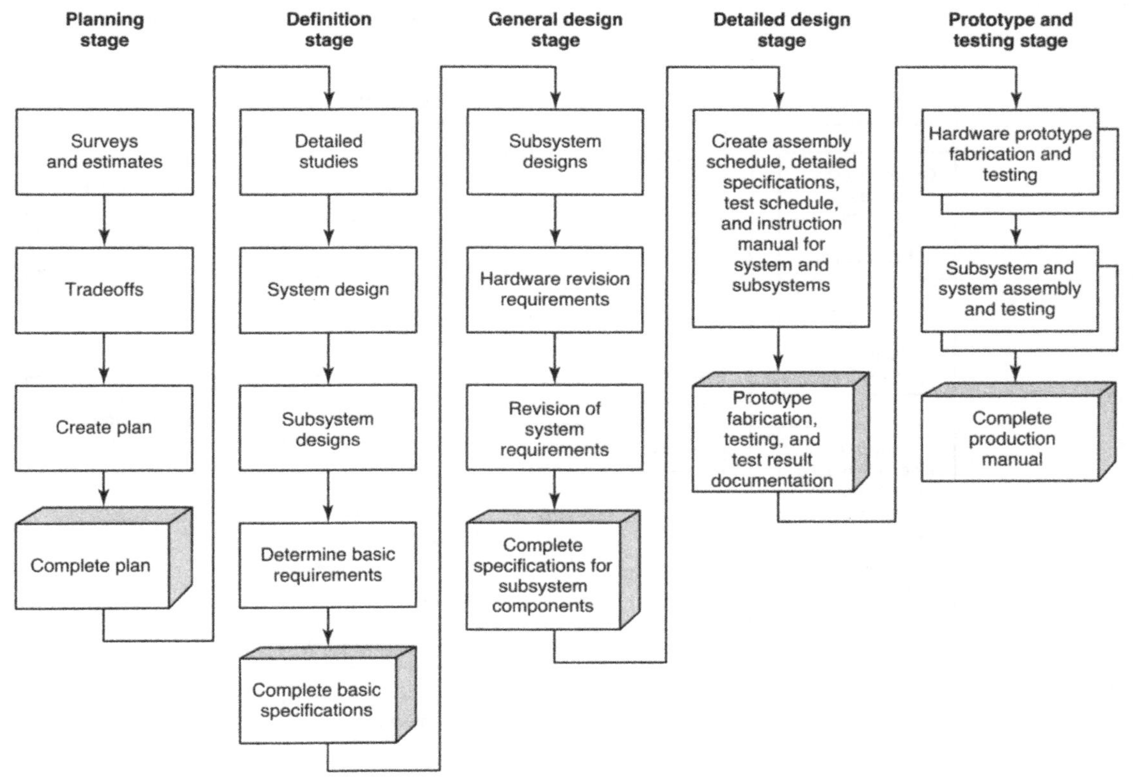

FIGURE 13-8. Specific Flowchart of Product Development Stages

DEFINITION STAGE

Here we generate the system design in line with the development plan. Studies and selection of subsystems, equipment and tooling, components, modules, and other parts should already be underway. This is also where we initiate detailed studies of production, sales, and operating conditions to establish basic specifications and, eventually, the specifications manual.

Preliminary design proceeds in three sub-phases as shown in Figure 13-10:

Phase I: Even though the development plan is already in place, designers arrange a meeting with target users, ordering customers, and our own top managers. At this meeting they revisit specific items to be included in the preliminary design and also examine current conditions for any recent changes.

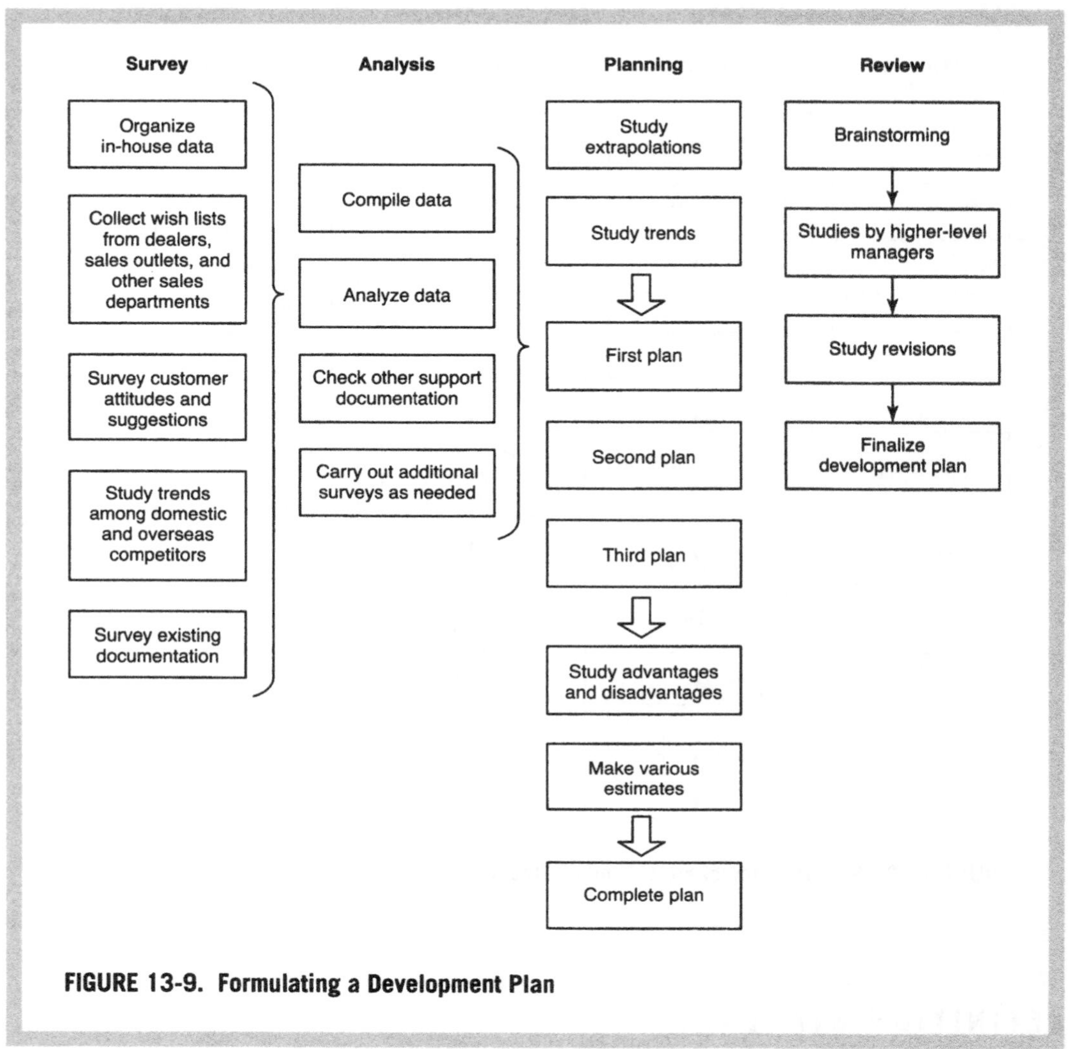

FIGURE 13-9. Formulating a Development Plan

Phase II: Designers complete the preliminary design according to the updated baseline, which incorporates the results from Phase I.

Phase III: We formally review the preliminary design.

While not necessary for small-scale development projects, these sub-phases are very important for high volume products and large systems. Even this early in the development process, a change in product requirements brings about enough design revisions to cause major scheduling problems and thus slow down the project. Table 13-3 lists system specifications associated with preliminary design.

TABLE 13-2. Development Plan Checklist

1. Product or system nomenclature
2. Overall description
3. Development basis or name of customer making order
4. Main factors and priority ranking (quality, cost, delivery, performance, reliability)
5. Market trends, previous results, related technologies
6. Required system configuration
7. DTBS
8. Analysis of development plan and schedule
9. Items for preliminary research, research project scheduling
10. Comparison of main items and values analyzed
11. Main performance factors
12. Persons in charge of development, test schedule, equipment setup, support organization
13. Costs (R&D, system development, production, overhead)

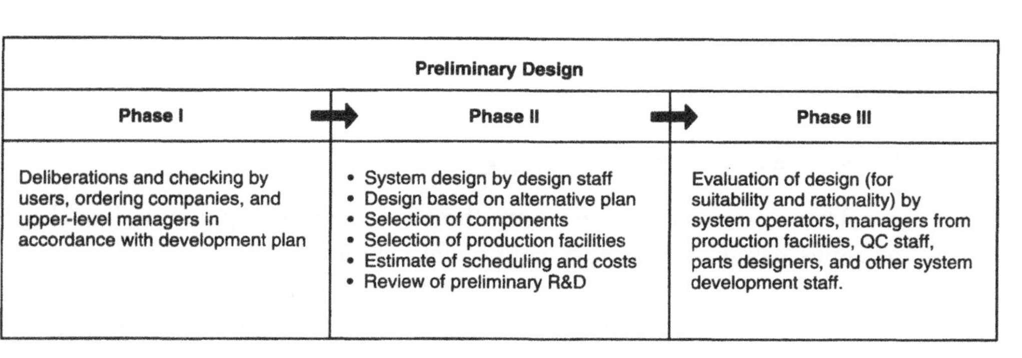

Preliminary Design
Phase I
Phase II
Phase III
Deliberations and checking by users, ordering companies, and upper-level managers in accordance with development plan
• System design by design staff
• Design based on alternative plan
• Selection of components
• Selection of production facilities
• Estimate of scheduling and costs
• Review of preliminary R&D
Evaluation of design (for suitability and rationality) by system operators, managers from production facilities, QC staff, parts designers, and other system development staff.

FIGURE 13-10. Phases in Preliminary Design

TABLE 13-3. System Specifications

1. Scope of application
   (Defines the limits of the target system's overall requirements)
2. Basic conditions
   (Associates the development baseline with an official plan number)
3. System requirements
   3.1 Configuration, related systems, configuration diagrams, function diagrams
   3.2 Basic operating conditions
   3.3 Performance features, dimensions, functions, characteristics, and limitations
   3.4 Product life, reliability, safety, and availability
   3.5 Manufacturing, handling, storage, transportation, and maintenance conditions
   3.6 Staff training, user manual, jigs and tools, test sets, repair shop setup, and spare parts
4. Quality assurance
   4.1 Development methods, development flow, test schedule
   4.2 Component QA
   4.3 System assembly and test requirements (durability, reliability, performance, function)
   4.4 Schedule for design qualification tests and transfer to production
   4.5 Manufacturing setup schedule
   4.6 Setup schedules for field service and maintenance systems
   4.7 Field quality verification plan
5. Production setup
   5.1 Requirements for plants and sales offices
   5.2 Requirements for maintenance and trade-ins

GENERAL DESIGN STAGE

These specifications now form the baseline for subsystem designs, hardware revisions based on in-house technologies (units, components, equipment, software modules), other revisions to meet system requirements, and the general assembly chart. This stage may involve a number of trade-offs, since one objective is to balance the product's performance features, functions, and other characteristics for optimum results.

Completion of the general design is accompanied by near-completion of the system's specifications. For small order-based projects, the last step is carrying out the customer's proposed revisions. At this point, subsystem and component designs are on track with their corresponding specifications. Of course, cost estimates are already in place, and schedules for prototype build and testing, the supporting facilities plan, the operations plan, and the marketing system are all complete or close to it.

Table 13-4 lists specifications for the subsystems and their hardware.

TABLE 13-4. Subsystem (Machine) Specifications

1. Scope of application
2. Basic conditions
3. Subsystem requirements
   - 3.1 Components, function chart, interface devices
   - 3.2 Dimensions, weight, external view diagram, mechanical attachments
   - 3.3 Performance, characteristics, functions
   - 3.4 Durability, reliability, safety
   - 3.5 Operating conditions
   - 3.6 Manufacturing conditions
   - 3.7 Management conditions
4. Quality assurance
   - 4.1 Development tests
   - 4.2 Qualification tests
   - 4.3 Test conditions
   - 4.4 Test items and methods
   - 4.5 Evaluation criteria
   - 4.6 Test data, evaluation, and analysis methods
5. Requirements for handover to system level
6. Other

DETAILED DESIGN STAGE

This is where we wrap up all the detailed design elements not already covered at the general design stage. Then we begin prototype setup by assembling the system and subsystems. While investigating ways to connect the components and wiring, organize the assembly sequence, and carry out reviews and tests, we also reevaluate the system design. Problems with the system assembly or machine design may surface in the process, and occasionally we find major defects. If the problems are critical enough, that can mean pushing out the development schedule, especially when additional prototypes and tests are required.

PROTOTYPE AND TESTING STAGES

This stage includes making and testing the system's hardware (and software where applicable). Now that we are moving from information to a physical product, any defects we find demand immediate and decisive attention. Some will be defects previously overlooked in documentation and drawings, which is why all documentation concerning parts, materials, processing, and assembly must be completed before this stage even begins. It is always far cheaper to make changes on paper than on the shop floor.

DEVELOPMENT SUPPORT ACTIVITIES

Various support activities parallel the main design work. For instance, we carry out preliminary R&D, fabrication, and testing for part prototypes, experimental prototypes, technical test models, and data acquisition models.

HARDWARE DEVELOPMENT

Figure 13-11 relates product development and hardware development. We distinguish among several types of hardware for project purposes:

- Hardware that uses only in-house technology and therefore does not require prototypes
- Hardware that uses slightly revised in-house technology, requiring prototype build and testing only in relation to the revisions
- Hardware that uses new technology based on preliminary R&D work and definitely requires prototype build and testing

Such development work usually falls under the categories of parts development, part prototype build and testing, or device/unit development. Like system development as a whole, hardware development should begin early enough to accommodate new or revised technologies in the schedule.

BBMs (bread board models), which represent completed segments of the product design, play an important role in hardware development. Originating in the electronics field, BBMs are generally associated with the planning or definition stage. But here the term refers to any experimental prototype that checks some part of the hardware design.

PLANNING FOR SUPPORT ACTIVITIES

Support activities must be in sync with the development plan. No later than the definition stage, project managers need to map out all critical paths and

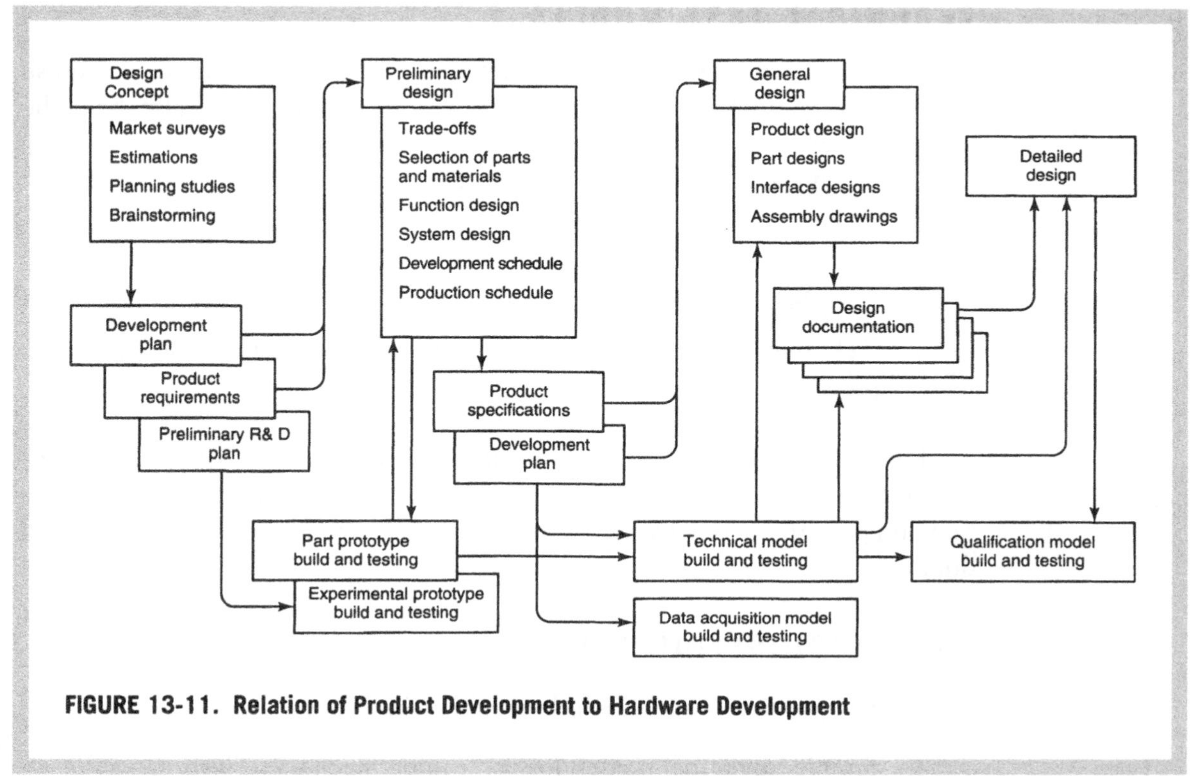

FIGURE 13-11. Relation of Product Development to Hardware Development

determine what preliminary research is required. Short of knowing the exact system specifications, they must prepare estimates for parts, materials, and component devices. If any of these items lie on a critical path, the system designer and parts developers should jointly identify them as high-priority and start any related research without delay.

PART PROTOTYPES

Once the system designers have determined basic requirements, those responsible for certain parts can create part prototypes. These parallel efforts are linked by ongoing coordination and review of results.

The preliminary design should include most of the specifications needed to build the product, as well as any R&D results available to date. Any untested technologies or other question marks will probably need to be earmarked for part prototype tests. Early identification of critical components allows more time to line up technical support. An ad hoc support system can provide experts from a variety of disciplines for in-house consultation. Supplier representatives are typically the best and most cost-effective alternative for any knowledge gaps your company cannot fill.

TECHNICAL TEST MODELS

Two more key support elements are technical test models and data acquisition models. Both test for design accuracy and feasibility and also help the designers prepare documentation for final qualification tests.

The technical test model has three specific objectives:

1. Checking design accuracy
2. Making sure the prototype accurately reflects design documentation
3. Determining where and how inspections should be made during production

Prototype builders refer to design drawings, reports, and instructions, revising these documents when necessary. The prototype tests look not only at function and performance but also at the user interface, operating environment, and durability.

DATA ACQUISITION MODELS

Data acquisition models include the following types:

1. Simple functional models for confirming mechanical layout, ease of assembly, and mechanical operating ranges such as the stroke range
2. Structural models for acquiring vibration, shock, and acoustics data
3. Thermal design models for acquiring heat and temperature data
4. Ergonomic models for confirming ergonomic layout, colors, ease of operation, and accuracy
5. Product life cycle models for acquiring data on life expectancy and durability
6. Maintenance models for confirming ease of maintenance and repair
7. Electrical models for acquiring data on electrical characteristics
8. Stress models for detecting weak points
9. System technology models for confirming all system functions

The first four are normally built as design prototypes, not experimental models per se. Since system technology models usually coincide with or immediately follow any technical test models, most companies classify them under that category instead.

PROJECT TECHNICAL DOCUMENTATION

The documentation on designs that have been confirmed via technical models is compiled into a single system design manual. After checking component-system compatibility, we submit this manual for approval. It will serve as the formal project technical manual for building and testing the final prototype models.

The facility or department that will be making the target system usually handles prototype build. That way they can easily spot problems and prepare for a smooth transition to full production. If problems remain in a technical model or if the formal manual contains errors or ambiguities, the engineering department should schedule design acceptance tests or initial production tests at that facility.

After building and evaluating the qualification model according to the project technical manual, we document all newly found abnormalities so that the manual can be updated. From this stage on, revisions to the production and testing manuals are managed via ECOs (engineering change orders). However, any changes to standards specification manuals, whether in-house or external, require an ECP (engineering change proposal) form to be submitted for management review and approval.

Once all documentation has passed through these processes to become official data, it is filed for future access by the production staff and other departments.

STANDARDIZATION

Standardization is an essential support element of both product development and DR. Design quality and efficiency flow not only from the designer's skill and creativity but also from well-defined standards and other guidelines. Since DR generally involves proprietary information, we want to make the most of in-house technology. This fuels a constant demand for current, accurate standards and documentation.

Table 13-5 lists various items that fall under the category of standardization. Your company's list may differ according to product type, project magnitude, and other factors. In any case, standardization makes the development process more reliable and efficient, as well as easier to carry out. These lists should not be seen as fixed and absolute, but rather as dynamic guidelines that can evolve with company needs and capabilities. I strongly suggest introducing the company's list of standards as part of new employee training.

TABLE 13-5. Types of Standards

Category	Standard	Description
Engineering standards Management standards	Drafting standards Specifications management standards Book and documentation management standards Operating manual management standards	Types, terms and expressions, units, drafting methods, revision methods Specification and revision formats Sorting and management of all books and documentation Management of documentation used in the plant
Design standards	Structural design standards Electronic design standards Mechanical design standards	Standards relating to structural design Standards relating to electronic circuit design Standards relating to mechanical design
Engineering standards	Soldering standards Gluing standards Coating standards	Technical instructions for soldering Technical instructions for gluing Technical instructions for coating and surface processing
Standard lists	Standard parts lists Standard hardware lists Standard materials processing lists	Lists of standard parts and specifications Lists of standard nuts, bolts and other common hardware Lists of standard materials and processing standards
Management procedures	Abnormality response procedures Design review procedures Development management procedures	Defines abnormalities and corresponding responses Describes design review steps Describes development management (configuration control) steps

CHANGE MANAGEMENT

No matter how much time and trouble go into preparing schedules, specifications, drawings, and manuals, we must not hesitate to correct and revise them when necessary. This is where ECPs and ECOs come in. Figure 13-12 illustrates some of the documents typically addressed by ECP and ECO forms.

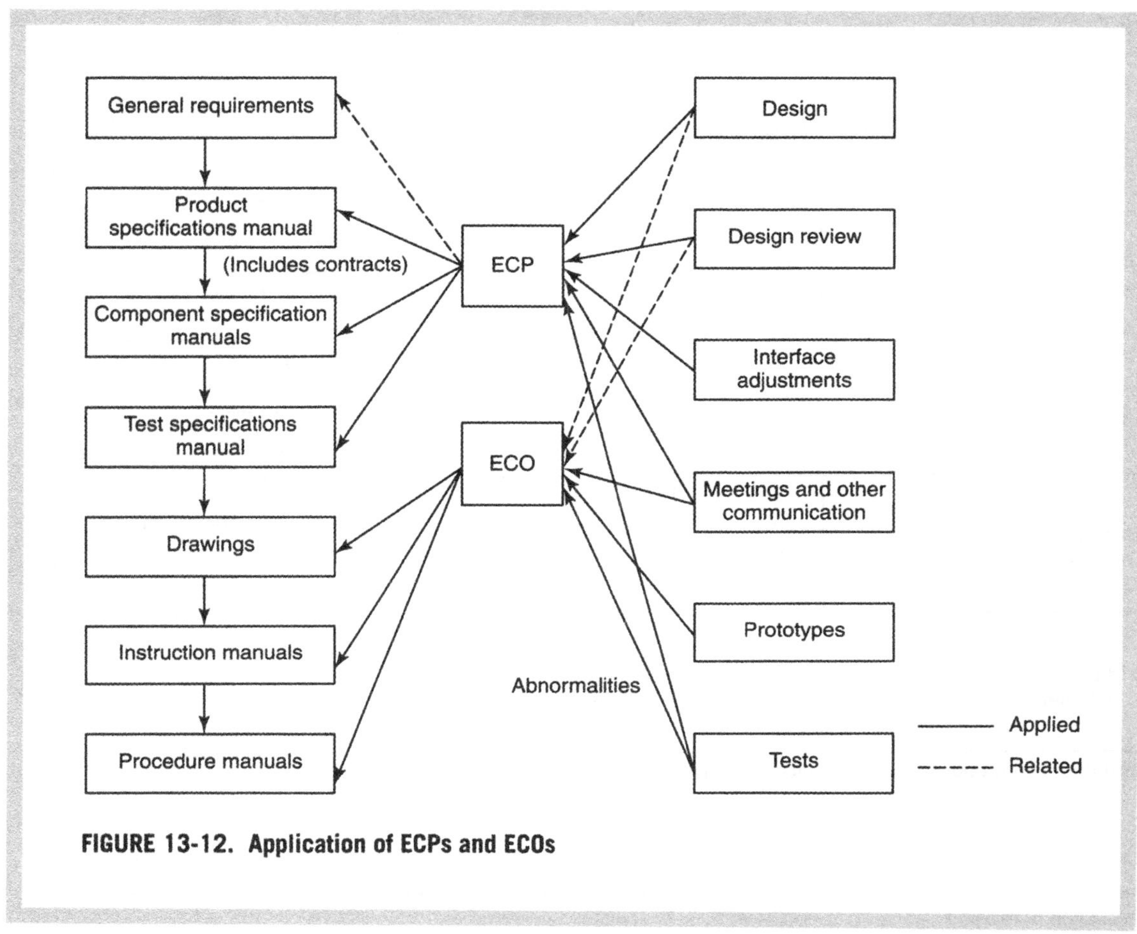

FIGURE 13-12. Application of ECPs and ECOs

ECPS

Most revisions during the initial stages apply only to the areas near the top of the figure. These generally involve revisions in requirements and are handled via ECPs. The usual sources are design reviews, other meetings, or technical memos, but rarely the designers themselves. Once approved, some of these revisions may force changes in the development plan or basic requirements manual.

Figure 13-13 shows an example of an ECP form. Our organization divides ECPs into two classes according to review and approval level. Class I ECPs affect the product specifications manual or other general documents, while Class II ECPs affect only lower-level specifications or schedules. This two-tiered classification helps streamline the change management process.

Engineering Change Proposal (ECP)				Category	Class I ECP Class II ECP
System name		Project name		Trace No.	
				Date	
Revision subject				Form filled out by	
				Department	
Baseline impact		Target subsystem(s)		Urgent?	Yes No Deadline:
Target document(s)		Scope of impact			
Background for proposal (design results, responses to abnormalities)					
Description of revision (Documents attached? YES NO)					
Impact factors Performance Safety Reliability Maintainability Interface Lead time Costs (for development and/or production) Other (please specify:)					
DR results			Impact on testing, development, and production		
CCB decision		Approval		Approval date	

FIGURE 13-13. ECP Form

ECOS

The main difference between ECPs and ECOs is in what they change. While an ECP affects system/product design and thus has strict approval guidelines, an ECO is targeted more at how the product is built and tested.

Drawings, instruction manuals, and other large documents are seemingly endless sources of revisions. No sooner are they published than we find something incorrect, inapplicable, or out of date. Moreover, much of the information used in prototype build and testing and general documentation can be difficult to capture accurately in a drawing. That is why we build and test prototypes, and we use ECOs to indicate where revisions are needed. ECOs are also convenient for managing revisions relating to interface adjustment or assembly.

QCD TRADEOFFS

Naturally, the whole point of reporting problems is to highlight the need for solutions, but during prototype testing, we do not always fill out ECPs on the spot. For instance, if an abnormality stems from a more fundamental problem, we may have to lower the requirements slightly rather than revise the prototype. This sort of classic QCD tradeoff (negligible sacrifice in quality for minimal impact on cost and schedule) is most common in the later stages of development. When this happens, the people who approved the initial requirements must also approve the ECP.

PROJECT COMMUNICATION AND COORDINATION

Our discussion so far has centered on determining project requirements and standards and setting up a system for making appropriate revisions. But requirements themselves tend to change as the design unfolds.

PROBLEMS IN COMMUNICATION

We cannot ignore the human element in the process. When a large number of individuals work together for an extended period, misunderstandings occur. The slightest misuse of terminology, difference in perspective, or lack of information can cause the same requirements to mean different things to different people. This can happen even within relatively common frames of reference, such as interface specifications.

You can minimize these problems by setting up a series of coordination meetings, either formal or informal, for everyone involved in a given project. However, if only some people attend, or if substantive discussions never carry over outside the meetings, most of the problems will remain.

CONFIGURATION CONTROL BOARD

Changes in one area often affect other areas, which is one of the reasons for convening a CCB (configuration control board). Chaired by the development project leader or another top manager, formal CCB meetings draw participation from the subsystem development, manufacturing, testing, QA, technical support, and sales departments.

CCB meetings are most frequent at the beginning of the project, later shifting from weekly to monthly or ad hoc meetings. Meeting minutes should record all deliberations for future review and approval and all planned adjustments and revisions for future follow-up. In the meantime, all verbal confirmation is considered unofficial. The administrative expense of maintaining all these written records is significant. However, it pales next to the costs of modifying user interfaces or other system components.

Figure 13-14 shows an example of a memo form for technical communications. CCB meeting minutes also follow a specified format which emphasizes traceability. It requires entry of a trace number, the date, the name of the person recording the minutes, and an approval signature. We make sure to document formally all proposed actions from CCB meetings, explaining every item that will be substantially affected.

DESIGN REVIEW

Any discussion of configuration control techniques should include DR. It brings together the company's knowledge and skills to initiate, evaluate, improve, and approve product development or other projects. From design concept to qualification tests, DR covers each stage of the development process. Starting with the project baseline, it corresponds to the "check" phase in the PDCA (plan-do-check-act) quality cycle.

Design work is creative work and, as such, requires as much flexibility as possible. While recognizing the normal constraints of time and money, we want to impose as few limits as possible. Hence product designers deal with only a very concise set of initial guidelines. These guidelines form the basis for DR evaluation, facilitating management decisions to adopt or reject new product proposals.

<table>
<tr><td colspan="6">**Technical Memo**</td></tr>
<tr><td rowspan="2">TO</td><td rowspan="2"></td><td rowspan="2">FROM</td><td rowspan="2"></td><td>Trace No.</td><td></td></tr>
<tr><td>Date</td><td></td></tr>
<tr><td rowspan="2">Subject</td><td colspan="3" rowspan="2"></td><td>Project name</td><td></td></tr>
<tr><td>DTBS No.</td><td></td></tr>
<tr><td colspan="4" rowspan="2">Description</td><td>Approval</td><td>Person in charge</td></tr>
<tr><td></td><td></td></tr>
<tr><td colspan="4" rowspan="2">Responses</td><td>Approval</td><td>Person in charge</td></tr>
<tr><td></td><td></td></tr>
<tr><td rowspan="2">Others to contact</td><td colspan="2" rowspan="2"></td><td rowspan="2">Project office</td><td>Received</td><td>Date</td></tr>
<tr><td></td><td></td></tr>
</table>

FIGURE 13-14. Technical Memo

OBJECTIVES

DR has two main objectives:

Evaluate design compatibility with project baseline. Does the design fully and consistently meet project requirements? Do the requirements themselves need reevaluation?

Evaluate design compatibility with in-house standards. Does the design meet all company design and technical standards, as well as national and international regulations? On top of all that, does it make good sense?

To answer these questions, reviewers must attempt to find and resolve all problems in either the system design or the development process.

BASELINE MANAGEMENT

The specific design goals embodied in the baseline are always subject to change due to cost or time constraints and customer requirements. Not surprisingly, reviewers often find a need to reconsider the current baseline. In our organization, baseline revisions must be initiated via an ECP. Since we cannot change in-house standards on a whim, there is a formal process for determining exceptions. This way we avoid compliance issues later in the project. Figure 13-15 shows the role of DR in baseline and standards revisions.

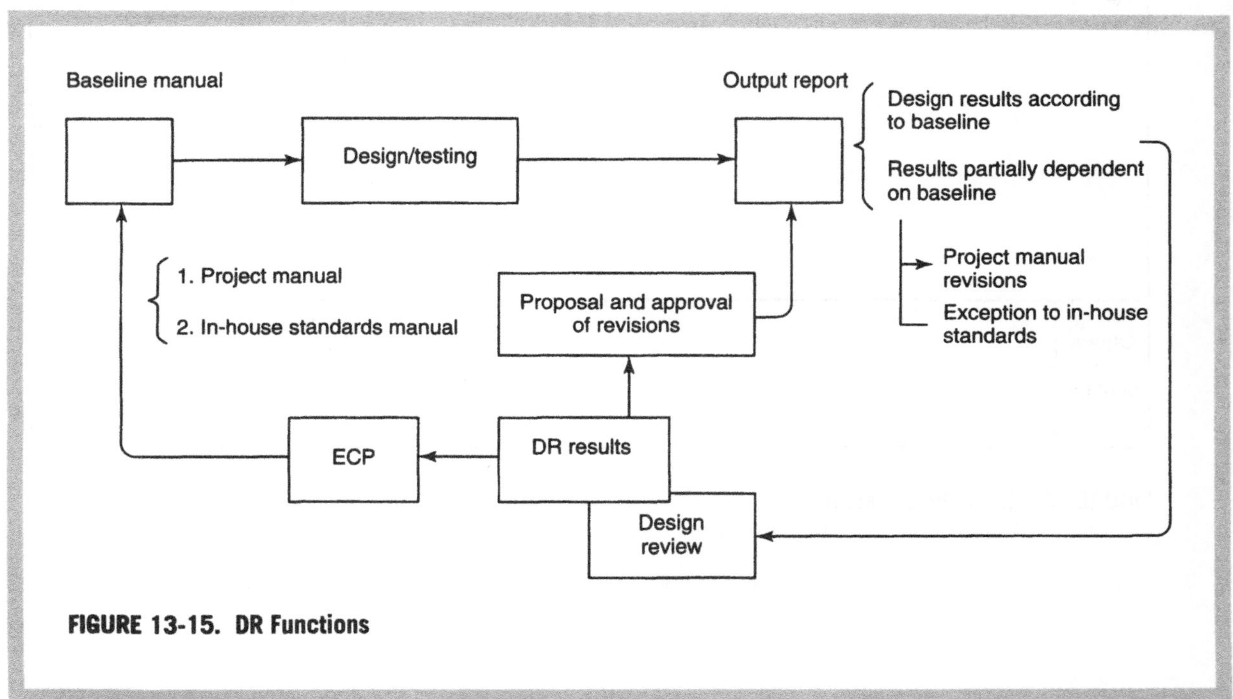

FIGURE 13-15. DR Functions

DR FLOW

Table 13-6 identifies review types by development stage.

TABLE 13-6. DR at Various Project Stages

Stage	Output	DR	Purpose
Planning stage	Design concept	System design concept review	Review the overall system to include estimating the project target feasibility and evaluating the development plan
Definition stage	Preliminary design	System requirement review	Review the suitability of specific requirements and evaluate subsystem development plans
General design stage	General design	General design review	Evaluate the suitability of the general design
Detailed design stage	Detailed design	Detailed design review	Evaluate revised portions of the previously completed manufacturing documentation
Prototype build and testing stage	Qualification tests	Final design review	Evaluate design and production documentation after qualification tests are complete

At the concept stage, DR's main target is the system design concept, while at the definition stage it focuses on specific system requirements. The general and detailed design reviews evaluate feasibility at successive levels of detail. Some people call the latter of these two the "critical design review" because it deals with documentation errors and scheduling problems. Following prototype build and qualification tests, the final design review looks back upon the completed project and confirms all the results.

KEYS TO SUCCESSFUL DR APPLICATION

DR should be tailored to the needs of each company, which is where the case studies earlier in this book can be helpful. At the risk of repetition, here are some points to remember about successful DR and configuration control.

PROMOTE DR FROM THE TOP

Upper managers who do not count DR among their everyday responsibilities will not give it the attention or support it deserves. Review committees start resembling report conferences or lecture meetings, accomplishing little. Companies can nip this in the bud by formally kicking off DR at a mandatory meeting for all top managers and then by ensuring adequate staffing and preparation for DR activities.

INTEGRATE DR INTO THE DEVELOPMENT PROCESS

As mentioned earlier, designers' need for freedom and creativity exempts them from many of the procedures and limitations we place on other staff. This complicates the application of configuration control to the design process.

The company as a whole must be cost conscious, and product development is no exception. That means eliminating design steps wherever possible, prioritizing new projects, and turning out cost-effective products. The following series of outline-style plans can help you tie DR into product development:

1. Configuration control plan
2. Baseline management plan (such as the one for product specifications)
3. Standards plan for creating and managing in-house standards
4. DR plan
5. Checklist management plan
6. Abnormality management plan

With ongoing changes in staff expertise, skill levels, and information resources, not to mention the products themselves, these plans help you manage projects efficiently while keeping pace with emerging technologies. But guidelines and standards can also work against project goals, so allow for exceptions to preserve design creativity, and cultivate a positive, constructive atmosphere at DR meetings.

USE DR TO IDENTIFY RISKS

Beyond its evaluation role, DR provides an excellent forum for identifying the risks in each new design.

You cannot manage design effectively with DR alone. It is just one aspect of configuration control, along with preparation and standardization. At the same time, the design department and other staff members need to see that DR is not just an exercise but a way to make sure their work is free of error and uncertainty. Once armed with this perspective, they will take DR far more seriously.

All original designs are fraught with risks. Furthermore, no one enjoys hearing other people pick apart his or her work. Even so, designers must live in the real world of profits and losses. After all, it is the company that carries the funding burden, not the individual. Managers must assess design risks in business terms, making sure other reviewers properly understand these risks when considering product proposals.

MAKE INFORMATION ACCESSIBLE

Even with the best people and organization, a project's success still depends on useful, available information. This means going to market surveys, data from outside sources, records of previous abnormalities and customer claims, advance R&D data, and reliability test data. Raw data must then be sorted, analyzed, and converted into checklists or some other in-house format. All this requires time and resources. The resulting documentation is critical not only to the actual design but also to the DR process.

FACTOR DR INTO PROJECT ESTIMATES

DR is not free. Development project estimates should allow for preparing documentation, conducting both preliminary and formal reviews, making revisions, and running the DR office. Companies also need to account for hours that non-design departments contribute to a project.

We can best judge DR by how well it prevents losses and preserves investments in technology. I know that without it, my company would struggle far more for consensus on development decisions and would not be as willing to invest in design quality assurance. Even if an initial DR meeting incurs large costs by involving a wide circle of participants, we consider it worthwhile if it promotes better understanding and cooperation during the rest of the project, prevents defects, and facilitates the development process.

RECOGNIZE INDIRECT DR BENEFITS

Designers have traditionally viewed DR as an unpleasant experience, but the trend is moving the other way. Many are realizing that the design itself is not the sole fruit of product development. Consider the variety of benefits—both direct and indirect—that companies routinely experience from applying DR:

- Participants learn better consensus-building and clarification of responsibilities.
- Data package materials provide a wealth of information for use in other projects.
- DR creates a system that facilitates future design revisions and procedural changes.

- Designers gain a clearer sense of direction, and even find ways to develop useful by-products quickly and efficiently.
- Designers gain confidence by explaining their work to management and staff.
- Designers take more care to ensure that their designs are viable and defect-free.
- Designers take better advantage of the supporting resources available to them, such as special expertise or survey data.
- On a deeper level, designers become less defensive and more receptive to outside help.

All these add up to the two greatest benefits:

- Better designs
- Better designers

CONCLUSION

DR's success at improving designers' activities and attitudes has addressed a sore spot for many design managers. As word gets around, more companies will want to try it for themselves. With that in mind, I would like to offer these final warnings:

1. DR is not the answer to all your development problems. (Nothing is.) It is one very important aspect of configuration control.
2. Do not approach DR as a magic formula for all the benefits listed above, and certainly not as a gimmick to motivate designers. That could easily tear apart the very fabric of design management and leave the company worse off than before.

DR is not a single method or technique but an overall approach to ensuring that new products deliver what the customer requires.

ABOUT THE AUTHOR

The late Takashi Ichida was professor of industrial engineering and management at Kanazawa Institute of Technology from 1979 until 1991. A graduate of Waseda University in electrical engineering, he previously served as chief director of the electronics department for Mitsubishi Electric Co., specializing in product assurance. Prior to that he was chief director of reliability in the management department of the Japanese National Space Development Agency.

Professor Ichida was coauthor (with Mr. Tetsuji Makino) of the 1981 book *Design Review*, which received the Nikkei Quality Management Literature Award.

INDEX

For Product Safety Concerns and Information please contact our EU representative GPSR@taylorandfrancis.com Taylor & Francis Verlag GmbH, Kaufingerstraße 24, 80331 München, Germany

Printed and bound by CPI Group (UK) Ltd, Croydon, CR0 4YY

08/05/2025

01864541-0001